The Gender Dance
in Couples Therapy

The Gender Dance in Couples Therapy

MARK WORDEN
Fairfield University

BARBARA DRAHUS WORDEN
Southern Connecticut State University

Brooks/Cole Publishing Company

I(T)P® An International Thomson Publishing Company

Pacific Grove • Albany • Belmont • Bonn • Boston • Cincinnati • Detroit • Johannesburg • London
Madrid • Melbourne • Mexico City • New York • Paris • Singapore • Tokyo • Toronto • Washington

Sponsoring Editor: *Eileen Murphy*
Marketing Team: *Margaret Parks and Jean Thompson*
Marketing Representative: *Michael Bushnach*
Editorial Assistant: *Susan Carlson*
Production Editor: *Marjorie Z. Sanders*
Manuscript Editor: *Becky Glenister*
Permissions Editor: *May Clark*

Interior Illustration: *Lisa Torri*
Interior and Cover Design: *Laurie Albrecht*
Cover Illustration: *David Ridley*
Art Editor: *Lisa Torri*
Indexer: *James Minkin*
Typesetting: *The Cowans*
Cover Printing: *Phoenix Color Corp.*
Printing and Binding: *R.R. Donnelley/Crawfordsville*

For more information, contact:

BROOKS/COLE PUBLISHING COMPANY
511 Forest Lodge Road
Pacific Grove, CA 93950
USA

International Thomson Publishing Europe
Berkshire House 168-173
High Holborn
London WC1V 7AA
England

Thomas Nelson Australia
102 Dodds Street
South Melbourne, 3205
Victoria, Australia

Nelson Canada
1120 Birchmount Road
Scarborough, Ontario
Canada M1K 5G4

International Thomson Editores
Seneca 53
Col. Polanco
11560 México, D. F., México

International Thomson Publishing GmbH
Königswinterer Strasse 418
53227 Bonn
Germany

International Thomson Publishing Asia
221 Henderson Road
#05-10 Henderson Building
Singapore 0315

International Thomson Publishing Japan
Hirakawacho Kyowa Building, 3F
2-2-1 Hirakawacho
Chiyoda-ku, Tokyo 102
Japan

Printed in the United States of America

10   9   8   7   6   5   4   3   2   1

Library of Congress Cataloging-in-Publication Data

Worden, Mark, [date]
    The gender dance in couples therapy / Mark Worden, Barbara Drahus Worden.
        p.   cm.
    Includes bibliographical references and index.
    ISBN (invalid) 0-534-34954-5
    1. Marital psychotherapy.   I. Worden, Babara Drahus, [date].
    II. Title.
RC488.5.W675   1997
616.89'156—dc21   97-15780
                                                              CIP

CONTENTS

Mark Worden, PhD, is Professor and Chair of Psychology at Fairfield University in Fairfield, Connecticut. As a licensed clinical psychologist, he specializes in couples therapy and working with adolescents and their families. Dr. Worden serves as clinical supervisor to community agencies and conducts workshops and training programs for school and mental health professionals. He is the author of *Adolescents and Their Families* (The Haworth Press, 1991) and *Family Therapy Basics* (Brooks/Cole, 1994).

Barbara Drahus Worden, PhD, LCSW, is an Assistant Professor of Social Work at Southern Connecticut State University in New Haven, Connecticut. As a licensed clinical social worker, she specializes in couples therapy and working with women. Dr. Drahus Worden is a clinical supervisor to beginning social workers and conducts workshops and seminars on women in midlife transitions and mother/daughter relationsips. She has authored several journal articles and is a contributing author to *Work and Well Being* (NASW Press, 1993).

PREFACE

In our individual practices we each work with couples. We occasionally refer to one another as the need arises. Sometimes the couple asks for a male or female therapist, or the nature of complaint (i.e., marital issues intersecting with parenting concerns) suits our individual areas of expertise. At other times, however, we may refer a member of the couple for individual therapy. It is during this cross-fertilization that we most seek the other's advice or assessment.

In addition, we supervise other therapists and graduate students who are doing couples work. These opportunities keep our focus on conceptualizing couples work and offer diverse lenses through which to view the therapeutic process. These viewpoints complement but may also challenge our personal perspectives.

As both the nature and function of marital roles have changed, particularly with the prevalence of the two-paycheck marriage, our perspectives have become increasingly colored by the influence of gender. Moving from viewing a couple as two individuals mutually shaping one another, we increasingly view a couple as two gendered individuals grappling with establishing a consensual intimacy. We may frequently ask each other about the couples with whom we work, "Why is he/she acting that way?" Or, "What is the best way of approaching him or her?" In our view, the influence of gender on a couple's functioning has assumed equal importance in relation to individual psychodynamics and systemic interactions.

Equally important, in our supervision and teaching we often find ourselves in abstract discussions of gender politics and the pragmatics of conducting couples therapy. Consequently, we feel the need to formalize our own understanding of gender influences and apply them to the treatment process.

The following book is our attempt to combine a discussion of gender while taking the reader through the labyrinth of couples therapy. In doing so, we will highlight basic steps and issues in treating couples from the first interview through termination. Our emphasis is on the process of treating couples or, more simply put, "what do I do now" and "what do I do next."

Therefore, the book has two goals: (1) to introduce the fundamentals of couples therapy, and (2) to consider gender influences in the treatment process. It is our hope that the reader will come away with guidelines for conducting couples therapy and a clearer lens through which to view gendered influences on clinical issues.

We would like to extend our heartfelt thanks to our manuscript reviewers: Thomas L. Millard, Montclair State University; and Elizabeth Sirles, University of Alaska at Anchorage. Their thoughtful critiques helped shape disjointed drafts into a more polished final manuscript. As always, we tip our hats to the staff of Brooks/Cole, whose encouragement and support were greatly needed at times. In particular, we wish to thank Eileen Murphy, whose positive affect was infectious, and Marjorie Sanders, for her patience in producing the book.

Mark Worden
Barbara Drahus Worden

Introduction

To knock a big girl down is a feeling I can't explain. You can feel the ground shake. Your head is spinning; you feel like you're floating on air. You can't hear anything but the cheering and you're thinking, "I brought her down."

(Longman, 1995)

Before anyone becomes too upset with this quote consider the source—a 115-pound, 5-foot, 3-inch coed from Penn State who was describing her feelings following a women's national collegiate championship rugby game. The article goes on to describe rugby as among the fastest growing sports for women and the only one to allow full, uninhibited physical contact.

The March 27, 1995, cover of *Newsweek* magazine pictures a woman with a series of electrodes and wires attached to her head, and under the lead title, "The New Science of the Brain," a subtitle proclaims, "Why Men and Women Think Differently." The subtitle is not asking a question but making a statement. Quickly flipping to the article, one is impressed with the bright, colorful positron-emission tomography (PET-scans) that clearly, it appears, demonstrate the differences in brain patterns between men and women.

A quick trip to a mall bookstore reveals that there are men who hate women, women addicted to love, men who cannot commit and fear intimacy, women who are codependent, and men who never grow up. Finally, we discover that men and women do not even speak the same language and, worse yet, are from different planets. The popularity of these books and the themes of talk shows would indicate that there is a mother lode being struck here. We argue over and are fascinated by the differences between women and men. Moreover, the age of political correctness heightens what we say and how we act toward the *opposite* sex (interestingly, *opposite* is defined as contrary or diametrically different).

What, you may ask, has this to do with a therapist conducting couples therapy? Everything, would be the reply. A therapist possesses a unique power when a couple enters therapy. In Torrey's (1972) cross-cultural study of healers, he refers to it as the "Rumpelstiltskin" (from the fairy tale) effect or the power to name the problem. Torrey states that the power to label the client's problem is common to witch doctors and psychiatrists. Basically, a client complains of a series of symptoms and the healer defines what the problem is—evil spirits or a chemical imbalance.

Similarly, couples seek out an expert to relieve their problems. As the expert, the therapist possesses the power to define the problem. For example, the couple complains of an endless cycle of arguments. He states or argues his point of view; she does the same. After half an hour of this heated Ping-Pong game the couple turns to the therapist for a judgment: Whose fault is it? Even if the therapist skillfully avoids this trap, assumptions are still rolling around in his or her head: Is the male partner afraid of intimacy? Is the female partner too dependent? Is he an emotional distancer? Is she an emotional pursuer? Is she a victim of a woman's submissive and powerless role in the culture? Is he a victim of paternal neglect that underlies his insecurity?

Even as the therapist keeps these assumptions silent, he or she must make an assessment and must implement interventions that may be guided by gender biases and cultural stereotypes. In order to be a purely objective therapist concerning the "battle of the sexes," one would have to be born and raised in isolation. Just as the couples we treat cannot escape cultural biases, neither can therapists.

This book developed out of our concern for our own gender biases. As clinicians who have been independently working with couples for many years, we have frequently been struck by our own contrasting views of couples. Sometimes we use different language to describe the same phenomena, sometimes we see things very similarly, and sometimes we view things quite differently. From our perspective, the impact of gender frequently underlined our viewpoints.

The book, therefore, reflects our attempt to focus on gender as a key issue in couples therapy. This is not to say that it is the central or dominant theme but rather a significant issue that exists within the couple, within the therapist, and within the therapeutic process.

In order to highlight and thus increase a couples therapist's sensitivity to the issue of gender, this book takes the reader through the treatment process while underlining the impact of gender on each phase of treatment. Because gender is seen as a process variable in couples therapy, specific theoretical discussions will be brief and serve more to orient the reader to various perspectives in the field. The main thrust of the book is to take the reader through the phases of couples therapy while emphasizing gender dynamics.

Before doing so, Chapter 2 provides a model to conceptualize the impact of gender on couples. Employing social constructionism, social learning theory, and social role theory, a distinction is made between sex (anatomical attributes that at birth divide babies into boys and girls) and gender (socially constructed role proscriptions). This is reflected in cultural views of traditional and egalitarian relationships.

Men and women frequently perceive the world and one another in different ways. Chapter 3 reviews psychological theories of men and women and empirical findings on the specific differences they experience in couples. Issues—for example, intimacy, communication, and conflict—are selected because they are directly relevant to the couples therapist.

Barring the luxury of an opposite sex cotherapist, couples therapy is conceptualized as an imbalanced gender triangle where the perceptions of the problems and the interaction among the participants are influenced by gender. Chapter 4 discusses the pitfalls in establishing a therapeutic alliance and views the therapist's role not as one of promoting traditional or egalitarian roles but as one of fostering the goodness of fit between the partners by balancing their reciprocity equilibrium.

Chapter 5 embarks on the pragmatic work of couples therapy beginning with the first interview. Besides taking the reader through this interview, the chapter underscores the ways in which men and women enter therapy differently.

As a prelude to intervention, assessment procedures consist of evaluating the influence of the past and the present on a couple's functioning. Specifically, Chapter 6 offers guidelines for assessing the impact of the families of origin on each partner's functioning. Object relations theory and Bowen's extended family systems theory serve as conceptual models to guide the assessment of past influences, particularly in terms of the partners' endorsement of traditional or egalitarian gender roles.

Chapter 7 assesses a couple's current behavioral patterns within general systems theory and cognitive attributions. General systems theory assists in identifying and understanding pursuer-distancer patterns while cognitive attributions frequently maintain and reinforce the current dysfunctional patterns. The assessment of a couple is also broadened to include the developmental stage of the marriage, environmental stresses affecting the relationship, and the couple's motivation for treatment.

The process of change in couples therapy is addressed in Chapter 8. Emphasizing a solution-focused approach over a problem-centered one, therapeutic interventions follow a logical sequence from first to second order. Specific techniques are discussed for each level of intervention.

It would be very gratifying and would certainly make a therapist's life easier if therapy followed a smooth logical progression from first interview through termination. Unfortunately, couples therapy may run into a series of impasses. These are conscious or unconscious themes acting as hidden agendas inhibiting the treatment process. Chapter 9 explores transference, countertransference, and content themes such as physical or drug abuse that contribute to stalemates in therapy.

Either through first- or second-order interventions or impasse resolution techniques, successful therapy renews the partners' commitments to the relationship. Chapter 10 discusses impasse resolution techniques and the movement toward termination. The specific process of termination is outlined.

In closing, a few footnotes are needed. To make the phases of therapy more alive, one case is introduced and followed throughout the treatment process. What we sacrifice in diversity we hope to make up for in consistency and clarity of presentation.

Finally, couples come in all forms: marriages, live-in arrangements, heterosexual, homosexual, and biracial. It is not our intent, nor our purpose, to address all of these various possibilities. Instead, we offer a generic view of couples therapy balanced with a respect for the power of gender. Consequently, in referring to members of a couple we may call them spouses, partners, or mates. This in no way reflects a bias one way or another. For example, we specifically address homosexual couples in Chapters 2 and 9 as a means of identifying societal issues that may be reflected in the treatment process. However, it is our belief that while each type of couple has its unique concerns, all couples struggle with building and maintaining a strong, intimate, and loving relationship.

CHAPTER TWO

Couples: Men and Women

Men are dominant, rational, objective, independent, decisive, competitive, aggressive, capable of leadership, good at science and mathematics, and interested in business, sports, and politics. Women, on the other hand, are submissive to others, caring, nurturing, affectionate, cooperative, emotional, relationship oriented, and good at domestic tasks and child-rearing.

Do you endorse all of these, some of these, or none of these statements? Do you take exception to the forced dichotomy between men and women? Do you believe the dichotomy is real and reflects innate biological, genetic differences? Do you believe the dichotomy exists but believe the reason is based in the inequity in status and power between men and women in our society, whereby women are relegated to a subordinate status position? Or, do you believe the difference exists because of unconscious, psychodynamic forces shaping masculine and feminine identification by age 6? If definitive answers existed for these questions, this and other books and articles would not be written. Instead, theoreticians, clinicians, and researchers struggle with the richness and complexity of our concepts of gender or the colloquial "battle of the sexes."

Gender is the most basic issue of diversity. Beginning at birth, we are divided into pink (female) and blue (male) categories. It is a differentiation that will greatly influence how we view ourselves, how others will view us, and how we will interact with our social environments. As such, our gender identity consists of an identification with our same-sex peers, a knowledge of where our sex stands in power and status in relation to the opposite sex, and proscriptive norms guiding each sex's behavior (Aries, 1996).

In the evolution of marital and family therapy, the issue of gender has grown in significance. Feminist critiques of the field argue that family therapy models have been blind to the impact of gender on family relationships and have not taken into account the differential in power and status between men and women in the cultures in which families are embedded (Luepnitz, 1988; Walsh & Scheinkman, 1989; Walters, Carter, Papp, & Silverstein, 1988).

In response to these critiques, the American Association of Marriage and Family Therapy (AAMFT Manual on accreditation, 1991) requires all approved programs to offer coursework in gender issues. However, in a study on the effects of gender training in reducing sexism in family therapy, Leslie and Clossick (1996) found that training in gender alone did not significantly affect sexism in clinical decision making but that gender coursework from a feminist perspective did significantly lower sexism. They define a feminist perspective as gender viewed from a social constructionist perspective and interplay of gender and power in families. Thus, they argue that merely addressing the areas of gender and sexism is not enough—what is taught and how it is taught are equally important.

In this chapter we attempt to place the discussion of gender within a theoretical framework. While Leslie and Clossick (1996) found social contructionism and power differentials to be key concepts in influencing clinical decisions, we build on a broader social-psychological perspective. From our perspective, gender is best understood as a social construction and a concept mediated by social learning theory that shapes one's gender schema and role definitions. Moreover, one's culture further defines and shapes the social construction of gender. Specifically, couples' relationships fall along a traditional–egalitarian dimension, and inherent in this dimension is the concept and distribution of power.

Finally, many of the concepts addressed in the chapter apply equally to homo- and heterosexual couples. However, because homosexual couples exist in a predominately heterosexual culture, there are issues unique to gay couples that warrant discussion.

Social-Psychological Construction of Gender

SOCIAL CONSTRUCTIONISM

Social constructionism views people as active participants in understanding their world. As such, there are no universal truths about human nature—that is, the innate differences between men and women—but instead beliefs are socially constructed, consensually held, and reinforced. These socially constructed, consensually held beliefs then become our definitions of "reality."

A social constructionist would endorse at least one of the following assumptions (Gergen, 1985):

1. An absolute reality does not exist. Instead, each culture defines its own reality. Cultural anthropologists have consistently shown that views of God, sexual norms, gender roles, and so on, are understood differently by different cultures.
2. Reality is defined through an interactive social consensus. That is, the members of a given society or culture actively cooperate in determining what constitutes and defines reality. Understanding is a social product. For example, popular media both reflect and reinforce our views of gender.
3. These definitions of reality persist because they are useful. For example, stereotypes serve as a means of categorizing people and therefore justifying existing cultural norms. If women are seen as emotional and men as

rational, then as a society we are justified in placing men in positions of power.

4. These socially constructed realities directly influence how members of a society are perceived and responded to. The rambunctious boy in the classroom setting may be seen as "all boy." A girl in the classroom performing similar acts would be quickly referred to the school psychologist.

Because of the consensual nature of these beliefs, the ability to define reality for a culture is strongly influenced by the majority and/or those with the most power. Accordingly, the constructed beliefs serve to maintain the status quo, particularly the culture's power hierarchy.

The power of a socially constructed belief system is that it serves as a lens to view all behavior. As an active process, we selectively seek information that reinforces our system while ignoring or "not seeing" contradictory evidence. For example, a little more than 100 years ago scientists demonstrated that a human female brain is smaller than a human male brain, thus lending biological support to the then cultural belief that women were physically and intellectually inferior to men (Gould, 1981). Hence, "scientific" evidence reinforced prevailing cultural views.

In meta-analysis studies on gender differences in cognitive abilities (Hyde, 1981), personality traits (Cohn, 1991), and social behavior (Aries, 1996), gender differences accounted for generally less than 10% of the variance and typically less than 5%. This means that there were greater differences within each group than between them. That is to say, men differed more from other men and women differed more from other women than men and women differed from each other. Or, more concretely, knowing the gender of the person was little help in predicting his or her behavior.

Still, gender differences are quickly trumpeted in the popular media. Rarely is the question asked, "Do men and women differ?" Instead, it is assumed that differences are real. But, as Bleier (1991) observes following her review of neurological gender differences, "Society, having carefully constructed a set of gender characteristics to be quite specifically and normatively different for girls and boys and men and women, ingeniously observes, through its scientists, that there are 'sex differences' and sets about assiduously to measure them and to find biological bases for them in our genes, hormones, or brain structures" (p. 67).

Human beings, therefore, are not passive recipients of gender roles; rather, we each actively engage our perceptions and thus "construct" our worldview as individuals and as a society (Beall, 1993). These socially constructed beliefs are very difficult to change because they support the culture's status quo and color our vision of the "facts."

SOCIAL LEARNING THEORY

Through social learning theory, socially constructed reality is reinforced in the individual. Briefly, social learning theory emphasizes the interaction between individuals and their environment in terms of observational learning, cognitive processes, and motivational beliefs. This interaction of the person and the envi-

ronment is called reciprocal determinism (Bandura, 1986). The social environment, a person's qualities, and his or her behavior form a circle in which all
elements mutually affect one another.

Social learning theory accounts for gender differences by examining socially
defined sex-typed behavior and how this behavior is subtly shaped through positive and negative reinforcement (Lott & Maluso, 1993). Shaping these sex-typed
behavior patterns is an essential element in the socialization process—defining
masculinity and femininity. Thus, one's gender identity refers to the cultural and
psychological attributes that children learn are appropriate for the sexes.

Mischel (1966) suggests that a person acquires sex-typed behavior by first
discriminating differences between male and female behavior, then generalizing
to new situations, and finally performing the behaviors and being rewarded for
it. For example, labeling clothing, activities, or behavior as male and female
begins the gender differentiation process. Rewarding the appropriate sex-typed
behavior in a given context further establishes the behavior.

In a study of teachers' reactions to "assertive acts" and "communicative acts"
of 12- to 16-month-old children, it was found that although there were no observable differences between the boys and girls in the frequency of these acts,
teachers responded far more often to assertive boys and talkative girls (Fagot,
Hagan, Leinback, & Kronsberg, 1985). Observing the same children 1 year later,
the researchers found an established "sex difference": boys were more assertive
and girls were more talkative to teachers.

By the age of 2 or 3, children develop a gender identity in that they have the
ability to classify themselves as male or female and can classify toys, behavior,
and people according to gender (Cross & Markus, 1993). Edelsky (1976, 1977)
asked third- and sixth-grade children and adults whether a man, a woman, or
both men and women would be likely to say a series of sentences. The sixth
graders agreed with adult ratings on all but one variable. Thus, Edelsky (1976,
1977) concluded that by the age of 12, children have incorporated norms for sex-
specific language.

It is not enough, however, to acquire the behavior—the sex-typed distinction
needs to be continually observed and reinforced. For example, gender differentiation is not only likely to be influenced by the parents' behavior (i.e., rewards
and punishments) but also by what the child observes. For example, how parents
relate to one another graphically portrays the cultural expectations for men's and
women's behavior (Meyer, Murphy, Cascardi, & Birns, 1991).

Social learning theory also emphasizes the situational context. It has been
found that boys and girls do not differ in the traits of passivity or activity but that
their behavior depends on the gender of the child with whom they are playing
(Maccoby, 1990). For example, preschool girls are seldom passive with one another but will let boys monopolize the toys in mixed-sex groups. Moreover, girls
in mixed classrooms stayed closer to the teacher not because they were dependent but because it gave them a chance to play with the toys. In fact, girls were
just as independent as boys in their play when they were in all-girl groups
(Maccoby, 1990).

Through social learning, sex-appropriate behavior is continually observed
and reinforced in the developing child. By 2 years of age, gender identity is
forming. But the developing child is not a passive recipient of environmental

shaping. Gender identity also signals developing cognitive abilities that fashion the person's interaction with the environment.

GENDER SCHEMAS AND SOCIAL ROLE THEORY

As we interact with our environment we attempt to make sense of our world. Cognitive schemas assist us in organizing our perceptions. Schemas are cognitive processes that order our perceptions, categorize our knowledge, and guides our behavior. Cognitive schemas also assist us in processing the continual flow of information we receive. Gender schemas divide people into male or female categories.

Spence (1985) argues that because gender distinctions are central and pervasive in our culture, gender identity is the most central and organizing schema of one's self-concept. Sexual stereotypes, therefore, serve as measures for our own behaviors, frame our view of others, and form our expectations of others.

Cross and Markus (1993) found that their subjects projected gender differences on even a very young child. Briefly, subjects observed a startle reaction in babies when the jack-in-the-box toy they were playing with popped open. If the observers thought the baby was a boy, they believed he was angry. If the observers thought the baby was a girl, they said she was afraid. In social-psychological terms this is referred to as an attribution error. We attribute or, in clinical terminology, project personality characteristics onto an individual. The error occurs when we attribute personality traits to behavior that is based within a social context. Moreover, prior beliefs—that is, gender stereotypes—are consistently applied in a self-fulfilling manner. He is a man; he is raising his voice; he is being assertive. She is a woman; she is raising her voice; she is whining.

Cultural gender schemas are also incorporated into our self-concept (Cross & Markus, 1993; Geis, 1993). The traditional, feminine gender schema involves caring, nurturance, and sensitivity. The expression of these behaviors requires another person. That is, a woman is caring, nurturing, and sensitive to others. Thus, her relationships with others would be a key element in her self-concept. Likewise, the male gender schema, which emphasizes independence, assertiveness, and competitiveness, requires a separation from others. As a result, men and women will pay attention to different areas: women to interpersonal relationships, men to competitive ones. This pervasive effect even affects memory. Men were found to have a better memory for information encoded with respect to the self, while women had a better memory with reference to others (Josephs, Marekus, & Tafarodi, 1992).

Social role theory postulates that people will behave consistently with their gender roles (Eagly, 1987). However, gender roles will dominate as long as they are not superseded by more salient roles. In the traditional view of women as submissive and passive, research has shown that men and women both know high- and low-status behavior patterns and that which set of behaviors is expressed depends on the context and not the personality (Geis, 1993). For instance, a high-powered male executive knows how to be submissive when his superior comes into the room. When assigned to the same role and status in the experimental conditions, men and women act in the same way. They are equally submissive or assertive dependent on their role assignments. Likewise, in an investigation of gender, authority, and leader-subordinate conversations, when assigned to a managerial role and given the same formal legitimate authority, men and women are quite similar in their communication patterns.

Thus, the "innate gender differences" disappear when social roles and situation context are manipulated. Following a review of the literature, Geis (1993) argues that the supposed dominant-submissive gender distinction more accurately reflects role assignments. Women act in passive and dependent ways because they occupy subordinate roles, not because of innate personality traits.

The gender roles and schemas are highly reinforced and thus are maintained through social interaction. For example, Carli (1990) found that in group discussions men agreed more with women who spoke tentatively than with women who spoke assertively. But the reverse was not found. Whether a man spoke assertively or tentatively had no bearing on agreement. Men were heard regardless of their language style. Consequently, the woman sitting in your office who begins every statement with a qualifier—"I don't know, I could be wrong but . . ."—or who rarely makes a direct statement may be accurately reflecting her gender role and schema. It is not that she is a dependent personality but that she is a person highly sensitive to status roles and is just trying to be heard.

Cultural Influences: Traditional and Egalitarian Relationships

The social-psychological construction of gender occurs within a cultural and ethnic context. Culture provides the overall context through which we organize and understand our experiences in the world (Saleebey, 1994). Specifically, ethnicity is a common ancestry through which individuals have evolved shared values and customs. "The concept of a group's 'peoplehood' is based on a combination of race, religion, and cultural history and is retained whether or not members realize their commonalities with one another" (McGoldrick, Giordano, & Pearce, 1996, p. 1). Ethnicity provides a sense of belonging and historical continuity (McGoldrick, Pearce, & Giordano, 1996; McGoldrick, Preto, Hines, & Lee, 1991). Moreover, ethnic heritage is steeped in norms and values transmitted over generations, norms and values that strongly shape one's gender identity.

Because ethnicity is also embedded within the broader societal-cultural context, specific ethnic values and norms may be supported or at odds with the broader societal norms. For example, an ethnic group may foster dependency in its young women. A young woman does not move out of the home unless she is to be married. The young woman, however, may identify more with the broader society norms of autonomy and independence. Thus, the seeds are sown for a family conflict.

But ethnic heritage does not necessarily imply ethnic identity. Phinney (1996) argues that ethnic identity is a complex cluster of factors that differs both qualitatively and quantitatively among ethnic group members. That is to say, a great deal of variability exists among the members of any ethnic group regarding an individual's identification with and commitment to the group. Thus, "the psychological correlates of ethnicity are likely to differ depending on the quality of this identity" (Phinney, 1996, p. 932).

Cultural transmission of ethnic identity occurs in several ways: (1) vertical transmission—through one's parents and extended family, (2) horizontal transmission—from one's peers and cohort groups, and (3) oblique transmission—from society in general (Berry, 1994). All forms of cultural transmission affect gender identity and role formation. It is beyond the scope of this book to address the various roles each type of cultural transmission plays in the development of gender identity and roles. However, it is safe to say that the assimilation of cultural identity affects one's behavior, attitudes toward familism, sex-role expectations, and cultural loyalty and values.

As a means of delineating gender roles within cultural contexts, researchers have differentiated between traditional and egalitarian societies. Traditional and egalitarian societies are distinguished along three dimensions (Haas, 1995). Traditional societies uphold a patriarchal hierarchy—father knows best. Egalitarian societies promote the beliefs that:

1. Women possess the opportunity to equally contribute to the family's financial resources, and this opportunity is supported by legislation.
2. Family and household work is shared across genders.
3. Public and private spheres are blended. There is an equal prioritizing of family and work. Both sexes combine breadwinning, housework, and child care responsibilities. Society recognizes that both sexes have family responsibilities.

(Please note that the definitions of traditional and egalitarian are based on the equality between the sexes on both the family level also in terms of societal supports.)

Investigating the effects of the broader societal-cultural context on gender roles, researchers in cross-cultural studies asked subjects to define ideal role relationships between men and women (Best & Williams, 1993; Williams & Best, 1990a, 1990b). The responses fell along a dimension of traditional to modern (egalitarian) gender roles. Traditional gender roles endorsed the view that men are more "important" than women and that it is proper for men to exercise control and dominance over women. Modern or egalitarian ideologies view men and women as equally important and the dominance of one gender over another is rejected.

In predicting a subject's definitions of ideal role relationships, the effect of culture was greater than the effect of gender. Or, in other words, there was more agreement among men and women within the same cultural group than among same-sex respondents across all cultural groups regarding the value of traditional or egalitarian gender relationships. Thus, attesting to the power of socially constructed gender roles, men and women within a given culture are more likely to share similar gender schemas.

Traditional–egalitarian gender ideologies are significantly related to a culture's social and economic development. As countries become more industrialized and urban, their gender roles become more egalitarian. To understand this, one must recognize two cultural tasks: reproduction and production.

In more industrialized countries with greater sexual knowledge and access to birth control methods, it is possible for women to reliably plan for and limit the number of children they will have. A woman's freedom to make choices with her life is greatly enhanced. Concomitantly, in more industrialized countries, production or work involves more people skills and brainwork that both sexes can do than production based on a strong back.

With the freedom to choose and a capacity to work outside of the home, women's status in a society increases. This is not to belittle or denigrate a woman's choice to be home with her children, but, for better or worse across cultures, people's value is often measured by their economic worth, and the financial value of work performed in the home is not recognized (Waring, 1988). For example, in the United States, studies have consistently shown that when women contribute financially to the family's standard of living, their status and power rise (Blumstein & Schwartz, 1991).

The personal effect of traditional and egalitarian gender roles is seen in men's and women's self-concepts. Defined by the difference between ratings for the "ideal" and "actual" self, the difference between men's and women's self-concepts were greater in less developed countries than in more developed ones (Best & Williams, 1993). That is to say, men endorsed a more positive self-concept than women in less developed countries.

Still, even in the modern, industrialized cultures, where egalitarian gender roles are more strongly endorsed, traditional gender roles change slowly. Across 25 countries, both men and women agreed substantially on characteristics differentially associated with men and women. Characteristics associated with men were: active, strong, dominant, autonomous, aggressive, exhibitive, achieving, and enduring. Characteristics associated with women were: passive, weak, abasing, deferential, succoring, nurturing, and affiliating (Best & Williams, 1993).

One possible explanation for the consistency of gender stereotypes across cultures is the traditional division of labor between reproduction and production. The capacity to bear children defines women's roles as care-givers, while men are assigned the task of providing the material necessities to sustain the family. For example, Darwin (1871) believed gender differences—men were aggressive and women nurturing—evolved because they were adaptive to the environment and thus more prevalent in the natural selection process. Men, in order to survive and prosper, developed abilities in hunting and tracking. Aggression played a key role in hunting as well as attacking one's enemies and defending one's home. Again, cultural beliefs are reflected in "scientific" findings. Darwin concluded that because of this natural selection process and the abilities required of men, men were superior to women because they had more highly developed reasoning skills.

Fisher (1992), an ethologist (one who studies the genetic aspects of behavior), believes that human beings share a set of unconscious tendencies or potentials that are the legacy of our ancestral forbearers. These potentials are encoded on our DNA and motivate behavior. Thus, gender differences and gender power differential are seen as expressions of a million years of evolution.

The origins of gender differences, Fisher (1992) argues, began with our descent from the trees onto the grasslands of Africa. We survived as a species by hunting game and foraging for seeds and berries. Role differentiation occurred because of anatomical differences. Hunting became men's domain because of their greater physical strength. Because of the ability to bear and nurse children, women were gatherers and in charge of child-rearing. Role differentiation gave order and specialization to the primitive culture as both men and women equally contributed to the survival of the species.

From a historical, socioeconomic perspective, while the division of labor—production and reproduction—was necessary for survival, men and women became relegated to distinct roles. These roles have specific behavioral requirements: production roles require aggression and mastery of the external world while reproduction roles require nurturing and affiliative skills. However, as we discussed, we frequently confuse role performance with personality traits. We begin to attribute personality characteristics to the people fulfilling those roles. (In social-psychological terms this is referred to as fundamental attribution error.)

Thus, the more a culture assigns production roles to men and reproduction roles to women, it is understandable that men would be seen as active, aggressive, and achievement-oriented and women would be seen as nurturing and affiliating because these attributes are needed to fulfill the respective roles. Through social learning, these respective behaviors are strongly shaped and reinforced to further define one's gender identity.

While initially based in anatomical differences, the differentiation of gender roles, in and of itself, is value-free. Both the roles of production and reproduction perpetuate the culture. However, the roles may not be equally valued, which leads to a power differential between the sexes.

Power

Despite endorsing more modern, egalitarian gender roles, in which law and ideology favor equal rights, men in more modern cultures still tend to have more power than women in the family and society (Best & Williams, 1993; Williams & Best, 1990a, 1990b). Even in intimate relationships, men are more likely to be listened to and have the decision-making power. What accounts for this?

Returning to Fisher's (1992) analysis, evolutionary and socioeconomic forces shaped early power differentials between gender roles. Following the Ice Age and the demise of large mammals, human beings were forced to hunt smaller game. In order to survive, humans domesticated wild animals and began to plant seeds—the beginnings of a farm. With the start of the agricultural society, women, as gatherers, were no longer equal partners in material survival. Particularly with the development of the plow—the heart of economic power in an agricultural society—women were relegated to home and children.

This drop in status was reflected in a society's laws. For example, in the law of codes of ancient Mesopotamia dating from 1100 B.C., women were described as child-producing property (Fisher, 1992). In colonial, agricultural New England communities before 1800 and through the early decades of the 19th century, male power was justified because men were seen as superior to women in both intellect and virtue. Men, through their reason, were better able to moderate passions such as envy than women and thus were best suited to head a household and democratically colead a community with other men. These "gender differences" were easily translated into laws that legalized male power (Rotundo, 1993).

As men held the power of economic survival in their hands, a woman's dependency on a man increased. Survival was tied to the relationship with a man because he controlled the resources. To support this argument, Fisher (1992) points to divorce rates and finds that the key factor in current divorce rates and marital instability is a woman working outside the home. For example, divorce is more frequent where the husband's income is markedly lower than the wife's. Likewise, educated women with high-paying jobs divorce more readily. Conversely, more stable marriages occur where the man is in a higher socioeconomic class and he has more money (resources) than his wife. Thus, a woman's sense of dependence or independence is tied to economic realities.

The traditional–egalitarian dimension is based on the concept of power. Who will influence whom? Who will control the resources? Who will make the final decision? Is all work, both in and outside the home, of equal value?

ECONOMIC POWER

"Historically, the distribution of power between men and women has been unequal in economic, political, and religious institutions, as well as in family life" (Low, 1990, p. 250). From an economic perspective, this unequal distribution of power has been based on the man's ability to provide a standard of living for the family. Traditional views hold that the man's job is to interface with the outside world and provide the basic, material necessities for the family. The woman's job is to tend to the home and children and maintain the expressive family functions, the quality of relationships both within and outside the family. Each gender measures self-worth by its ability to fulfill its respective role assignments.

Within this economic schema, the covert agreement is that the man's job takes priority because it provides the family's basic needs. Even when the couple is a two-paycheck relationship, women still take on the lion's share of domestic responsibilities (Blumstein & Schwartz, 1983). Subsequently, in many couples' discussion of priorities, the man feels justified in assuming that his job and the status this provides should come before the woman's job or her needs. In many couples, women share this assumption and therefore repress their own needs or minimize their success to maintain the established power/status balance.

In the unstable economic times of the late 20th century when families of all economic strata face layoffs, downsizing, and job eliminations, traditional role expectations place an often untenable burden on both sexes. Tied to financial performance, a male's self-worth may be highly vulnerable to fluctuations of the economic marketplace. Unemployment signals failure. The traditional feminine gender role places women in a subordinate, dependent, and vulnerable economic position.

Current employment statistics challenge traditional gender roles since two paychecks are usually needed to provide for a family. Often individual familial and role changes lag behind broad social changes. When people search for reference points and examples of how to be a husband or wife, they often rely on family of origin models. For example, people in their 20s marrying in the mid-1990s were raised by parents who grew up in the 1950s. Their parents' cultural gender realities are quite different from the gender realities of the 1990s. Still, as a psychological buoy, the parents' marriages serve as a beacon we head toward or away from.

Economic inequality translates into interpersonal power inequities. While members of a couple may not consciously endorse such differentials in power, gender roles affect our behavior and spill over into psychological perspectives of power. As Low (1990) points out:

> The woman has to consciously and unconsciously defer to her husband because he is the man, even though at times such deferences may do violence to her own self-image. She may also have to idealize him, to exaggerate his talents and abilities, in order to justify her less powerful position. By marrying a man who is typically older, taller, smarter, and more educated, a woman places herself in a position in which it seems natural to be less powerful. The converse is also true: Most men marry younger, smaller, less intelligent, and less educated women, which helps them to maintain their more powerful position. (p. 252)

As a footnote and attesting to the power of economic roles, Beer (1993) found that when wives earn the family income and their husbands stay home with the children, the husbands complain of not feeling listened to or loved enough.

PSYCHOLOGICAL POWER

Power is the capacity to influence and affect our environment. Power is enhanced by the possession of resources. Broadly defined, resources are anything that can be used to satisfy or frustrate the needs of others. The more resources one has in a family, the greater his or her power will be. For example, studies in the United States consistently show that when women contribute financially to the family's standard of living, their resources and power will rise (Blumstein & Schwartz, 1991).

Besides the obvious effects of economic power discussed above, there are psychological resources that are used to influence one's partner and that may be controlled by either partner—sexual attraction, affiliation, and anger. Gender roles also shape our views of power.

Sex

The power of sexual attraction is most evident in dating situations. Here we may be attracted to someone but them not to us. This person's attractiveness may wield considerable power over us as we attempt to woo and win his or her affections. Even the financially wealthy individual may be powerless in attracting the object of his or her dreams.

Unfortunately, in established relationships sex may be used as a powerful resource. For example, the partner with the low sex drive may have power over a more highly sexed partner. Moreover, sex may be used as a reward or a punishment for the partner's behavior. Suffice it to say, once sex is employed as a form of psychological power to influence or control one's partner, the couple's capacity for intimacy severely suffers.

Affiliation

Affiliation needs are formed early in childhood and family experiences. Mothers teach daughters to be empathic and responsive to the needs of others, while sons are encouraged to leave and loosen attachments (Chodorow, 1978).

Women often keep connected with those who are important to them through a continuity of thoughts and attention to the relationship between them. These qualities are emphasized early as daughters and their mothers develop the capacity to flow back and forth as both the giver and receiver of emotional supplies (Stiver, 1991). This emotional flow is easily transferred to the adult female–male relationship.

Autonomy and objectivity are not a woman's primary goals within a relational context. Women often fear that if they were less "in tune" with relational needs and more "in tune" with their own needs they would hurt or distance themselves from those they love. Therefore, fulfilling affiliative needs is highly valued within the context of the feminine gender role.

In addition, passive, affiliative behavior has often been conveyed as the hallmark of successful femininity (Lerner, 1988). This behavior serves two relational needs: (1) The dependence of one spouse (female) assures the independence of the other spouse (male); (2) greater efforts at autonomy can connote a betrayal to the relationship.

The male gender role, however, values autonomy and objectivity. Because mothers perceive their sons as different from them, they seek to affirm this difference within the context of a strong masculine identity. Fathers and the surrounding culture support this difference by encouraging the young males to seek separateness and autonomy.

Women fear the loss of connection while men fear the loss of autonomy. Given these differences in affiliation, conflicts appear inevitable in male-female relationships. Low (1990) argues that this conflict is so basic that only a rare couple is free of it.

The male "doing" versus female "talking" is most graphic on the affiliation dimension. For example, a man shows his commitment through action: "I bring home a good paycheck." "I have worked long and hard this week." "Look, I fixed the doorknob." Or, in the heat of an argument, "What do you mean I don't love you? I am here, aren't I?" For a man, action is clear, tangible and speaks for his caring. Women, however, are most comfortable with talking about the relationship and sharing one's feelings.

Within this gender dynamic, a man may view his mate as engulfing and/or emotionally demanding. Or, he may experience a chronic sense of criticism that he does not measure up to his partner's expectations. He is accused of not caring about the relationship or of being selfish, while he believes he is working very hard to take care of things. In his mind, he is fulfilling his gender role and he doesn't understand his partner's dissatisfaction. He works, brings home his pay, and is faithful—what more does she want? She is always creating problems.

In contrast, the woman who feels responsible for the quality of family relationships is hurt and fears she is failing in her gender role. A typical interchange in your office goes something like this:

She: We fought this morning and I couldn't get any work done all day. I thought about the argument and our relationship all the time.

He: I leave my problems at home. I forgot all about it until she reminded me just now.

She very often concludes that he is withholding feelings and rejecting her and the relationship.

But, a hidden affiliative dimension exists in couples' relationships. While a man is to be independent and strong, there is also an unfulfilled need for nurturing and approval (Gordon & Allen, 1990). This need results in a man's hidden dependence on a woman. Male jealousy, for example, is in direct proportion to the perceived threat to his dependency. Masculinity does not permit the acknowledgment of this dependency; rather, it is expressed through controlling his mate, particularly with regard to her expressions of autonomy. In these cases, it is not uncommon for each attempt by a woman to move outside of the home to be countered by sabotage. "How can I go to school at night if when I come home nothing has been done and it's all sitting there for me?" laments a wife and mother trying to earn her degree in the evening.

In summary, even though both partners may not be contributing financially to the relationship equally, both partners may be equal in power because affection and nurturance are highly valued within the marital relationship (Balswick & Balswick, 1995).

Anger

Popular opinion and clinical anecdotes offer that women have trouble with anger and men do not. Popular myths aside, a review of the research literature found: "Neither sex has the advantage in being able to 'identify' anger when they feel it or in releasing it once it is felt" (Tavris, 1982, p. 185). While men and women become angry at the same offenses, for example, condescending treatment, injustice, and attacks to self-esteem, they differ in their perceptions and meanings of these events. Or, in other words, men and women do not always feel angry about the same things. (Tavris, 1982).

Imagine a scene in which the husband is demanding to know why his wife spent so much money on groceries last month. Who will be angry and why? Or, he sits down in front of the television while she spends an hour and a half getting the kids to bed. Or, while paying bills, she points out that he is not making enough money. Or, he tells her she is gaining weight. As we can see, gender roles influence and define what makes us angry.

Gender roles also shape the expression and meaning of anger. Lerner (1988) observes, "The expression of legitimate anger and protest is more than a statement of dignity and self-respect; it is also a statement that one will risk standing alone, even in the face of disapproval of the potential loss of love from others" (p. 63). For women, this statement is contrary to a gender role that values connection and the quality of relationships. Anger not only creates distance but also may threaten connection. Many women deny or minimize their angry feelings because they not only fear hurting their partner but fear they will disrupt this important relationship. When a women expresses her anger, she often also expresses guilt and fear.

The *expression* of anger is a different signal for each sex. For a woman, anger signals that the relationship is in trouble. Her anger is both a concern for the relationship and a fear that her partner has not noticed or is not taking the issue seriously (Low, 1990). Thus, her anger seeks to reconnect or strengthen the connection.

For men, however, anger is a signal for the conflict to stop, his assertion that a boundary has been crossed. It is an attempt to break off contact and increase the separateness (Gottman, 1994). Moreover, his anger may be an attempt to control the interaction—when he gets angry she backs off. In addition, many men fear an escalation of anger because they do not want to be seen as a bully. They, too, are socialized not to explode, especially at women. This explosion and subsequent loss of control can be seen as vulnerability, which is threatening to their manhood or, in the reverse, reaffirms their masculinity.

As a source of power, anger by either partner may influence the partner in unintended ways. The woman's anger attempts to connect and point out a problem in the relationship, and the man's anger attempts to neutralize the disagreement and create distance. For couples particularly vulnerable to this dynamic, their arguments spiral out of control, creating hours or days of silence in the house. For these couples, the expression of anger comes easily, but the resolution of conflict does not.

Conversely, there are couples who "never fight" and who express their anger in passive and often manipulative ways. For these couples, anger is the hidden subtext that simmers beneath a falsely placid surface. When couples hold back anger or express it in counterproductive ways, it is a disempowering, ineffective feeling that can undermine the very fabric of a relationship. However, therapists must not respond to their own interpretations of anger but must carefully listen and appreciate how each partner (1) experiences and (2) communicates his or her anger. Likewise, a therapist only confuses matters by setting an ideal standard for the expression of anger.

Gender Views of Power

Lastly, gender roles shape differential views of power. The masculine perspective of power is associated with competition, domination, and assertiveness. There are winners and losers in the masculine framework. Each man strives to be the winner, even in interpersonal relationships. Winning enhances his position within a relationship.

The feminine power perspective is often conceptualized from a very different point of view. Feminist writers speak about power as an inner strength, or the ability to self-determine. When others are involved, the notion of power then becomes interactional or one of empowerment. Women are often uncomfortable with the notion of "winning" over another person. As each individual in a relationship is empowered (mutual empowerment), only then is the relationship empowered (relational empowerment) (Surrey, 1991).

From a feminist perspective, power is not about winning or losing or about maintaining a status differential. Power (1) is interactional, (2) it enhances mutuality, and (3) it is a status equalizer.

Miller (1986) proposes that women often have a difficult time enhancing their own personal power for three reasons:

1. If women are powerful, they are not enhancing others and therefore may see themselves and be labeled by others as being selfish.
2. If women release their power they will be destructive to their relationships and the environment in which they reside.
3. If women become too personally powerful, the need for others may be diminished. This ignites a fear of abandonment.

Therefore, from a gender perspective power is both conceptualized differently and used for different purposes. For example, when a therapist encourages a partner in couples therapy to become more powerful in the relationship, the therapist and the client need to *clarify exactly what defines power and weigh the effects of a shift of power for the relationship.*

Effects of Power

Men and women attempt to influence others in different ways. Women are more likely than men to use indirect methods of influence, such as pouting, crying, manipulation, or "soft" strategies such as acting nice or flattering the other person. Men, on the other hand, are more likely to use persuasion and reason, and force if necessary (Falbo & Peplau, 1980; Hatfield & Rapson, 1993). These gender differences in communication, however, may have less to do with "innate" differences than with the social norms for expressing power (Carli, 1990; Lakoff, 1990; Lips, 1991).

For example, Carli (1990) found that women used different strategies when speaking with men than when speaking with women. Perceiving men as more powerful, women use indirect strategies to influence a decision. In group discussions, women frequently hesitate and qualify their statements—"I could be wrong, but maybe . . .." Again, this did not reflect passive personality traits but when they qualified their statements and used indirect strategies, women were more likely to be heard by male group members. In doing so, women are careful to not challenge men's status or power (Carli, 1990).

Power imbalances also affect perceptions. Snodgrass (1985) paired men and women in work teams and alternated the assigned leadership role between the men and the women. Regardless of gender, subjects occupying the subordinate's role were more sensitive to the leader's nonverbal signals than the leader was to the follower's cues. Or, in other words, a subordinate develops empathy for superiors. Is a man sensitive and perceptive of others? Of course, when the other is his boss or supervisor.

In reviewing Snodgrass's study, Tavris (1992) observes that because of the power inequity in gender roles, women are intent observers of men, empathic to men's moods and actions. It is a skill that is necessary for survival. In occupying a higher status role, men, on the other hand, have little motivation to empathize with women. Thus, the feminine, relationship-oriented trait that some may argue is biological may instead reflect a social, "self-protective" skill. Or, as Snodgrass (1992) argues, "women's intuition" should really be called "subordinate's intuition."

Finally, returning to the traditional–egalitarian dimension, cross-culture studies show that the happiest marriages are those in which decision-making authority is equally shared (egalitarian) (Gray-Little & Burks, 1983). But power inequities change slowly, despite the evidence that marital satisfaction and stability are associated with relatively equal power in decision making. Proponents of traditional gender roles believe marriages are happiest when the husband "rules the roost" (Hatfeld & Rapson, 1993).

Gay Couples

Although this discussion is based primarily on heterosexual couples, the concepts apply equally to homosexual ones. For example, gender schemas and role theory, traditional and egalitarian relationships, and power have specific relevance to gay couples.

GENDER SCHEMAS AND ROLE THEORY

Gay couples are not immune from the social-psychological construction of gender. Appleby and Anastas (in press) make a distinction between gender identity and sexual orientation. Gender identity, as used above, refers to one's sense of being, male or female. Sexual orientation, however, is the identification with being a *homosexual* male or female. It is an orientation that integrates into a coherent whole one's sexuality, emotionality, and social functioning. Thus, one may possess a homosexual sexual orientation but also be quite traditional in terms of gender role.

In a culture that defines heterosexual sexual orientation as the norm for gender identity, the gay man or woman must construct a homosexual sexual orientation without broad cultural supports and in the face of possible discrimination. At the very least, this may take the form of an absence of support from family and heterosexual acquaintances to, at its worst, a sense of condemnation in terms of job and housing discrimination. Lesbian couples, in particular, face the double discrimination of being both woman and lesbian in our society (Ussher, 1991).

Thus, the very societal pressures that may keep a heterosexual couple together—"What will our families and friends think?"—are the same pressures pulling same-sex couples apart. Even establishing and maintaining a religious involvement becomes an issue for gay and lesbian couples because most religions condemn homosexuality (Keller & Rosen, 1988).

Likewise, the effects of discrimination influence an individual's and couple's decision to remain in the "closet" (Fisher, 1993). Staying in the "closet" eliminates a public statement of one's identity and demonstration of the couple's relationship. The simple act of going to an office party with one's partner must be weighed against the consequences of potential discrimination.

Cultural views of homosexuality range from mild tolerance to condemnation. In a homophobic society a continual message sent to the homosexual is deviance and inferiority. Depending on a number of factors—that is, friends, family, and community support—a sense of inferiority may be internalized (Fisher, 1993; Friedman, 1991). These internalized homophobic attitudes injuriously affect gender identity.

> Among the major deleterious consequences of unconscious homophobia are a sensed lack of entitlement to give and receive love, resulting in irrational efforts to undermine the relationship; and projection of the devalued self-image to the partner who is then made the scapegoat. Internalized homophobia is always organized around shame, guilt, anger, and anxiety. (Friedman, 1991, p. 488)

Homosexual couples by no means avoid the impact of gender roles, particularly with regard to sexual functioning. In same-sex couples, each partner mirrors the other regarding socialization concerning sexual roles. In lesbian couples neither partner is fully comfortable with being sexually aggressive nor with their partner's sexual aggressiveness. Likewise, each gay male partner may want to be the initiator of sex, as defined by the male gender role, leading to a sexual competition where each partner vies to instigate sex (Blumstein & Schwartz, 1983).

TRADITIONAL–EGALITARIAN RELATIONSHIPS

Underlying all discussions of gay and lesbian relationships is the question of whether or not same-gender relationships can or should resemble the cultural norms embodied in heterosexual marriage (Appleby & Anastas, in press). For example, in contrast to traditional heterosexual couples where gender roles define relationship patterns, same-sex couples are able to build relationships based on role equality. Unfortunately, the lack of traditions and role models for such a relationship provide few guidelines for same-sex couples. Consequently, gay and lesbian couples may model their relationships on their families of origin (Fisher, 1993). Thus, the same-sex couples may struggle with their personal definitions of role equality based on the strong influence of family of origin themes.

Freed of the restraints of traditional gender roles that define heterosexual relationships, each homosexual couple defines new egalitarian roles, particularly in the area of sexuality. In the age of AIDS and safe sex, the question of an open or an exclusive sexual relationship is at the heart of the trust issue. Will we be faithful to one another? Do we want a more open relationship?

In their study of American couples, Blumstein and Schwartz (1983) found that women in relationships were the "keepers of fidelity." For women both in heterosexual and homosexual relationships, sex functions as a strong emotional as well as physical bond. Both heterosexual and homosexual men, on the other hand, were less inclined to the emotional side of sex and were thus more likely to seek sexual variety. Serial monogamy is more common in gay men's relationship patterns than in the heterosexual population (Ussher, 1991). Again, without traditional boundaries of gender expectations, gay couples evolve their own definitions of egalitarian sexual practices.

POWER

More specifically, money and property for all couples serve as means of defining power in a relationship. The traditional, breadwinning husband's job comes first because it pays the bills. The husband's needs come first because he pays the bills. The husband works and supports the family while the wife takes care of the home. While these traditional stereotypes place women in a subservient position of power, the roles do provide guidelines for behavior.

In gay and lesbian relationships without the formal sanction of legal marriage and the accompanying laws defining joint property, the issue of finances and ownership of property becomes more precarious. Without the guidelines inherent in the marital relationship, the issues of money and property may divide a couple. For example, because earning power is central to a man's identity, gay men's relationships suffer when one partner has a larger income than the other (Blumstein & Schwartz, 1983). It is as if a higher income gives one partner a symbolic advantage, thus creating tension regarding providing for and being provided for.

Lesbian couples, on the other hand, are in a double bind. They value a sense of mutual dependency but do not want a partner who is completely relationship-centered. Instead, lesbians want a partner who will be relationship-oriented but also strong and ambitious in the outside world (Blumstein & Schwartz, 1983).

Overall in gay relationships, although there is no expectation based on gender that one person will be the decision maker, the partner who has more resources—in particular, a higher income—tends to have more power.

Summary

To summarize, while sex is genetically determined, gender—our definitions of masculine and feminine—is socially constructed. Gender divides our society by contrasting what we label male and female and proceeds to attribute qualities based on the differentiation. But it is not just differences we are describing, because in those "differences" are the norms for relationships, role requirements, and political and economic distinctions.

Bem (1985, 1993) argues that hidden assumptions about sex and gender are embedded in the culture and systematically reproduce a male status hierarchy generation after generation. These "lenses of gender" take three forms:

1. *Androcentrism or male centeredness*: The male experience is the norm or the standard by which to measure normality.
2. *Gender polarization*: Men and women are fundamentally different and the differentiation of roles evolves accordingly.
3. *Biological essentialism*: To rationalize and legitimize the above lenses, the biological differences between men and women are emphasized lending "scientific" credibility to gender roles.

In a key distinction, Bem (1993) does not deny biological differences between men and women but points out that these "facts" have no meaning in and of themselves. Rather, society imputes meanings to these facts. For example, society may value intelligence and logical abilities. To maintain the power structure, we attribute these qualities to men. To rationalize our position, we create an artificial dichotomy and point to incidences where men are logical and women "emotional." To further legitimize and reinforce our position, we will search and find biological sex differences.

Investigating the belief of innate sex roles—men are born to be ambitious and aggressive and by nature women are happiest when making a home and caring for children—Mirowsky and Ross (1987) found that this belief is greatest in individuals who prefer the traditional system of sex roles and sex stratification. And, not surprisingly, the average husband believes in innate sex roles more than his wife does. The researchers concluded that the belief in innate sex roles provides an ideological justification for a sex-based hierarchical system and since men benefit from the system more than women, husbands tend to believe more than wives. Interestingly, context again appears in that the findings showed a correlation within the couples—that is, the more one partner believes in innate sex roles the more the spouse also believes. This correlational finding, however, does not explain the causes. Perhaps men and women marry someone who is similar on this value dimension? Perhaps a woman adopts her husband's belief to minimize conflict and preserve the relationship? Or, perhaps the husband and wife mutually shape one another's views over time?

Overall, despite popular beliefs, few sex differences have been empirically demonstrated in the literature. Instead, the context in which the behavior occurs overwhelms any supposed "differences" (Tavris, 1992). In terms of intimate relationships, men can be sensitive to others, women can speak assertively, men can express emotion, and women can effectively problem-solve. These behaviors, therefore, become dependent on the context and the couples' motivation and ability to nurture satisfying behaviors.

The behavior of men and women around us merges with cultural beliefs and values to form our personal gender schemas. Do all men think about all women the same way? Or, do all women think about all men the same way? Of course not! We each have our unique thumbprint. From a macro to micro systems viewpoint cultural biases influence social (ethnic) values that impact family of origin dynamics that underlie a couple's personal history. Thus,

GENDER SCHEMA = CULTURE + ETHNICITY + FAMILY OF ORIGIN + COUPLE HISTORY

From a therapeutic perspective, a therapist does not stand outside of his or her culture. Cultural gender biases are our biases to one degree or another. As we saw from the previous review, even "scientific" opinion is embedded within cultural contexts. But, this is not to leave the discussion of gender differences on an academic plane. Couples therapists struggle daily with gender "differences" in their offices to the point where, as we will discuss later, stereotypic gender roles produce stereotypic couples' conflicts. But, first and foremost, a therapist, in the role of mental health expert, possesses the power to define the problem.

In couples therapy, the power to define the problem assumes great significance. More often than not, couples present dichotomous views of their problem. "He is cold and unemotional. He never discusses what he is feeling." "She gets emotional at the drop of a hat. I never know what mood she will be in and she always wants to talk, on and on and on." At these moments, the couple may be trapped in their own gender biases, but the therapist's own gender beliefs and biases also enter the picture. Is the man too unemotional and uncommunicative? Should therapy focus on his inadequacies in these areas? Is the woman too emotional and dependent? Should therapy foster her independence and more appropriate assertiveness? Without realizing it, a therapist may fall prey to the polarity view of gender differences.

As a means of conceptualizing the discussion of gender, Figure 2.1 (p. 24) views the definition of gender as a series of embedded circles of influence. The outer circle represents the influence of the culture to define gender. Cultural norms pervade the media, business, legal, and family hierarchical structures. The next circle represents ethnic influences. (Again, ethnicity is a combination of race, religion, and cultural history [McGoldrick, Giordano, & Pearce, 1996; Phinney, 1996].) Ethnicity may be a powerful influence in defining and reinforcing gender roles, particularly the role of women (McGoldrick, Anderson, & Walsh, 1989; McGoldrick et al., 1982). The next circle refers to the couples' unique families of origins. Did gender divide family chores? Did gender define responsibilities? What was the relationship like between each set of parents? The circle closest to the center represents the couples' unique history. Over time, each member of a couple influences the other. Each has taught the other about gender on a personal level. Finally, each member of the couple is represented by an individual circle, because each member carries into the relationship a personal history of gender, a personal history that includes experiences and opinions about masculinity and femininity.

In summary, from a social-psychological perspective, gender is an arbitrary, ever-changing, socially constructed set of attributes. The quote from the coed rugby player in Chapter 1 attests to changing definitions. We doubt whether a similar quote could have been found 10 years ago. Still, socially ascribed roles are powerful predictors of behavior and change slowly—or, some might say, not at all. Perhaps Tavris (1992) captures it best when she identifies an inherent paradox in socially constructed gender roles, "Both sexes play their gender roles to perfection and then lament their consequences and fight over them" (p. 268).

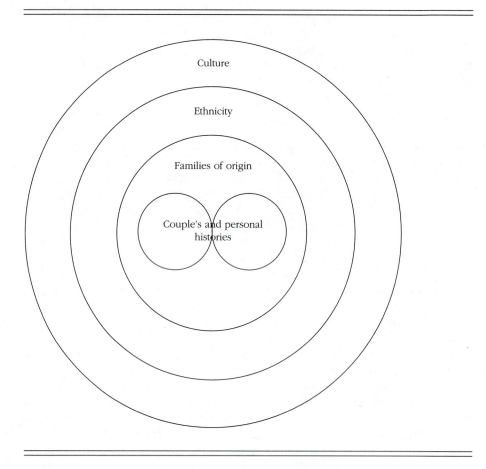

F I G U R E   2.1   Social-Psychological Influences on Gender

CHAPTER THREE

Differences in Experience

As referenced in the previous chapter, egalitarian relationships emerge in industrialized societies in which women have equal opportunity to education and employment. However, even in cultures endorsing egalitarian roles, traditional gender roles exert considerable influence over interpersonal behavior. Specifically, men are still more likely to make decisions of importance and have the "last word" (Best & Williams, 1993).

Furthermore, cultures socially construct masculine and feminine gender roles. Even though culture may dictate via laws that males and females should be treated as equals in all areas, gender roles are still internalized in terms of gender identity (schemas). These gender identities define what it means to be male or female and influence our views of ourselves, our behavior, and others' reactions to us. Thus, socially constructed gender roles lead to different experiences for each sex. Identifying and understanding these different experiences highlights what couples bring into therapy.

The following chapter introduces the reader to these different experiences. First, a sample of clinical theories conceptualizes the differences in experience; next, results from empirical studies identify demonstrated differences.

Psychology of Men and Women

PSYCHOLOGY OF MEN

Because of its extensive influence on later thought, the work of Freud offers an early 20th-century, "scientific" perspective on gender differences. In his *Three Essays on the Theory of Sexuality*, Freud endorsed Krafft-Ebing's view that each individual is born with a bisexual disposition and is endowed with masculine and feminine brain centers (Gay, 1989). These masculine and feminine traits are easily recognizable in childhood, but at puberty a sharp distinction is established between masculine and feminine personality characteristics. The origins of these distinctions can be found in the anatomical sex differences discovered in early childhood. (The following briefly summarizes Freud's ideas based primarily in his *Three Essays on the Theory of Sexuality* and his 1925 article *Some Psychical Consequences of the Anatomical Distinction Between the Sexes* [Gay, 1989]. The reader is specifically referred to the latter article because it elaborates on Freud's views of the difference between men and women, but it also puts forth his controversial view that anatomy powerfully shapes gender differences.)

Both boys and girls progress in similar ways through the early oral and anal psychosexual stages of development. About the age of 4, however, the genitals become the source of sexual pleasure and curiosity. For Freud, this is the beginning of the phallic stage of development. At the completion of this stage, the boy identifies with the father's masculinity.

Briefly, Freud's emphasis on sexuality places the mother as the first and central figure in a child's life; consequently, she is the initial sexual object for the boy. The father, on the other hand, is viewed as a rival for the mother's affections, a rivalry so intense that the son wishes to do away with the father. The intensity of the rivalry spawns a fear that the father is too powerful a rival and that he will castrate the son. The son, recognizing the futility of his struggle, relinquishes his obsession with mother and affectionately identifies with father.

This fear of castration, or castration anxiety, destroys the Oedipus complex. The emotional, sexually driven attraction to mother is broken. During this process, the boy separates from the infantile bonds with his mother and embraces the masculinity of his father. In so doing, the primitive, infantile sexual attachment to mother is replaced in the boy's psyche by a higher order superego—our conscience, our sense of right and wrong. The boy has obtained a higher level of maturity as reason now rules over primitive impulses and emotions.

Freud, however, had a theoretical dilemma. If the mother is the first and primary attachment and sexual object, how does one explain the girl's sexual desires for her father and the resolution of those feelings and the development of femininity? His solution was the differences in anatomy.

When the boy first observes a girl's genital area, he interprets this as his worst fear, the result of castration. For the girl, the boy's penis graphically displays her own inadequacy and inspires her envy. "They [girls] notice the penis of a brother or playmate, strikingly visible and of large proportions, at once recognize it as the superior counterpart of their own small and inconspicuous organ, and from that time forward fall a victim to envy for the penis" (Freud in Gay, 1989, p. 673).

This desire for and envy of the penis may result in several outcomes (to be fair, Freud believed the penis was biologically essential to sexual functioning and propagation; thus its importance). For some women, penis envy is a block to their development of femininity—"Thus a girl may refuse to accept the fact of being castrated, may harden herself in the conviction that she does possess a penis, and may subsequently be compelled to behave as though she were a man" (Freud in Gay, 1989, p. 674). Or, what is more likely the case, the girl recognizes her anatomical inferiority and gives up her wish for a penis, instead wishing for a child by her father—the beginnings of femininity.

Anatomical differences also serve to justify "character" differences between men and women. As was stated above, for the boy the resolution of the Oedipus complex motivated by the fear of castration is replaced in his psyche by a more highly developed superego—one that emphasizes reason and control over impulses and feelings. Within Freud's theoretical framework, however, girls enter the world castrated and therefore never fully resolve the phallic stage. That is to say, a woman does not have to renounce her attachment to her mother and thus never develops a superego equal to a man's—a superego that would overrule emotional impulses.

Given Freud's theoretical line of reasoning, it is easy to understand the context for the following quote concerning the differences between men and women. "Character-traits which *critics of every epoch have brought up against women* [our italics]—that they show less sense of justice than men, that they are less ready to submit to the great exigencies of life, that they are more often influenced in their judgments by feelings of affection or hostility—all these would be amply accounted for by the modification in the formation of their super-ego" (Gay, 1989, p. 677). The quote, although couched in "scientific thought," clearly reflects the cultural norms of Freud's time. Freud, it would seem, developed a scientific justification for the status quo of socially constructed gender relationships.

In summary, from a Freudian perspective, masculinity and femininity are rooted in anatomical sex differences and infantile sexuality. A boy's original, sexually laden attachment to his mother is severed through his competition with his father and his fear of castration—a castration that is visible in girls. This fear motivates his renouncement of his attachment to his mother and strengthens his identification with his father. He will be like his father and will incorporate his father's masculine behavior into his own.

Shifting to more contemporary writings, current opinions of masculinity carry hints of Freud's ideas blended with recent sociological views of men. From a social historical perspective of American society of the past 250 years, current gender differences are rooted in the late 18th-century and early 19th-century social and economic shifts from an agricultural-based economy and social life to changes placed in motion by the Industrial Revolution (Cancian, 1989; Rotundo, 1993).

In colonial, agricultural New England before 1800 and through the early decades of the 19th century, contemporary gender wisdom supported inequality before the law and in the household. Men were expected to be pleasant, mild-mannered, reasonable, and devoted to their communities. Women were seen as susceptible to more base passions such as ambition, defiance, and envy. Because men possessed greater reasoning abilities as opposed to women who were seen as ruled by their emotions, the power of the community was entrusted into their hands (Rotundo, 1993).

Despite the accumulation of power within men's hands, gender roles were not polarized (Cancian, 1989). Both men and women were equal contributors to the economics of the home. Husbands and wives performed similar economic tasks and shared the job of caring for family members. Men and women were dependent on each other materially and emotionally with the family closely integrated into the agricultural community. All tasks were essential for the family's economic well-being.

Overlapping this time period and extending into the middle and later decades of the 19th century, the Industrial Revolution and the development of a middle-class market economy produced significant shifts in gender roles. Male identity was no longer defined as the benevolent head of the household and upholder of the common good but as the individual man out to prove his worth in the world, in the marketplace.

As fathers left the home, their vacuum was filled by women. Women became the guardians of the common good and were in charge of socializing the children (a woman's identity was thus tied to the behavior of her children) and running the home. In this redefinition of roles, women were now seen as possessing inherent virtues. Women were not inferior to men as much as *different* from them—a difference that would still justify inequities in the law.

With the father gone, home became an increasingly domestic world where women set the tone. Close, expressive relationships developed between women within the household and in cooperation with other women in the community. Women's identity evolved within this setting of mutually supporting relationships. In contrast, the individualistic, capitalistic work world placed a premium on shifting male alliances to further individual gain. Friendships and supporting relationships were secondary to business networking. Thus, men were trained in power and influence and women cooperated and submitted.

By the 1840s the split between "the home" as the feminine sphere and "the work" as the masculine sphere was deepening (Cancian, 1989). Men carried the economic burden for the home into an impersonal, competitive marketplace, while women focused on the care of their children and their husbands. Men developed "public" relationships based on cooperation and competition for personal gain. Women fostered "private" relationships where love and compassion ruled.

Even though a man's identity was equated with success in the material world, he could still long for a respite, a castle to which to retreat. His spouse, therefore, was valued for running a good home and for being different from the outside world—that is, submissive. A woman's submissiveness was appealing and was a sharp contrast to the struggles for dominance in the marketplace. The docile, submissive wife would be rewarded with economic security (Rotundo, 1993).

Thus, by the mid-19th century gender roles were shaped that better fit the Industrial Revolution and free market society. Men would be independent, rational, aggressive, and in control of their emotions—traits rewarded in the work world. Women would guard the heart of the family; they would provide a respite for men from the competitive marketplace and would raise the children. Men and women were no longer equally involved in child-rearing. The wife's duty was to develop the children's character. To reinforce this mission, motherhood became the ultimate definition of being a woman (Cancian, 1989).

Recent writings on the psychology of men echo the consequences of the loss of the father figure to the Industrial Revolution and the creation of the emotionally confining male role needed to compete in the marketplace. It appears that an underlying question in recent literature is "What's wrong with men?" Characteristically the problem is portrayed in the stereotypical view of the emotionally repressed, noncommunicative man—the man who throws himself into work, is emotionally cut off from his own feelings, and fails to nurture those around him, especially his mate and children. More specifically, he is the man who completely resists therapy and is always the empty chair in family sessions. From reading the literature one gets a sense that all men suffer from the disease of maleness to one degree or another. To highlight these themes, we offer the mythopoetic men's movement and revisions of the masculine gender roles as examples.

In the late 1980s and early 1990s the mythopoetic men's movement captured the public's imagination. Led by Iron John (Bly, 1992), men discovered the Wild Man within—a Wild Man who could integrate nurturing and aggression. For Bly (1992) the love unit most damaged by the Industrial Revolution was the father-son bond. In an agricultural community, jointly working a family farm created a bond between a father and son. Not only were they engaged in a cooperative enterprise, but the son had the opportunity to learn from his father, succeed in his father's eyes, and be recognized accordingly (the farm was passed on to the son). With the onset of the Industrial Revolution, however, economics pushed men off the farms and into factories. Bly believes the young boys lost not only the emotional security of their father but also the participation of older males in their lives as they were left at home in feminine hands.

Without the participation in initiation rites with older males, men became increasingly insecure and longed for their fathers. Because this was to be an unmet hunger, men denied their accompanying feelings of grief and anger at the loss of their fathers, threw themselves into work and began the cycle of emotional detachment (Bly, 1992). Emotional detachment—denying and isolating oneself from one's feelings—protected men from their psychic wounds. Unfortunately, the consequence was the legacy of stoic, emotionally repressed masculinity. Thus, men may be accused of not expressing their feelings when in actuality they may not know what their feelings are or how to access them. As Bly stated, "Some women feel hurt when a man will not 'express his feelings,' and they conclude that he is holding back, or 'telling them something' by such withholding; but it's more likely that when such a man asks a question of his chest, he gets no answer at all" (Bly, 1992).

According to the mythopoetic men's movement, a man must grieve the loss of his father, celebrate and in the process affirm his masculinity, and discover his hidden, emotional side—an emotional side that allows him to care deeply and passionately, combining tenderness and strength.

This unmet hunger for a father's involvement and affirmation, or father hunger, is a frequent, contemporary theme in the psychology of men. Pittman (1993) viewed it as the root of the disorder he calls masculopathology, or the masculine role taken to excess. For men who long for and lack the love and approval of their father, adopting an excessive male role is a defense against their own fears of inadequacy—an inadequacy based on the lack of affirmation of the man's maleness by a father. (It is assumed that only a man can give this affirmation of masculinity to another man.)

This fragile male identity has direct consequence for the couple. Borrowing an underlying Freudian theme, a boy who has not had the involvement of a father never fully resolves the oedipal crisis. The struggle to separate from the mother is never complete because of the father's absence. Consequently, a fragile, tenuous self-identity evolves that masks the fears of dependence on and dominance by the mother figure. To defend against these fears, a veneer of masculinity is created borrowing from cultural models of masculinity. The fears, however, exaggerate and distort masculine behavioral patterns. Macho behavior and having others react to the "manly" behavior reassures the jerry-built sense of masculinity.

Consequently, feminine-defined qualities or interests are avoided by these men. Intimacy with a woman is risky because she may engulf and threaten the fragile male identity. Not only is emotional intimacy avoided, but a woman's anger cannot be tolerated; it is as if the man's mother has come back to take his puberty away (Pittman, 1993).

To compensate for these fears, masculopathology turns boys into one of three types: philanderers, contenders, or controllers (Pittman, 1993).

1. Philanderers fear women but depend on them to define their masculinity. Seducing or pursuing one woman after another is a way of managing the fear and continually reaffirming one's masculinity. A long-term intimate relationship, however, is avoided, because it risks engulfment and the subsequent loss of masculinity. Love them and leave them is the battle cry.

2. Contenders have not given up the desire for a father's approval and dedicate their lives to competition with other boys. On the field of battle they will win the king's approval, even though the king is only a creation of their mind and therefore no victory is truly satisfying. Competition thus becomes an end in and of itself. Women basically are there to nurse the men's wounds and keep the home fires burning, essential for nurturing but not for sharing intimacies.

3. Controllers will protect their masculinity by controlling all that they purview. No area is left unnoticed, be it work, spouses, or children. Through an active sense of control, power bolsters and protects a fragile male identity. Women pose no threat as long as they can be controlled.

In summary, from the individual psychological perspective, a boy incorporates, observes, identifies with, and imitates the older men he sees around him. The key emotional relationship, however, is the father-son bond. For Freud, this was a rivalry essential to resolving the boy's oedipal attachment to mother and fostering masculinity. The importance of the father's involvement in a son's life is underlined by contemporary writers, who portray father hunger as a primary motivational force in men's lives. Taken together, however, the development of a sense of masculinity and the definition of what is masculinity is passed from father or father figure to boy, a male chain of affirmation.

PSYCHOLOGY OF WOMEN

Sigmund Freud

As was just outlined, Freud's view of gender differences strongly reflects a historical-sociological context. He saw differences between men and women and employed his developing theory of psychoanalysis to explain these differences. Women, however, did not fare well in his analysis.

Believing that both boys and girls progress in similar patterns through the early oral and anal psychosexual stages of development, Freud theorized that masculinity and femininity are dramatically shaped in the phallic stage. In short, as the child begins to discover the genital area as a source of pleasure about age 4, girls discover that boys possess a penis, which becomes a source of envy, an envy Freud referred to as the "masculinity complex of women."

This masculinity complex must be resolved if the woman's development is to progress. To do so, the girl must accept the fact that she is castrated and that she will not be and is not a man. This recognition and acceptance of anatomical differences between the sexes forces the girl away from masculinity and toward femininity. Consequently, the girl gives up her wish for a penis and replaces it with a desire for a male child—and, in her fantasies, a male child fathered by her own father. Thus, the father has now replaced the mother as the love object and the girl's feelings toward her mother are now ones of jealousy, a jealousy that Freud believed persists as a character trait in women.

This transition is not without additional costs to women. As Freud stated:

> After a woman has become aware of the wound to her narcissism, she develops, like a scar, a sense of inferiority. When she has passed beyond her first attempt at explaining her lack of a penis as being a punishment personal to herself and has realized that that sexual character is a universal one, she begins to share the contempt felt by men for a sex which is the lesser in so important a respect, and, at least in holding that opinion, insists on being like a man. (Freud in Gay, 1989, p. 674)

In light of all that we have discussed to this point, it is difficult to avoid editorializing on Freud's quote. Words such as *inferiority, contempt,* and *lesser* when referring to women jump right off the page. We chose this quote not to demean Freud's work or to belittle his brilliant accomplishments and insights into the human mind, but to emphasize that no one escapes his or her cultural context and that the subtlety of gender roles pervades clinical theory and practice.

Freud developed his theories from direct clinical observations that were embedded in a specific cultural context. His societal influences emphasized an upper middle-class clientele with an intense maternal relationship and an equally intense and powerful, but distant, father figure. Within this limited sociodemographic sample, Freud pronounced his findings to be universal. This pronouncement and the early popularity of psychoanalysis as a basis for personality structure helped entrench this theoretical system as the bedrock for many contemporary theories.

That Freud gave short shrift to female development, and then only as an analog to male development, has long been a feminist criticism of psychoanalytic theory. Scholars and students of the psychology of women distinguish themselves by debating two broad issues in the body of psychological literature: (1) the valuation of the male phallus as a developmental concern for both sexes, challenging the assumption that anatomy is destiny, and (2) the inequality (political, social, intellectual, and emotional) for the feminine gender role.

Attempting to redress traditional analytic thinking on the development of femininity, more recent psychoanalytic theorists have developed differing views of early female sexual development and its effect on the young girl's conceptualization of her feminine gender identity. (For a short but thorough summation of the development of psychoanalytic thought and feminine development, see Chehrazi, 1987.) For example, as opposed to the masculinity complex, little girls between the ages of 2 and 4 develop a sense of their own genitalia that is grounded within a more general sense of gender identity. This identity formation results not in a sense of trauma and inadequacy but in a growing awareness and appreciation of "femaleness." In other words, a little girl experiences early on a valuation of what she has and not an undying envy for what she does not have (Chehrazi, 1987).

Contemporary theorists also broaden the lens to weigh the influence of society in general and more specifically, cultural and familial influences. Thus, personality and ego development are not merely a consequence of innate biological drives but emerge through the interaction of biological drives and the social environment. For instance, if the parental (and by extension, familial) environment is supportive, the little girl is encouraged to value her own genitalia within the context of her femininity. However, if the surrounding environment (familial and cultural) devalues the female and the feminine experience, then the little girl will learn to devalue herself.

Finally, ego psychologists added two additional perspectives relevant to the psychology of women: (1) the individual has the capacity to receive and organize environmental stimuli to adaptive capacities and (2) individual development is viewed as an adaptive social-relational experience. Thus, with this outlook, all ego and personality development is that of a self in relation in which social and interpersonal experiences have various psychological meanings and interpretations. Males and females experience different interpersonal environments and family practices that, in turn, create different relational needs and occupy them with different issues (Chodorow, 1978). These interpersonal experiences begin with the earliest caretakers and parental figures and transpose themselves to other family members and, in later life, to lovers, mates, and one's own children.

The above is a rudimentary summation of the psychoanalytic treatment of feminine development. In addition we have outlined generally what a feminist theoretical framework might encompass. The next sections present several major feminist scholars who have profoundly affected the development of feminist theoretical perspectives and therapeutic approaches. We realize this choice of theorists is selective and is certainly not meant to be exhaustive, yet we hope that the broad themes of feminist thought are clearly outlined.

The feminist writers discussed in the following sections asked a series of questions that are important for practicing clinicians to keep in mind when working with couples. Chodorow (1978) asked not why women do mother, but why men do not. Miller (1986) examined models of mental health and asked not why women don't separate and individuate, but why men are not more relationally focused. Gilligan (1982), in examining women's moral development, asked not why women are so concerned with helping others (the logic of care), but why men are so unconcerned with cooperation and mutuality (the logic of justice). Finally, Lerner (1988) supported the work of feminist psychoanalytic theorists but challenges their linear focus on the mother-child dyad by highlighting women's development within multiple contexts.

Nancy Chodorow

Chodorow (1978) broadened the psychoanalytic lens to include socioeconomic variables. She argued that all societies have a social organization of economic production that feeds some form of sex/gender system in which the organization of gender is socially constructed and systematically reproduced in a way fundamental to the organization of that particular society. By and large, the division of labor is centered around two genders and an assumption of heterosexual marriage. Moreover, this division of labor is reinforced by creating appropriate gender roles at two levels: (1) within society and (2) within the family.

While recognizing that the assignment of caretaking duties to females has been present historically throughout all societies and remains closely linked to the uniquely female capacities of birth giving and lactation, Chodorow (1978) believed that women's mothering had been the defining issue in male dominance and female submissive gender roles:

> Women's mothering is a central and defining feature of the social organization of gender and is implicated in the construction and reproduction of male dominance itself . . . domestic and public aspects of social organization can be distinguished in all societies . . . with mothers and children forming the core of domestic organization . . . with these ties assumed to be natural and biological . . . men are also involved with particular domestic units, but men find a primary social location in the public sphere. (p. 8)

Returning to our earlier question—why men don't mother—Chodorow argued that mothering is a psychological process encouraged in women and not men and that it affects not only women's individual lives, but the ideology that is constructed about women. This ideology centers on the concept of women "as mothers" and therefore fosters sexual inequality through a division of labor engendered by societal expectations. If women are seen as biologically preordained to bear and raise children, then domestic duties should be their assignment—the private sphere of home.

The public sphere, therefore, is reserved for men. This defines society as masculine—that is to say, masculine values dominate—which in turn sustains men's power behind institutions of social and political control. From this viewpoint public domain dominates private, which is biological and natural, and because men dominate in the public domain, therefore men dominate women.

Chodorow also claimed that social role expectations alone do not account for mothering behavior. Instead, mothering is an internalized psychological phenomenon for women, built through developmental experiences with their own mothers in their own families. For example, a girl does not absolutely change her love object but remains in connection to the mother and merely adds the father to form a type of love triangle. Males, therefore, become the primary "erotic" object, but not the primary "emotional bond." The intensity of the early mother-daughter relationship precludes severance by the presence of the father. Moreover, the intensity of the mother-daughter relationship creates complex relational needs in women.

Because of the socialization differences between men and women, women's complex relational needs are more likely to be met through supportive relationships with other women, through a desire for a child, or through both means. A child completes the emotional triangle women initially experienced with their own mothers and fathers. The early experience of being mothered by a woman produces in daughters: (1) an identification with their mothers, (2) an expectation that women naturally take care of children, and (3) a belief that women's maternal qualities extend to all women's work. Thus the cycle of women as primary parent is regenerated and reproduced with each succeeding generation. This cycle sets a woman's place in the domestic domain of emotional life and relationships within the family.

Finally, when women idealize men and fashion their lives around them, it is not because of intense love and devotion, but more from a need to survive as a member of a subordinate group. A need exists, therefore, to believe that their man is strong and competent enough to protect them and continue their dependency, both economic and emotional.

Jean Baker Miller

Miller (1986) wrote simultaneously on two levels about women's development. On a macro level, she addressed societal and cultural characteristics that she believes perpetuate the status of women as unequal. On a micro level, she assessed the impact of social inequality on the individual.

Unlike Chodorow, Miller did not analyze the how or why of social inequality; instead, she began from the premise that it exists. For example, because males are the dominant group in society, the masculine gender role defines what is culturally, sociologically, and psychologically "normal." As a result, individuation and separation are valued processes. Furthermore, maturity lies in successful recognition and repression of excessive dependency needs.

Within this context of domination and subordination, the issues of power and conflict are paramount. Unequal power relationships are inherent within the paradigm. The dominant group is often unaware of and therefore perpetuates the inequality under the guise of the "natural" or traditional way of relating and accomplishing tasks. Furthermore, because the dominant group defines acceptable characteristics and roles for the subordinate group, women are assigned psychological characteristics that both please men and perpetuate weakness and immaturity. Women, in order to survive with the dominant culture and to appear well adjusted, become very aware of and reactive to men's needs and wants.

Occupying a subordinate position within the dominant (normal) male culture, women are in a permanent position of inequality, reacting to and nurturing the dominant group's needs. Women as individuals do not have direct integration with reality, but for them, reality is mediated by serving others' needs. Women, therefore, develop a sense of self through maintaining those connections and affiliations.

A sense of self through relationships is Miller's micro and second level of analysis:

> Women's sense of self becomes very much organized around being able to make and then maintain affiliations and relationships . . . affiliation is valued as

highly as, or more highly than, self enhancement . . . individual development proceeds only by means of connection. (Miller, 1986, p. 83)

As women develop themselves through serving others' needs and maintaining those connections, they begin to see their own needs as mirroring those of significant others: parents, spouses, children, and employing organizations. Women learn to not recognize their own needs or to act as an independent agent to meet those needs.

A woman, however, may face a dilemma. If serving others is woven into a sense of self, then recognizing her own needs may raise several fears. First, she may lose the position of "weakness" that offers her "protection"—"If I do what I want, he will be angry and reject me." Second, when she is serving others she knows she is "pleasing" and therefore aspiring toward perfection and more connection in her relationships. Striving to meet her own needs diminishes her illusion of perfection and her self-esteem. Finally, meeting her own needs sets in motion a feeling of separation and aloneness that diminishes the feeling of connection necessary for her continued development. This separation can connote not just a loss of a relationship but a serious threat to the integrity of a sense of self.

In summary, in occupying a subordinate role in the male-dominated culture, women gain protection by ascribing to their assigned roles and develop a sense of self through relationships. This "other" orientation mitigates against a woman recognizing and acting to fulfill her own needs while being judged by the quality of her relationships.

Carol Gilligan

As detailed above, Freud believed that because women do not experience castration anxiety and thus do not realize a clear-cut oedipal resolution (separation from the mother figure) as men do, women possess a less developed superego (our sense of morality). Later theoreticians and researchers (Kohlberg, 1981; Piaget, 1965) proposed theories of moral development based on observations of boys and young men and extrapolated these conclusions to apply to women (Gilligan, 1982). To correct this imbalance, Gilligan (1982) investigated women's sense of morality.

Gilligan described the making of a moral decision as making a choice and taking responsibility for that choice. When women feel excluded from participation or power in society, they often do not see the choices before them. They instead rely on a consensus made by those men on whom they depend for protection and support. In this way women hope that by pleasing those men who offer support, the women will be loved and cared for. For Gilligan, a woman's moral choices arise from conflicting responsibilities to others, in contrast to men who focus on what is right based on logic, reasoning, and absolute rights.

In making a moral choice, women must separate the voice of self from the voice of others. Because of their role in society, women must learn to balance care for the self and care for others and acknowledge the fear that this balancing may cause hurt to someone. Any moral conflict resolution requires a mode of thinking that shifts the criterion for judgment back and forth from goodness (to others) to truth (the needs of the self). Where men may rely on abstract conceptualizations of right and wrong, women weigh the impact and consequences to others. Or, in other words, men separate themselves from a moral decision and make it an abstraction, whereas women must consider others and thus personalize that decision.

In moral development, women demonstrate a continuity of relationships in their lives. This presents a deviation from the norm in categories that are based on the male experience of separation. Women will change the rules of a situation to preserve the relationships involved; men abide by the rules and often see relationships as replaceable.

Harriet Goldhor Lerner

The richness of psychoanalytic theory permits its application to a host of areas and a variety of interpretations. Much of the contemporary psychology of women literature, as reviewed above, applies psychoanalytic principles but from a feminist perspective. For example, the importance of the mother-daughter relationship is central in traditional psychoanalytic thought and feminist psychoanalytic thought. Both perspectives accept the developmental differences between boys and girls whereby boys are differentiating from the maternal figure and developing a "self" apart from her, while girls are developing a sense of self in relation to mother. Thus both agree that gender differences are polarized. Men and women are different because of the divergent psychosexual paths each one takes.

Although she applauded the contributions of feminist psychoanalytic theorists, particularly for bringing the value of empathic relatedness and the description of the relational self to the forefront, Lerner (1988) raised several thoughtful concerns. First, psychoanalytic thought views development as a linear process whereby the actions of the mother directly shape and influence the child. Instead, Lerner believes this to be a reciprocal process—the mother influences the child, and the child influences the mother. For example, a mother with a colicky baby will react differently to the baby than if the baby had an easy temperament. Lerner then broadens the lens, viewing a child growing up within a family, within a community, within a society. How can a mother-child dyad be understood without appreciating the broader context?

The consequence of viewing a woman's development from a psychoanalytic, mother-focused, linear viewpoint is that the child's behavior is implicitly the mother's responsibility (Lerner, 1988). Endorsing this position not only lays the foundation for blaming mother for all ills, but it also absolves the father and other family members from any responsibility.

Second, emphasizing the differences between the sexes as a result of "separate but equal" lines of development inadvertently reinforces traditional gender roles. Women are more nurturing and relationship oriented. Men are more independent and function better in the broader world. Women are made to be at home taking care of children and men are meant to bring home the bacon.

Finally, supporting traditional gender differences also supports dominant and subordinate groupings. The public, economic sphere belongs to men and the private, economic-dependent, child-centered home belongs to women. This sociopolitical context sharply contrasts with basing gender differences primarily on early childhood stages of development.

Overall, Lerner (1988) supported the work of feminist psychoanalytic theorists but questioned their linear focus on the mother-child dyad. For Lerner, women's development takes place in the multiple variable world of family and sociopolitical contexts, contexts involving reciprocal interactions. Furthermore, by presupposing that men's and women's development is inherently different, psychoanalytic thinking emphasizes the differences between the sexes and fails to address the differences within each sex. For example, some men may be relationship oriented (male therapists?), and some women may be fiercely independent. In summary, the psychoanalytic position continually places the mother at the center of a woman's development to the neglect of broader sociocultural factors.

Specific Differences in Experience

Although differing in their explanations, the above theoretical perspectives would agree that men and women traditionally occupy separate roles within the society. These roles reflect the broad societal-cultural tasks of production and reproduction. Specifically, men's domain is the public, production sphere where independence, assertiveness, and control of emotions are valued. In part because of the ability to bear children, women have been assigned private, reproductive roles in which relationships are valued and fostered. (Feminist theorists, discussed above, have sought to redress the cultural imbalance of gender biases that favor men's development as normal by underlining and praising women's relational abilities.)

Traditionally, this role differentiation has resulted in power differences, or what is commonly referred to as the "Golden Rule": He or she who has the gold makes the rules. Cancian (1989) argued that with the split between home—a woman's place—and work—a man's world—what women did at home was defined as love. Love and home were private, disassociated from the public world. Love was thus associated with tenderness, expression of emotion, and vulnerability: the jurisdiction of women. Cancian (1989) points out that equating women's home-based activities with love and men's activities with work widens the perceptions of gender differences. Not only were men's activities more highly valued—"Hey, who do you think pays for all of this?" —but women's labor was not labor but love. Hence, tending children, cleaning the house, and making the meals were labors of love.

Despite movement toward egalitarian roles, traditional role differentiation is still prominent. Jensen, McGhie, and Jensen (1991) gave 56 couples a list of adjectives and asked them to circle those that described characteristics they felt were important for a person to possess. Women preferred compromise to power, mercy to justice, feelings to facts, and cooperative ability to competitive ability. As for the emphasis on relationships, when men and women were asked to identify events considered distressing, women reported distress regarding life crises occurring in family members, friends, and neighbors, while men seldom mentioned such events (Kessler & McLeod, 1984). However, when crises affect one's spouse or children, men do appear as distressed as women, but they do not show concern in the same way for individuals beyond the immediate family unit. A woman's empathy for others sharply contrasts with a man's immediate emotional concerns.

Because of the separate socialization paths and the subsequent roles ascribed by society to them, men and women experience the same event in different ways. The following sections highlight these differences in areas directly related to couples therapy: intimacy, communication, response to conflict, and satisfaction/dissatisfaction with marriage.

INTIMACY

From the historical, socioeconomic perspective, boys growing up need to break away from the domesticated women's world of the home and develop individualistic skills to succeed in the outside world. Relationships are based on competition and cooperative alliances. Sports, for example, provide ideal training for men. They not only foster a competitive spirit, but they also provide an opportunity for men to be close with one another—a context where intimacy can be expressed through nonverbal communication. Men can compete, joke, touch, and share accomplishments. Where else can men slap high fives, bump chests, hug one another, and even pat one another on the rear end? In this active style of intimacy, men empower one another with the skills necessary for problem solving and gain a sense of engagement (Swain, 1989).

Men's and women's different ways of expressing intimacy reflect a "doing-versus-talking" distinction (Tavris, 1992). For men, love is action. If you care about someone, you do *things* for them. For women, love is talking, be it about the relationship or the other person's feelings. The obvious difficulties ensue.

The husband fixes the doorknob his wife has asked him about for the past 2 months. Completing the task he proudly turns to her for acknowledgment and approval. She points out the leaking faucet in the bathroom. Later that day the wife says, "We never talk!" The husband replies, "Fine, what do you want to talk about?" In all probability it will be a long night.

Tavris (1992) attributed these differences to emotional styles fostered in childhood. Boys develop "side-by-side" relationships, in which intimacy means sharing the same activity, whereas girls prefer "face-to-face" relationships, in which ideas and feelings are shared. With little training or experience in face-to-face relationships, a man may be confused about his partner's request for intimacy. All the talk about feelings is anathema to him. She, on the other hand, is hurt and confused by his seemingly double message. He says he cares but does not elicit her feelings or listen to her.

When he says he has a close friend, it means the friend and he share activities and can count on one another for tasks or problem solving. When she says she has a close friend, she means she and her friend share a great deal of empathy for one another's feelings and provide support by listening.

Unfortunately, these different, socially constructed patterns of intimacy frequently fuel the marital crucible. If a man cares for someone, he expresses it by doing things for him or her—by being a good provider, by fixing the doorknob, by making sure the car is running, by protecting the family. But if a woman cares for someone, she listens to and acknowledges his or her feelings and mutually shares feelings about the relationship. Given the potency of these distinct socially constructed patterns of intimacy, it is no wonder that the marital crucible over-flows into the therapist's office.

COMMUNICATION

Nowhere do gender differences, excuse the phrase, speak so loudly than in men's and women's communication styles. Tannen's (1990) book *You Just Don't Understand: Women and Men in Conversation* struck such a popular chord that it became a number 1, national bestseller. Men and women now had an explana-tion for the misunderstandings, disagreements, and arguments that plagued their relationships: We do not speak the same language!

A woman begins to tell her husband about the problems she had that day with the children. The husband half-listens while he flips through the mail, and then he quickly offers advice on how to solve the problems. The wife, who is at the point of exasperation, has to choose between hitting him over the head or leaving the room. She decides to break off the exchange and walk out of the room. "What's wrong with you?" he shouts to her back as she exits.

Tannen (1990) found this a perfectly understandable exchange. The husband hears a request for advice and offers it. The wife, however, is not asking for advice but wants a response to her frustration, perhaps a simple, "I'm sorry to hear you had such a bad day." Or, as Tannen observed women do with one another, the husband could offer matching troubles, "My day was not too good either." From a conversational analysis perspective, offering advice is an asym-metrical pattern creating a one-up/one-down distancing effect. Thus, for the woman the above exchange is a failure not only in communication but also intimacy; he has rejected her. But for a man, offering advice is a means of problem solving and helping the other person. He is left confused; "Didn't she ask for help?"

In terms of communication differences, the above exchange highlights gen-der differences in the training men and women receive via socialization (Tannen, 1990). For success in the public world, men are instructed in public, or "report," talk. Report talk emphasizes one's knowledge and skill, serving as a means of gaining the center stage and thus influencing the group. Most importantly, report talk is a means of establishing and maintaining status in the groups.

Conversely, if talk is a means of establishing oneself in the pecking order, then listening is not a valued skill. Listening would be too passive an activity and risks losing status. When listening does occur it serves as a means of gaining ammunition for a reply, "Well, you have a good point, but . . . ." For a woman to understand this phenomenon, a simple piece of advice (a male thing) is to listen to about 15 minutes of a radio sports call-in show. There she will hear point-counterpoint and no one will be listening to anyone. Listening is unimportant; who has the better opinion and who knows more is the goal.

Women, however, will talk less in public settings—that is, group meetings—because they do not use talk to assert status and because they fear they will be judged negatively (Tannen, 1993). Instead, women will talk more than men in private settings—that is, with family and close friends—in order to maintain and nurture relationships. Private communication or "rapport talk" emphasizes sharing similarities and matching experiences. And in contrast to report talk, rapport talk may emphasize listening. If you take the time to listen to me, I believe you care about me, and, in the reciprocal nature of the exchange, I will listen to you.

The difference between public talk and private talk, again, underlines the importance of the context. The question "Who talks more, men or women?" is unanswerable without considering the context. Men will talk more in public forums, and women will talk more in private relationships.

James and Drakich (1993) focused on how status differences organize interaction or what is termed *status characteristics theory*. For example, groups establish status roles. High-status roles are central to a group performing its task—for instance, an architect is a high-status role in the construction of a building. Lower status roles tend to support the work of the higher status roles. In this differentiation, each role is attributed with characteristics. Individuals in high-status roles are viewed by themselves and others as more intellectually competent. Individuals in lower status roles are judged more by what they lack than their personal competencies.

Specifically, the greater one's skill in problem solving and furthering the group's task, the higher one's status. Thus, men succeed in the world by possessing problem-solving skills and being skilled in public, or report, talk. Women, relegated to a lower status position, speak less in public. But context again is crucial. If constructing a building is the group's task, then problem-solving skills are central and rewarded. However, if the group has a social goal—that is, a family whose goal is to nurture and support its members—then building and maintaining relationships is a priority. Consequently, private speaking or rapport talk is valued. Unfortunately, these task and socioemotional roles are not equally valued in the overall society; public talk is more highly rewarded.

To summarize, gender roles powerfully shape our communication patterns and underlie the "gender differences" in communication. Because they focus on their place in the power hierarchy, men are practiced in the art of public talk. Women, who focus on maintaining, building, and nurturing relationships, are the masters of private talk. On the emotional, expressive level, women are well practiced in verbalizing thoughts and feelings in close relationships. Men, in contrast, are well-schooled in dismissing their feelings or keeping them to themselves. For men, there is nothing about the expression of feelings that will determine status or help them compete in the outside world. Thus, rather than discussing innate differences between the sexes concerning communication, it is more important to become aware of the context and the power of gender roles to powerfully influence what we hear, what we say, and the purpose of our communication.

CONFLICT

Considering the differences in expressions of intimacy and communication patterns, it is no wonder men and women struggle to connect with one another.

Conflict would appear inevitable, but even in conflict gender differences have been identified.

Conflict is a threat to connection for women, whereas for men it is a means of negotiating status (Tannen, 1990). For women, maintaining connection may mean conceding an argument or placating her mate rather than risking the male's further anger. Or, maintaining connection may mean pursuing the emotionally withdrawn partner or attempting to provoke her mate's anger to at least engage involvement. Even if the woman is hurt in the exchange, she opts to maintain the relationship rather than sever it.

For men, conflict may be perceived as a threat or challenge. A disagreement means someone is right and someone is wrong. Consequently, in an argument all is fair, from beginning with logic to raising one's voice to threatening anger.

Besides the different meanings of conflict, men and women differ in physiological responses and behavioral responses. During negative exchanges with their partners, men become physiologically flooded far more easily than women. For men, stress measures rose far faster during a negative marital exchange than they did for their wives. Moreover, as measured by heart rate and blood pressure, men reach a state of emotional overload faster and stay at that level long after their wives have calmed down. Even criticism was sufficient to elevate the physiological measures in men, whereas women reached similar levels when contempt entered the picture (Gottman, 1994a).

This physiological profile suggests the origins of the classic presenting couple's problem of a wife seeking or pursuing emotional contact from a distant, aloof husband. For example, in the course of a negative exchange, the man becomes rapidly, physiologically distressed and responds by withdrawing or stonewalling. From a physiological perspective, his withdrawal or stonewalling is not necessarily a sign of rejection but rather an attempt to reduce his physiological arousal. He shuts her out to shut out the stimuli.

In the exchange, however, the wife feels ignored and rejected. If she is still invested in the relationship, then she will continue to pursue her husband, which only serves to ignite his need to withdraw. As she becomes less invested in the marriage, she too may begin to withdraw to protect herself.

Gottman (1994a) attributed these differences in physiological arousal to biological differences and the effects of socialization. For example, some evidence indicates that men have stronger, more intense physiological reactions to certain emotions than women. These differences may be shaped in the socialization process, but they are most certainly exacerbated in traditional roles in which boys are taught not to cry and to suppress feelings whereas girls' emotional expressions are fostered.

A vicious circle occurs as men withdraw into stonewalling as a means of calming themselves down. Stonewalling, however, shuts down expression of feelings and temporarily ends the relationship. For the woman, this cessation of communication only serves to increase her own physiological stress state.

Gottman (1994a) believed that these different socialization patterns and physiological vulnerabilities explained the pursuer–distancer pattern in many troubled marriages. Males and females learn separate patterns in the management of emotions. Because men are less adept at managing conflict in intimate relationships, they respond much faster physiologically than women and thus seek to diminish their arousal by distancing themselves from their partner. Rationalization and intellectualization are two chief ways of establishing the needed distance. For the woman, maintaining contact reduces her stress symptoms. Thus, she pursues emotional contact as a means of lowering her physiological arousal. At this point a vicious, circular pattern exists with no winners—she pursues and he distances.

Over time, stonewalling and emotional isolation take their toll on men's and women's health. Women in particular, confronted with chronic emotional isolation from their partner, reported greater health problems in a 4-year follow-up study (Gottman & Levenson, 1992).

Ironically, and perhaps not surprisingly, in happy marriages there are no gender differences (egalitarian roles) in emotional expression (Gottman, 1994a). The obvious clinical question is what explains the difference between healthy and dysfunctional couples? Do the men and women in healthy couples enter their marriages with the same degree of emotional expressiveness and thus are more compatible with one another from the beginning? Or, have healthy couples managed to develop effective problem-solving styles and, therefore, successfully avoid the negative cascades? And what about the family of origin influence? Are the basic male-female gender-role patterns enhanced or modified by the family of origin? If so, to what degree?

In a study of sex differences in marital communication, Burggraf and Sillars (1987) found that personal conflict styles were based more on reciprocal, mutual influence than gender differences. That is to say, over time couples evolve unique conflict styles, a mutual shaping process as it were. Some couples evolve conflict-avoiding patterns; for others, conflict-confronting acts may characterize their relationship. The point is that regardless of gender influences—for example, women avoiding conflict—each couple constructs its own pattern of communication and conflict management.

In summary, healthy couples appear to transcend traditional gender roles regarding the expression of emotion and the care of intimate relationships. Troubled marriages frequently present as caricatures of masculine and feminine gender roles. Men accuse women of being too emotional; women accuse men of being cold and aloof. Men withdraw into stony silences; women pursue emotional contact. Men respond with intellectualization; women respond with emotion. Yet the unique personal conflict style that evolves over the course of the couple's relationship transcends gender roles.

MARITAL SATISFACTION: GENDER VIEWS

Who benefits most from marriage? Who takes the responsibility for the care and maintenance of a marriage? Do men and women experience marriage differently? Bernard (1972) argued that marriage is better for men than it is for women. When first proposed, Bernard's thesis stirred a controversy in the "battle of the sexes." Feminists seized the issue as further proof of male domination. Nonetheless, later research supported the basic thesis and more fully illuminated the concept of marital satisfaction.

In a nationwide survey of 7,261 couples, Fowers (1991) found that men generally reported greater marital satisfaction than women. Specifically, husbands rated their marriages more positively than wives did in terms of finances, parenting, family and friends, and their partner's personality. Wives, however, more often expressed a desire for more egalitarian roles than did husbands. Women's satisfaction ratings of their marriages also are directly related to the degree tasks are shared in a marriage (Whisman & Jacobson, 1989). The more equitably the tasks are distributed, the more positively women rate their marriages.

Broadening the lens in viewing gender and marital satisfaction, investigators explored the ups and downs of satisfaction over the length of a marriage. Earlier findings indicated a curvilinear, inverted U-shaped path in marital satisfaction over the course of marriage (Anderson, Russell, & Schumm, 1983; Dougherty & Jacobson, 1982). Marital satisfaction was highest in the early years of marriage, lowest with children in adolescence, and returned to higher ratings as the children left home.

The fact that marital satisfaction is the highest in the first years of marriage comes as no surprise given the euphoric glow of love and the hopes and expectations that begin a marriage. Nevertheless, marital satisfaction reaches an all-time low when the children are adolescents. During this time period, not only does the adolescent challenge the family norms but differences in parenting attitudes and styles come rapidly to the forefront. The parent-adolescent triangle is a potent source of disagreements. (As a primer in working with adolescents and their families, see Worden [1991]). As the children leave home, however, and couples approach retirement, marital satisfaction increases. The child-rearing years are over and financial responsibilities have become more manageable. A couple's differences generally have been resolved or are at least tolerable. Differences are more likely to be accepted than fought over.

Levenson, Carstensen, and Gottman (1993) specifically looked cross-sectionally at long-term marriage and at the relationships of age with gender and satisfaction. Employing self-report measures, the researchers measured two groups: (1) spouses in their 60s and 70s who had been married at least 35 years and (2) middle-aged couples (age 40–50) who had been married at least 15 years. Although different cohort effects exist—the older couples were children of the Great Depression, married toward the end of World War II, and raised families during the 1950s; the middle-aged couples were baby boomers who grew up during times of relative prosperity and began families during the late 1960s and early 1970s—the two groups did not differ in age at time of marriage, amount of marital counseling they had obtained, or their consideration of separation and divorce. As predicted from earlier studies, the middle-aged couples reported greater conflict and less pleasure in their marriages, with the children being a chief source of conflict. Health issues, however, revealed significant gender differences.

In general, wives in both groups reported greater signs of physical and psychological distress. In dissatisfied marriages, wives reported more symptomatology than husbands. Is marriage potentially hazardous to a woman's health? Because the research is correlational, the best that can be said is that a relationship exists between women's health and their satisfaction with their marriage, which leaves a question of directionality. For example, does marital satisfaction decrease because the wife is ill, or is she ill because the marriage is dissatisfying?

Expanding the view of the problem, Gottman and Levenson (1992) found that in highly dissatisfying marriages, in times of conflict women took the initiative and were more physiologically aroused than men. Moreover, in a follow-up 4 years later, these same women reported greater health problems compared to men. Thus, the data suggest that in dysfunctional marriages, women will assume the responsibility to confront and repair an ailing relationship but at a physical and emotional cost to themselves.

In an attempt to compare disaffected and nondisaffected spouses, Kayser (1993) collected a random sample of 354 married individuals (59% female, 41% male) who responded to a mailed questionnaire. The respondents' mean length of marriage was 20.8 years. Although not a focus of the study, certain gender differences in marital disaffection became apparent while analyzing this data.

Of the 354 respondents, only 19% felt even some degree of marital disaffection. Nevertheless, of this group, women rated higher for disaffection than men. The data and the research reviewed above suggest that women are more likely to be dissatisfied with their marriages. The chief areas of dissatisfaction were emotional intimacy and inequities in household responsibilities—areas that mirrored the findings with disaffected spouses. Conversely, men in marriages with inequities in housework and child care are more satisfied with their marriages and less critical of their wives.

A related study that compared the effects of employment (employed husbands, unemployed husbands, employed wives, and unemployed wives) and social support on marital satisfaction and dissatisfaction found that employed wives were most concerned with equity in their marital relationship (Vanfossen, 1986). Equally important, however, was the social support they received from their husbands via affirmation. Affirmation was defined as being shown appreciation for one's efforts, recognition of one's abilities, encouragement in one's work, or, in simpler terms, having someone in your corner. Couples counselors should note that women working outside of the home valued this type of support more than intimacy, which was defined as having a sympathetic listener. To modify an old saying, perhaps behind every good person is a good person who affirms him or her.

Men and women suffer alike when disaffection strikes. Once disaffection began, there were no significant differences between men and women on the level of disaffection or psychological well-being. Kayser (1993) concluded her discussion on gender differences by stating, "Men and women may differ in the way they express intimacy, but the desires and needs for a close, self-enhancing relationship exist for both sexes" (p. 135).

The above data would appear to indicate that his and her marriages are a norm. In general, men are more satisfied with marriage and benefit from it. Women find marriage more dissatisfying, particularly regarding the inequity in task sharing. Also, when dissatisfaction in the marriage increases, it is most likely the woman who feels it the most intensely and who will try to confront the problem, but at an emotional and physical cost to herself.

What exactly does all this mean? Are women so finely tuned to emotional/ relationship issues that they are the first to pick up problems in the relationship and therefore they confront the issues long before a man is even aware of them? Or, are women too highly attuned to relationship subtleties and, with their need for dependency, place too many demands on a marriage? Are men just fat, dumb, and happy because they are oblivious to relationship issues and do they benefit from marriage because they hold the power? Or, are men fulfilling the cultural gender roles assigned to them and do women confuse men when they ask more of them? These questions may seem like abstract topics to be examined in future studies, but as a clinician you will have to continue working with your clients without the luxury of waiting for researchers to answer these and other questions relating to gender and marital satisfaction.

Summary

Assuming that conflict is part of every intimate relationship, how the inevitable conflict is managed is crucial to a couple's life. Unfortunately, gender differences, particularly traditional gender roles, exacerbate these conflicts. First, on a societal level, a differentiation of duties still persists: The man will take care of the outside of the house while the woman takes care of the inside. The man barbecues and the woman cooks. Despite the dramatic increase in two-paycheck families, the burden of household chores still falls on the woman. The research shows that this is a chief reason for a woman's marital dissatisfaction. She attempts to elicit more support from her partner but to no avail.

In resolving differences, men, poorly trained in expressing and confronting intimate issues and more quickly physiologically aroused in a negative exchange, respond to intimate conflict by attempting to control or withdraw from the partner. One way a man controls the exchange is by presenting logical argument after logical argument to reduce his partner's emotional reaction. If he can dominate the discussion through long logical monologues, then the woman sits in silence. This method is particularly effective if the logic implies that the woman is misperceiving or is thinking illogically about the situation. If, however, the man has reached a point of emotional overload then he can attempt to control the discussion by bullying his partner into silence. Sometimes an angry stare will do it, sometimes raising the voice will do it, or sometimes an angry accusation is enough. A man's final option is to withdraw into stony silence or, better yet, leave the situation.

In the peculiarities of gender roles, the man's withdrawal is a loss of contact for the woman. She pursues him to close the emotional gap he is creating. Even if that pursuit leads to increased arguments, that is preferable to the aloneness of silence for some women.

Healthy couples appear to transcend these traditional gender roles—for example, household chores are not necessarily divided along gender lines. And as we will see in later chapters, in healthy couples the roles of pursuer and distancer are interchangeable, dependent on the issue and the importance of the issue to each individual. On one issue the man may pursue the woman, on another the woman may pursue the man. Emotional intimacy is valued by both parties.

The two basic ingredients in emotional intimacy are love and respect (Gottman, 1994), but the mix of these ingredients may take several forms. Summarizing 20 empirical studies involving over 2,000 couples, Gottman (1994) identified three healthy marriage styles:

1. Validating marriages are marked by compromise and rational problem solving to reach a mutual satisfaction.
2. Conflict-avoiding marriages agree to disagree and, fearing conflict, avoid direct confrontation.
3. Volatile marriages erupt in passionate and heated disputes.

Thus, we do not have one single definition of an intimate, healthy relationship to guide us. Instead, in intimate relationships, people struggle with very basic issues: a desire to be loved, a desire to be respected, a desire to be valued and affirmed, and a desire to be heard. Through the lenses of gender roles, however, these issues may mean different things to a man or a woman. For example, a man may feel valued when nothing is asked of him when he comes home from work, while a woman values him when he pitches in to help bathe the children. Or, a man is heard when someone does what he requested, while a woman is heard when a man sits and listens to her feelings.

In closing, although we are focusing on the differences, we do not wish to overly exaggerate them. Men and women are not from different planets. We believe that our similarities, particularly in the human struggle for intimacy, far outweigh our differences. We all struggle with being cared for, caring for others, building our hopes, reaching our dreams, expressing our wants, meeting our desires, being understood, understanding others, and loving and being loved. Couples therapy, therefore, is an intimacy crucible. However, because gender roles and internalized gender identities may stand as roadblocks to the intimacy we seek, we turn now to the assessment and treatment of couples while highlighting the role of gender in these processes.

CHAPTER FOUR

The Imbalanced Gender Triangle and Reciprocity

Imbalanced Gender Triangle

Financial and time constraints give few therapists the luxury of working in a male-female cotherapy team. More often than not, it is one therapist meeting with a couple alone. Thus, other than when working with gay couples, the therapist creates an imbalanced gender triangle when forming a therapeutic alliance with a couple. Regardless of the therapist's sex, one member of the couple is outnumbered. Viewed from this perspective, the therapist's sensitivity and awareness to gender issues are at a premium as each type of therapeutic triangle contains its inherent liabilities.

It would be nice to believe that because of their training and experience therapists are free from traditional gender roles and are capable of viewing each client not as a male or female but as a person. But, can we be immune to social influences? We are each embedded in our own unique cultural, ethnic, and family of origin gender frames. Thus, all three parties—the couple dyad and the therapist—carry gender liabilities and biases into therapy, liabilities expressed through transference and countertransference (issues more completely discussed in a later chapter) and conscious and unconscious gender role enactments.

For example, a male couples therapist may be pulled in two separate directions. On the one hand, he may compete with the husband for status and hierarchy in the session. Picking up the gauntlet, the husband challenges the therapist's competency—"Where did you get your degree and how long have you been doing this?"

The therapist's countertransference response may attempt to gain or maintain a superior position through (1) using psychological interpretations of the husband's behavior, (2) negatively judging the male's behavior, or (3) simply discounting his questions.

Or, the therapist's behavior toward the wife may stand in direct counterpoint to the husband's failings as a mate. The therapist will be sensitive and caring and will truly listen to her. In response to the wife's feelings, a male therapist's understanding nod of the head or soothing "that must be difficult for you" goes a long way in undermining the husband's involvement in therapy. Why should the husband come to therapy in order to feel more inadequate in the relationship?

On the other hand, the male therapist may inadvertently play out a number of male gender roles in relationship to the women in couples. For example, the male therapist may wish to protect the woman but in reciprocal ways will require the woman to be compliant and acknowledge both his gender and professional authority. He must perform a balancing act to present himself as both strong and competent—to meet the masculine projections—and nurturing enough to "hear" the feminine concerns. As Lerner (1988) observed, "Because women themselves have enormous unconscious fears regarding their own destructiveness and the related fragility of the male ego, both client and therapist may fail to recognize the subtle ways in which the woman is being 'a good patient' at the expense of her own autonomy and growth" (p. 119).

The female couples therapist also experiences opposing forces. For example, her presence as the authority in the room may throw the husband into unfamiliar waters. Does he relate to her as a woman (as an equal or someone to be seduced) or as a superior? Does he defer to her judgment or challenge it?

In addition, the female therapist must judge how to relate to the husband. If she assumes too much control early in the session, the husband may feel threatened and withdraw. This could undermine his commitment to the therapy. He could also adopt one of two extreme positions: He could submit and respond to her as a mother figure, possibly duplicating the role he assumes with his wife. Or, if the female therapist allows the first interview to become laissez-faire and structureless, she is inviting the husband to fill the perceived vacuum and assume control. Either way the female therapist can unconsciously cement rather than change the gender pattern of interaction.

In relation to the wife, the female therapist assumes several ongoing roles and must maintain a continuing balance. The same-sex therapist must always be wary of "outperforming" the dysfunctional spouse. For women this plays out in fears about the therapist being too understanding or supportive of the husband. In addition the wife has her own fantasies about how the therapist functions as a woman—for example, how does the therapist perform in all her feminine roles? The therapist's balancing dilemma is inherent in concurrently validating the feminine experience without alienating the masculine presence or diminishing his frustrations with the relationship. The male client gains comfort with the female therapist as a competent professional who will remain objective. The female client gains comfort with the therapist as a *woman* (an ally, not a competitor) who will remain objective.

Each member of the couple also carries gender into therapy. For example, both the husband and wife project their own views of gender expectations onto the therapist, and they expect the therapist to fulfill his or her assigned gender role (Newberry, Alexander, & Turner, 1991). At least initially, the therapist's gender guides the couple's behavior. The husband may compete with a male therapist, but with a female therapist he may assume dominance over the session. The wife may be compliant with a male therapist and more assertive or competitive with a female therapist.

But perhaps most importantly, the therapist's personal beliefs strongly influence the role of gender in couples therapy. A therapist is not separate from nor free of the cultural context of gender. Therefore each therapist brings to his or her work an implicit concept of normality for men and women. These implicit concepts influence every part of the therapeutic process from assessment through termination.

PERCEPTIONS OF THE PROBLEM

Social roles are the convergence points between the culture and the individual. The roles not only prescribe acceptable forms of behavior but also serve as our personal lenses through which we view ourselves and others. Our sense of our own masculinity and femininity is to a large degree dependent on our view of the male and female role and how well we are fulfilling our specific gender role. Problems we experience may reflect a conflict between ourselves and our gender role or with behavior required of us that is incompatible with our perceived role. Within the therapeutic context, perceptions of gender roles may influence the process in three ways: (1) the couples' perception of the problem, (2) the therapist's perception of the problem, and (3) the interaction between the two.

Couples' Perceptions and Reactions

In an article reviewing gender differences in cardiovascular responses to stress, Polefrone and Manuck (1987) argued that the supposed biological differences between men and women in physiological reactions to stress were more a reflection of social roles than biological differences. For example, in an experimental condition where female subjects were forced to be competitive in a game situation and male subjects were coerced to cooperate in a competitive game, both sexes experienced similar heart rate elevations. One interpretation of this finding is that the performance of behaviors incompatible with one's social role induced stress. Another possibility is that performing unfamiliar behaviors raised one's anxiety.

Regardless of the interpretation, the studies reviewed strongly suggest that the experience of stress is correlated with our social role, our commitment to and acceptance of the role, and the context of the behavior (Polefrone & Manuck, 1987). For example, men were found to be more depressed than women by strains encountered at work. Women, in contrast, were more depressed by marital problems (Aneshensel & Pearlin, 1987). This finding makes perfect sense in light of our earlier discussion on the psychology of men and women (see Chapter 3). If the male gender role is primarily based on success in the outside world, then work-related problems most certainly induce stress. Likewise, if a woman endorses the role as the emotional caretaker for the marriage and family, then family difficulties would produce the most stress for her. Thus, the male member of the couple in your office may minimize the marital problems yet be quite animated when discussing his work problems. If the woman is selfless and compliant, she may experience his absorption in work as a deficit in her. If she has an intact sense of self, or is more in touch with her anger, she may assume something is missing in him. In either case, she may wonder what she (or the therapist) can do to engage him in the marriage and family.

In dual-earner marriages, both the male and the female may be highly stressed in the workplace, yet women more than men continue to focus on the home and relationships therein.

Often the reluctant or resistant male sees no problem in the marriage because he is not attending to the social cues—"You've got the problem; I don't."

Because women have a greater involvement in the lives of others, interpersonal problems greatly increase stress. Women more often reported distress due to crises occurring with their family and friends, while men seldom mentioned such events as sources of stress (Kessler & McLeod, 1984). Again, it is a matter of roles and perception.

Multiple roles also mitigate the perception of stress. Marital stress was perceived differently by women who were homemakers than by those employed outside the home. The latter reported less depression in response to marital stressors (Kandel, Davies, & Raveis, 1985). The authors of this article concluded that the more central a role is to our identities, the greater the potential for stress in this area. Likewise, the extent of a woman's interrole conflict and stress between work and family was dependent upon the demands experienced within each role and the personal investment in each role. That is, problems outside the home produce stress dependent upon both a man's and a woman's investment in the role. A man may perform a job simply for a paycheck but may measure his worth more by his role as a husband and father. A woman may be invested in a career and may share home responsibilities and stresses with her spouse.

Research further supports a gender distinction regarding the interaction of roles and the impact on one's well-being. Barnett and Baruch (1987) found that men could offset dissatisfactions with their marriage with satisfaction in their parental role. Women, however, did not compensate for marital dissatisfaction in any other role. They were primarily defined by the marital role.

Finally, men and women will present different styles in response to their marital dissatisfaction. White (1989) found that men assume a coercive stance toward their partners, and women take an affiliative position. During times of marital conflict, men analyze, attempt to take control, and use coercion to distance themselves from the situation. Women assume an affiliative position in an attempt to maintain the relationship until resolution may be reached.

Drawing upon gender-different worldviews, White (1989) speculated that men regard conflicts as potentially emotionally explosive situations that need to be controlled. Thus they move to create distance and disengagement. For women, however, conflict risks dissolution of the relationship and raises the fears of isolation and vulnerability. Therefore, due in large part to the influence of gender roles, each sex's approach to conflict directly threatens the other.

Therapists' Perceptions

Focusing on the therapists' gender lenses, Zygmond and Denton (1988) asked therapists to offer prognostic judgments on clinical profiles of couples seeking marital therapy for inhibited sexual desire. The identified patient's gender did not influence either male or female therapists' clinical judgments, but male and female therapists used different clinical cues in formulating their prognosis. Female therapists attended to the seriousness of the presenting problem for the couple, the other spouse's satisfaction with sexual intercourse, and the other spouse's desired frequency of sexual intercourse. Male therapists focused on the wife's desired frequency of sexual intercourse and the husband's sexual satisfaction. Although the authors presented their findings tentatively underlining the limitations of the study—that is, the study did not control for other therapist variables such as level of education, years of experience, and sex-role attitudes—they conclude that the data highlights gender influences in clinical assessment.

Sherman (1980), after reviewing the literature on therapist attitudes and sex-role stereotyping, concluded that a therapist's sex-role values are operative during therapy. Specifically, male therapists were found to stereotype via gender roles more than female therapists. When a client's behavior was at odds with the person's gender role, he or she was judged more maladjusted by a male therapist. A man crying uncontrollably through the interview was judged more harshly than a woman exhibiting the same behavior. Again, what is normal and what is abnormal would seem to be at least partially dependent on one's sex and fulfilling one's gender role, even for therapists.

Tavris (1992) underscored the role of gender in assessing another's behavior in a discussion of the codependency movement. She observed that the symptoms of codependency—that is, worrying about other people's problems instead of your own, taking on more responsibility than you should in relationships, ignoring your own needs to meet someone else's, and concern about what others think about you—are the hallmarks of the female role. The feminine gender role values the caring for others.

One may argue that the concept of codependency is not deriding the feminine gender role but pointing out the consequences of the role taken to the extreme. Tavris (1992) added that a recovering codependent has to learn to become independent and self-reliant, to say no to the demands of others, and to not become hooked by the problems of others, or, in other words, to become the "stereotypical" male. In this topsy-turvy world of gender roles, a woman may be negatively judged for possessing the very qualities she was raised to cultivate.

The Interaction

Finally, the therapists' and clients' genders interact to shape the therapy process. Couples seeking marital therapy were asked to complete protocols on potential therapists. The experimental conditions varied the marital status and sex of the potential therapists. Although neither variable had an effect on the subjects' perceptions of the therapists or therapy expectations, female subjects viewed the potential therapist as more trustworthy, attractive, and expert, and had higher expectations for therapy than did male subjects (Campbell & Johnson, 1991).

Even though this was an analog study and the authors recommended follow-up studies after couples had begun actual therapy, the influence of gender was readily apparent. Both therapists' expectations and attitudes about their clients and clients' expectations and perceptions of their therapists mutually influenced the process of therapy (Marecek & Johnson, 1980).

SUMMARY

Because subsequent chapters will focus on the specifics of couples therapy, we close this section with a summary of stereotypical, traditional gender-role differences that are likely to surface in work with couples. This is not an exhaustive list, but it reflects common themes presented by couples. (The complete list appears in Philpot's [1991] article on gender-sensitive couples therapy.)

1. Autonomy Versus Affiliation

Man: Hey, sometimes I just like going out with my buddies. So what's the big deal? Why do you make such a fuss about it?

Woman: I would like it if you spent time with me—if you thought about me and planned for us to do something together.

Man: I'm home all the time and we do a lot of things together. So what if I come home a little late from work because I stopped for some beers? I'm entitled.

Woman: But you don't call. You don't let me know when you will be home.

Although a man may be extremely controlling, he is also hypersensitive to being controlled by a woman. His childhood and adolescent struggle of separation from mother may be ongoing in the current relationship. The perpetuation of this struggle comes at a high cost. After a few years, marriage, a few children, and a mortgage may feel suffocating to the man who believes he was robbed of his independence. To not call and stay out late after work may be the man's message that he will not be controlled, delivered in a passive-aggressive style.

For the woman, her mate's behavior strikes at the heart of her need for affiliation and connectedness. Problems in the relationship threaten her sense of self and level of self-esteem. Worse yet, she feels to blame for what is going on. Is she too possessive? What has she done to make him reject her?

The conflict between autonomy and affiliation frequently presents as a *battle over time*—who controls the couple's time and how will it be spent.

2. Instrumental Versus Expressive

Woman: We never talk. I never know what you are feeling. You never share those things with me.

Man: Well, I'm not going to sit around all night like you and your friends do and just yak-yak-yak.

Woman: I just want to know what you feel about things.

Man: *(No reply. He sits in stony silence.)*

The masculine role proscribes that if you love someone you don't talk about it, you *do*, you protect, you provide. For men, actions really do speak louder than words. Talking and reflecting about problems are perceived as feminine activities for which men have little training. A man will share a problem with another man but only to brainstorm solutions. The idea that just expressing your feelings is helpful is anathema to most men. Consequently, when she says she wants to talk, a red flashing light appears in a man's head signaling dangerous ground ahead. He may perceive the potential conversation as a test he is bound to fail.

Unfortunately, in a relationship with a noncommunicative man, a woman may die a slow, emotional death. Not only does she experience chronic rejection by his inability to share his feelings, but she also assumes the responsibility for this state of affairs. In the extreme, she is left with the choice of either accepting the status quo and suffering the longing of the loss of contact or pursuing her mate until an argument ensues—at least an argument is contact. For many women, the third choice is to accept the status quo and meet her intimacy needs through her children or her friends. Women in this position are often vulnerable to the attentions of other men to whom they can feel emotionally connected.

3. Assertiveness Versus Accommodation

Woman: I think we need to talk about our sex life.

Man *(in a somewhat irritated tone)*: What do you mean?

Woman: Well, I don't think we have sex often enough.

Man *(now in an angry tone)*: Why do you always have to bring that up? You pick the worst times.

Woman: *(No reply. She sits in silence.)*

Stereotypical gender roles say men can be assertive and go after what they want, but women need to accommodate to the needs of others. An assertive woman is seen as pushy; sexual assertiveness is the man's prerogative. A reversal in role is threatening to most men.

Despite the instrumental versus expressive dichotomy just discussed, men can be quite comfortable with the feeling of anger, especially as a useful tool for controlling others. Anger in a woman, however, is traditionally deemed inappropriate and a challenge to the man's authority.

4. Family Versus Career

Woman: Do you have to spend so much time at work? Sometimes I think you care more about the job than you do about me and the kids.

Man: Well, what do you think pays the bills so that we can live like this. You think I enjoy going to work? I do it for you and the kids!

Being a good provider is fundamental to the male role. One's self-esteem and sense of competency come through a job. In the extreme, success at work can compensate for a poor marriage. In a job, one's success is tangible and recognized as opposed to the murky emotional water of intimate relationships. Consequently, a man's identity will more often than not flow out from his work.

In the dichotomy of home and work, a woman's identity is tied to relationships. Even though she may work outside the home, her gender role dictates that job is not as important as the family relationships and their "success." Along with her outside job she is still responsible for the cleaning, cooking, and laundry, and if the man decides to help with some of that, she should be appreciative. This couple's presenting problem is a conflict over commitment and priorities.

5. Emotion Versus Logic

Man: Why do you have to get so emotional every time we have a discussion?

Woman: Because it's the only way I can get through your coldness.

The woman in this couple finds the man's logical approach to problems maddening. He never gets upset; he never lets his emotions show; therefore, she doesn't know what he really cares about. He, on the other hand, cannot believe she has a feeling about everything. And what is really upsetting is that her emotions influence her decisions. Why can't she just use logic like he does? Why can't she just act like the people at work do when there is a problem?

Unfortunately, the emotion versus logic dichotomy is not limited to a problem-solving plane; it becomes personal. The woman experiences the man's logic as cold, possibly rejecting, aloofness—it is a sign he does not care for her. The man experiences the woman's emotions as overwhelming. All he wants to do is get away from them.

Androgynous Therapeutic Role

The therapist's role requires a range of behaviors that may cross gender role stereotyping. On the one hand, the therapist is creating an atmosphere of trust and warmth, empathetically connecting with others, and responding to another's feelings and moods. At other times in therapy, the therapist needs to structure and control the session, offer directives, and confront when necessary. Overall, the therapist walks a fine line in emotionally responding to his or her clients while remaining detached "enough" to maintain objectivity. No small task indeed!

To function most effectively, a therapist combines masculine and feminine behaviors using the appropriate response at the appropriate time in therapy. Empathy may be the best response one moment, while confrontation facilitates progress the next. Assuming that a therapist is made and not born, he or she may need to develop the full range of gender-coded or androgynous behaviors.

Newberry, Alexander, and Turner (1991) argued that the therapist role requires both instrumental and expressive behavior. Instrumental behaviors are more stereotypically male—task oriented, controlling, directing—and expressive behaviors are more stereotypically female—expressing warmth, offering emotional support. Because socialization patterns of gender roles lead to different learning experiences, male therapists may have less experience with expressive behaviors and female therapists may have less experience assuming the authority position.

To investigate these hypotheses, male and female therapist trainees were observed conducting psychotherapy sessions and were rated on the frequency of instrumental and expressive behaviors. While no difference was found between the frequency rates—that is, both male and female therapists were similar in their response patterns—there was a difference in the response of family members to the therapist's gender and behavior in two ways.

First, fathers in the study rated their experience in therapy more positively than did mothers when therapists, male or female, used structuring, or instrumental, behavior. The findings suggest that when the process of therapy more closely reflects masculine behavior, men are more responsive than if expressive behaviors dominate. Instrumental behaviors are familiar to men. As the therapist structures and directs the course of therapy, men are on more comfortable ground.

The second pattern that emerged was the different responses of family members to the same behavior from male or female therapists. For example, if a female therapist offered a supportive response, she was more likely than a male therapist to receive a supportive response in return. (This is reminiscent of the discussion in Chapter 3 of gender differences in communication where it was observed that women engage in reciprocal "rapport" talk [Tannen, 1990].) The researchers concluded that family members expect gender-stereotypical behaviors of the therapist and respond in gender-defined patterns (Newberry et al., 1991).

Just as family members carry their gender biases into therapy, the therapist may be limited by his or her gender role. This is particularly true in cross-gender relationships: male client–female therapist, female client–male therapist. Bograd (1990) observed that female therapists struggle with balancing the power of their professional, expert position with a woman's more traditional role of nurturer and caretaker. Particularly with male clients, female therapists have great difficulty being assertive, commanding, or challenging, because as women they have been taught to influence men indirectly. Likewise, male therapists may fall into a paternal, protective mode with female clients at the expense of the woman's growth. Instead of confronting or empowering female clients, a male therapist may inadvertently foster dependency and give directives.

Forming the Therapeutic Alliance

Each sex may approach the initial stage of treatment in different ways. Women may seek to affiliate with the therapist. Some sense of an emotional connection with or understanding from the therapist may be an essential element in establishing rapport. Men, on the other hand, may at first sit back, evaluating the therapist, or may attempt to control the sessions.

The therapist, in turn, may err by not accepting and instead responding to these initial behaviors. For example, the therapist may spend too much time connecting and understanding the woman's position. Although this may enhance the therapeutic relationship with the woman, it does little for the man. The husband was reluctant to begin therapy in the first place, and now the first several sessions are dominated by dyadic conversations between his mate and the therapist.

Likewise, a therapist may initially accept the man's stoic repose and attempt to connect with him via his work or interests. As one woman complained, referring to the first couples therapist she saw, "The sessions would always digress to a discussion of golf. That's what my husband and the therapist seemed to share."

That therapist may have been trying to form a therapeutic alliance with a very reluctant husband. Still, the therapist had erred by not broadening the area of contact beyond golf and by neglecting the affiliative contact the woman desired.

Without sensitivity to gender issues and in the heat of an emotionally charged context, a therapist may attempt to change one or the other partner with little success. The male partner may resist being pulled closer to sensitive issues and the woman may feel isolated if the therapist pulls away from the exchange. In the imbalanced gender triangle of couples therapy, the therapist walks a fine line between the gender sensitivities. Not surprisingly, the successful couples therapist is able to establish positive, affiliative relationships (feminine) while also structuring the therapeutic process toward established goals (masculine).

In examining outcome factors in family therapy, Gurman and Kniskern (1991) stated, "A reasonable mastery of technical skills may be sufficient to prevent worsening or maintain pretreatment functioning, but more refined therapist relationship skills seem necessary to yield truly positive outcomes in marital-family therapy" (p. 875). Green and Herget (1991) echoed Gurman and Kniskern (1991), finding that the therapist's relationship skills and the strength of the therapeutic alliance are the most powerful predictors of therapeutic success. In their empirical study, Green and Herget (1991) found that clients improved more on their main treatment goals when their therapists were warmer and more actively structuring.

With an emphasis on the therapist's relationship skills and keeping in mind the imbalanced gender triangle, we offer the following guidelines for establishing a therapeutic alliance in couples therapy:

1. *Respecting different styles of relating*—As has been reiterated throughout the book, men and women will present different styles of relating. A couples therapist, therefore, is called upon to engage each member of the couple differently. Initially, this may mean discovering and validating mutual interests with the man and connecting with the woman's pain of the relationship. This does not mean colluding with the couple's respective styles but rather recognizing (and respecting) that they're different.

2. *Establishing a nonjudgmental atmosphere*—Along with a respect for different styles of relating, establishing a nonjudgmental atmosphere furthers the development of trust. Partners in distress may manifest their pain in any number of ways—that is, intellectual defensiveness, seeking control, passive-aggressiveness, domineering behavior—however, there will be little movement in therapy if either member of the couple feels judged. Women may be told they are dependent, needy, emotionally explosive, or suffocating. Men may be told they are aloof, cut off from their feelings, or intellectualizing. Although the therapist may feel confident in his or her judgment, therapy bogs down as one or both partners defensively withdraw from the therapeutic alliance.

3. *Being aware of the influence of gender roles in each partner's presentation*—Implied in these points is the therapist's awareness of the influence of gender roles. It may be impossible to separate the clients' personal presentation from the impact of gender roles. Is the husband's stoicism a reflection of childhood, family of origin patterns, or gender roles? Does the therapist attempt to

explore the husband's family of origin to "change" the behavior or to help the client see the power of gender roles to limit one's behavior? Or, does the therapist accept the behavior but help the husband "discover" the impact these patterns have on his wife?

4. *Developing consensus on the goals of therapy*—A significant part of actively structuring the treatment process is establishing clear goals for therapy, with an emphasis on *consensus* between each member of the couple and the therapist. Not only do goals serve as a destination point, but they are also measuring sticks of progress. Ironically, sometimes therapy is successful by just completing this step. For some couples, identifying and establishing goals clarifies their issues and from there they can make steps toward change on their own.

5. *Developing consensus on the structure of therapy*—An additional step to actively structuring the treatment process is establishing boundaries, such as the length of the sessions and the frequency of the meetings. Couples entering therapy for the first time are understandably anxious and unsure of what to expect. Will we be judged? Will we be told there is something wrong with us? What is this counseling stuff all about? However, as the therapist and the couple actively structure the early stages of therapy together, couples' anxieties rapidly decrease and the clients are reassured that the therapist knows what he or she is doing.

6. *Maintaining accurate empathy*—As opposed to individual therapy where one is in an ongoing dialogue with the client or in a large family session where the therapist focuses on the interaction between the various family members, the imbalanced gender triangle of couples therapy is a constantly shifting series of dyadic conversations that always leaves one member of the triangle in the outside position. For example, as the therapist engages one partner, the other partner may be listening intently and interested in what is being said or may feel left out and worried that the therapist is "buying" the opposing view of the problem.

Couples therapy demands that the therapist maintains accurate empathy with both partners. The therapist cannot assume he or she knows what either member of the couple is thinking and feeling without continually asking for feedback. In so doing, not only is the therapist solidifying the therapeutic alliance, but he or she is also communicating an interest and respect for each point of view while modeling effective communication.

7. *Being aware of one's own gender biases*—As someone also embedded in the cultural context, a therapist cannot escape his or her own gender biases. They may be evident in one's perceptions, judgments, and style of relating, but equally important is their influence on one's behavior in couples therapy. Is my therapeutic style more reflective of masculine or feminine gender roles? How do I respond to masculine or feminine gender-role behavior in my clients? What are my beliefs concerning men and women?

8. *Developing both masculine and feminine relationship skills*—Although unable to offer empirical support for this statement, we assume that the highly successful couples therapist possesses both masculine and feminine relationship skills. These skills enable the therapist to empathize and engage each gender style. Moreover, change is more probable when clients feel understood and when new behavior is proposed with respect to established gender roles.

Therapeutic Change
from a Gender Perspective

The influence of gender roles is viewed by some therapists as the source of men's problems (Meth & Pasick, 1990). Specifically, the male concern for independence and control masks fears of dependency and vulnerability. Problems in relationships, therefore, need to be controlled or ignored. In addition, the denial and repression of feeling further encumber men's personal development. Thus, the restrictions of the male role rob a man of his ability to know himself and to develop satisfying interpersonal relationships (Meth & Pasick, 1990).

Meth and Pasick (1990) stated that their goal in working therapeutically with men was to change their beliefs about masculinity and to make a connection between these beliefs and the problematic behavior. They viewed this in several stages. First, men's beliefs about masculinity were explored. The topic areas included messages from their fathers, cultural and ethnic expectations, and personal beliefs. Then, the harmful results of these beliefs were examined. Next, a connection was made between these beliefs and the presenting problems. Finally, the therapist emphasized that these beliefs were not freely chosen and could be consciously changed. Meth and Pasick's (1990) underlying assumption was that if beliefs change, then behavior will change.

Meth and Pasick (1990) acknowledged, however, that challenging these core beliefs is difficult and that the process of therapy—that is, a sacrifice of autonomy and an increased sense of vulnerability—raises anxiety in men. To combat this, they emphasized active strategies that provided the male client with some control over the process. For example, setting goals, delineating tasks for the session, and assigning homework moved the male client into a coparticipant position.

Whereas these clinical observations are offered as a current perspective on treating men individually, we would be remiss if we did not place their comments within our gender-role perspective. For example, once you begin to place some sort of value on gender roles—that is, that one is better than another or that one needs to be modified—you are entering a political and phenomenological arena.

A political stance judges the correctness of behavior. Instead of "Why can't a woman be more like a man?" the question is recast to "Why can't a man be more like a woman?" Thus, in a specific cultural shift valuing political correctness, male gender roles may be seen as harmful to couples' health.

Likewise, the subject or phenomenological experience of a gender role may contrast with the therapist's view. For example, a male client may believe he has very satisfying relationships, particularly with other men. He loves hanging around the bar with friends after their team's softball game and as the client might add, "I know I can count on my friends whenever I need help with something." The therapist who attempts to challenge this belief faces an uphill battle because it contradicts the client's experience and masculine role.

The political and phenomenological perspectives assume even more relevance in the imbalanced gender triangle of therapy in which a therapist is making judgments concerning behavior. Is the male gender role harmful to a couple's life? Does the male need to forsake his ingrained role if couples therapy is to be successful? Will the female partner and therapist consciously or unconsciously collude to change the male partner? Will the woman's complaints about her mate's aloofness resonate with the therapist's perspective? However, from a broader perspective, does the therapist support traditional gender roles or advocate equal, egalitarian roles?

THERAPIST: ADVOCATE FOR TRADITIONAL OR EGALITARIAN ROLES

As discussed earlier, as the nature of work changes and the choice of reproduction exists, the justification for traditional roles is significantly challenged. Egalitarian ideology argues that the traditional gender roles are interchangeable and thus antiquated. Women are fully capable of performing production roles, and men, although unable to bear children, are fully capable of nurturing a child's growth. Thus, not only do traditional gender roles support an inequity in power between the sexes, but they also narrowly confine the expression of one's desires and abilities.

Given the above reasons, one could easily argue that a couples therapist's job is to be an advocate for egalitarian roles. These roles would redress the power imbalance between men and women. Freed of restricting gender roles, men and women would be in a position to assume equal responsibility for the relationship. Unfortunately, two roadblocks exist in the successful execution of this assignment: (1) traditional roles change slowly, and (2) from a gender identity perspective, a person must answer the question, "What does it mean to be male? Female?"

The movement toward egalitarian roles reflects a change in public opinion via laws and opportunities, but equally important it reflects a change in personal attitudes via redefinitions of what it means to be male or female. Personal attitudes are woven by the culture, the family of origin, and personal experience. Although egalitarian ideology is increasingly dominating the broader society, traditional views of gender roles change slowly and present almost schizophrenic pictures. For example, in the 1996 presidential campaign, both candidates' wives spoke at the respective conventions. This not only sent the message that they are supportive wives, but their very presence as speakers subtly defined them as equals.

We are not condoning or advocating traditional gender roles but instead are accepting them as facts of life. Perhaps a woman will be president in the near future, but a long time will have passed between that event and when women were "given" the right to vote. Furthermore, specific ethnic groups within the culture may greatly differ in the value placed on traditional or egalitarian roles. Thus, the influence of personal history and ethnic identity may supersede the therapist's advocation of egalitarian roles.

For better or worse, traditional gender roles do provide guidelines for behavior that lead to clear interpersonal boundaries regarding expectations and responsibilities. Although the egalitarian position would argue for equal power and shared responsibilities, egalitarian roles by definition do not designate differences between men and women. Instead, egalitarian ideology emphasizes the similarities between the sexes in terms of qualities common to all people. Thus, a person, male or female, may be strong, dependent, assertive, independent—the full range of human emotions and behavior.

Still, men and women are anatomically different. Sex is one of our most basic identifications. Egalitarian roles, however, do not facilitate a gender identity. In a world of equals, what does it mean to be male or female? By cutting our moorings to traditional roles, we drift into unfamiliar waters. When a man and woman form a relationship, what do they each expect of the other? What does he want and expect in a woman? What does she want and expect in a man? Thus, until egalitarian ideology can articulate gender-specific but equal roles between the sexes, traditional gender roles will still exert considerable influence.

As therapists, therefore, rather than advocating for traditional or egalitarian gender roles in couples therapy, we focus on two concepts in evaluating and treating couples: (1) the goodness of fit and (2) reciprocity.

The Goodness of Fit

The concept of the goodness of fit is drawn from developmental psychology (Chess & Thomas, 1986; Thomas & Chess, 1980). Briefly, healthy development occurs when there is a goodness of fit or compatibility between a person's capacities and characteristics and the demands and expectations of the environment. For example, if parents value and reward athletic abilities and their son is a good athlete who loves sports, then the good fit between expectations and abilities will foster positive development.

On the other hand, psychological problems are directly related to a poorness of fit or incompatibility between the person and the environment. For example, if parents push academic performance but their son suffers from severe learning disabilities, then the poor fit between his abilities and his parents' expectations will probably lead to behavioral problems.

When faced with a poorness of fit and in order to reduce it, a person may (1) attempt to modify or change environmental demands and expectations or (2) modify his or her behavioral patterns to achieve an optimal goodness of fit with the environment. In psychotherapy, a person's presenting problem may be put within the context of a poorness of fit. Therapy, therefore, attempts to modify the environment or change a person's behavior to enhance a better fit. (The concept of goodness of fit applied to therapy with children is detailed in Chess and Thomas, 1986, and Worden, 1991, applies it to the treatment of adolescents and their families.)

Applying the goodness of fit model to couples, we may first conceptualize traditional and egalitarian gender roles on opposite ends of a linear dimension and then place each partner and the relationship at points along the dimension.

TRADITIONAL .... EGALITARIAN

From this perspective, goodness of fit is defined by the distance between each partner's position on the scale and the relationship's position. The closer the three points cluster together, the better the goodness of fit. For example, in one couple both the man and woman may endorse traditional gender roles. In that case, each partner is in agreement concerning differential expectations and responsibilities. Another couple, however, may endorse egalitarian roles and agree to equally share all responsibilities. She will contribute economically to the home; he will equally share in child care.

But two other partners may greatly diverge in their positions. He endorses traditional roles, while she believes in egalitarian ones. This couple's goodness of fit is poor. Their arguments, in all probability, reflect the struggle over which ideology will dominate the relationship. Will she be the traditional wife he expects? Or, will he become the equal partner she desires?

But as mentioned here, egalitarian roles contain the pitfalls of unclear boundaries. If a couple agrees to equality, then (1) what are the psychological/emotional expectations of involvement in the family, and (2) how are the tasks of living divided? The couple may divide shopping, paying bills, and other task allocations more equally than ways to mutually nurture each other and coparent. Once traditional roles are thrown out, the couple is left to define and negotiate both roles and tasks with only the vague concept of equality as a guide.

Thus, without the benefit of culturally defined gender roles, each couple begins anew to define egalitarian responsibilities and expectations. The concept of equity may be agreed to, but implementing it in daily life requires successful negotiations. These negotiations may also lead to conflict.

Reciprocity

We prefer to work with the concept of role reciprocity rather than the concept of a traditional–egalitarian dimension when examining the intricacies of a couple's relationship. (By reciprocity we mean the mutual and complementary exchange of roles in a couple's life.) Reciprocity is a broader conceptual tool because it is fluid. It is framed by cultural expectations, developmental phases, and often changes with age and the interrelationships between the couple. For example, with today's fluctuating economy and the preponderance of two-paycheck families, roles and role expectations are more fluid and changeable. One partner may be out of work for several weeks, months, or years, and the other may need to assume more of the financial responsibilities. As children move through the developmental stages, different responses are required of the couple as parents. The man or woman may need to be more involved with the children.

Thus, as time goes on, what each partner needs or wants from the other may change. One partner may take on the majority of household tasks while the other partner pursues a degree in night school. Once that partner has graduated, the roles may be reversed. A couple's strength lies in establishing reciprocal patterns of responsiveness to one another. One partner may have to postpone his or her needs while the couple's resources go to his or her mate. This is done in good faith because the partner knows that at some point in the future this consideration will be returned.

However, reciprocity should not be confused with a tit-for-tat mentality or with each partner keeping score of what the other one has received. It is a recognition by both parties that a relationship ebbs and flows and that at any given time one partner's needs may take precedence, but ultimately a balance will be maintained.

The concept of reciprocity has its roots in sociological and social-psychological exchange theory within a feminist framework. When working from a social systems perspective, we understand that all forms of social organizations are composed of interdependent parts. A marital couple is no exception.

Exchange theory is based on the assumption that all people need others. The exchange of all types of goods, services, emotions, and benefits is the medium through which need satisfaction occurs. The theory, which applies psychological generalizations to sociological phenomena, was initially developed to study small groups (Kelley & Thibaut, 1978; Thibaut & Kelley, 1959). From an exchange theory perspective, relationships are satisfying and fair when both partners make approximately equal contributions and receive approximately equal positive rewards (Sabatelli & Shehan, 1993). When one partner does not believe the relationship is fair, then he or she may either decrease his or her investment in the relationship or attempt to change the other person. Within this context, reciprocity refers to situations in which partners, taking each others' needs into account, negotiate exchanges that not only benefit themselves but are mutually rewarding. Gottman (1994a, b) observed that couples may absorb negative exchanges if for every one negative exchange there are five positive ones.

It is not, however, the quantity or quality of the items exchanged but the value we place on them that determines the rewards and costs of the exchange. For example, partners offer one another resources in exchange for needs satisfaction. She walks the dog, and he cleans the kitchen. As a couple's relationship evolves, exchange patterns become established. You do this, and I will take care of that. The value, however, placed on the various resources is unique to each couple. For example, the wife greatly values the husband getting up early on Saturday morning and taking the kids out of the house to play so that she may sleep late. He values the extra hours she works to help pay the bills. She values being held in bed.

What if he also hates getting up early on Saturday morning? Or, in the words of exchange theory, the cost of getting up on Saturday is high. He may decide to do it because it avoids an argument between them, but in his mind he will be looking for a reward of equal value from his wife—for example, she does not complain about him playing softball with his buddies during the week (equal value in his eyes).

The balance of value is a central force in maintaining the equilibrium in the couple's relationship—the rewards and costs of the relationship are in balance. Reciprocity describes a means of mutual exchange that establishes and maintains the equilibrium. When it is maintained, both partners' needs are being met, but when the process of exchange is imbalanced, individual needs are not being met and the costs of being in the relationship are too high—the steady (homeostatic) state of the system is upset.

A couple entering therapy presents an imbalanced equilibrium. Perhaps one or both parties feel that their needs are not being met and that the costs of the relationship outweigh the rewards. Or maybe one partner's needs dominate over the other's. What each partner values or needs may not be understood by the other. Or, perhaps the couple is not able to evolve mutually satisfying, reciprocal exchange patterns. Whatever the case, the therapist is being asked to establish or reestablish a reciprocal exchange pattern.

The concept of reciprocity is congruent with an ecological approach because to define the meaning of reciprocity *for the couple,* the therapist must consider not only the psychological influence of their families of origin, but the cultural and ethnic influences that frame this couple's reality. Because culture provides an interpretive system for behavior, the therapist must consider not only the couple's individual cultural heritage, but also the degree of acculturation of the ethnic group in general.

For example, McGoldrick et al. (1991) observed that ethnicity intersects with class, religion, politics, and the length of time a group has been in a country. Traditional Puerto Rican families are patriarchal, and the relationships of African-American couples tend to be more egalitarian. However, gender roles may change as the ethnic identity assimilates into the dominant culture.

This acculturation process influences the perception of proper role expectations and the distribution of power. The perception of proper role expectations influences the couple's definition of reciprocity within the relationship. For instance, when a couple with a strong cultural, traditional influence that scripts that women stay at home with young children have their first child, they may *both* decide that the new mother will stay home and the new father will procure a second job. They may *both* perceive a good deal of reciprocity in this situation. Even though an economic power imbalance occurs, it may not upset the couple's homeostatic balance, because they *each* endorse the cultural norms and believe they are doing what needs to be done to care for their baby.

Summary

Without the luxury of an opposite sex cotherapist, therapists form an imbalanced gender triangle with heterosexual couples. It is within this context that gender biases on both the therapists' and couples' part affect the therapeutic process. All three members of the triangle enter therapy with their respective views of male and female roles and criteria for judging how well one is fulfilling his or her role.

A therapist is by no means immune to socially constructed cultural definitions of male and female behavior. As couples explore their family of origin influences and current gender-role expectations, many subtle and overt examples of sexist behaviors and power imbalances emerge. Consequently, the therapist must avoid two pitfalls: (1) intruding with one's own sociopolitical views of family, gender, and marriage and (2) aligning with the same-sex client concerning the partner's accusations and role expectations.

In order to avoid these traps, particularly those related to traditional and egalitarian ideology, a therapist first assesses a couple's goodness of fit. Where does each partner fall along the traditional–egalitarian dimension and how satisfied is each partner with the other's position?

Embedded within cultural and family of origin influences, individual positions along the traditional–egalitarian dimension may prove difficult to shift. However, even if a couple presents a poor goodness of fit where there are significant differences between the two positions, modifying the reciprocity equilibrium offers an alternative means of improving the relationship.

Above all else, what a therapist can most definitely be aware of is his or her own position on the traditional–egalitarian dimension. Not only is it valuable self-knowledge, but it is an awareness that hopefully sensitizes one to the issue of gender in couples therapy.

Our belief is that each therapist must construct his or her own gender-sensitive guidelines for the androgynous therapist's role. However, as food for thought, the following is a list of guidelines toward a feminist family therapy perspective formulated by Walters, Carter, Papp, and Silverstein (1988) in their book *The Invisible Web: Gender Patterns in Family Relationships*. Based on the notion that "gender is the essential wellspring of all behaviors" (p. 26), we hope this list will stimulate the reader's own construction of guidelines for couples therapy:

1. Identify gender message and social constructs that condition behavior and sex roles.
2. Recognize the real limitations of female access to social and economic resources.
3. Be aware of sexist thinking that constricts the options of women to direct their own lives.
4. Acknowledge that women have been socialized to assume primary responsibility for family relationships.
5. Recognize the dilemmas and conflicts of childbearing and child rearing in our society.
6. Be aware of patterns that split the women in families as they seek to acquire power through relationships with men.
7. Affirm values and behaviors characteristic of women, such as connectedness, nurturing, and emotionality.
8. Recognize and support possibilities for women outside of marriage and the family.
9. Recognize the basic principle that no intervention is gender-free and that every intervention will have a different and special meaning for each sex.

CHAPTER FIVE

The First Interview

We now turn to the process of therapy proper. The remainder of the book follows a case presentation from the first interview through assessment, planning interventions and the middle phases of therapy (which involve change, impasse and commitment) to termination. Keeping with the theme of the book, we highlight the influence of gender at each of these phases.

The importance of the first interview cannot be underestimated because this is when each member of the therapeutic triangle (therapist and couple) forms individual impressions and assessments. Each member of the couple evaluates the therapist as much as the therapist evaluates the couple. The couple want to know if the therapist is reliable, trustworthy, and knowledgeable and if he or she will understand them or judge them, Overall, the couple want to know what this therapy business is all about. The therapist, on the other hand, begins two critical processes: engagement and assessment (Worden, 1994).

Structural Sequence

In order to introduce the case presentation, as well as to underscore the progression of a first interview, the following sections take the reader through the structural sequence of a first interview: initial contact, greeting, defining the purpose of the first session, defining the problem, establishing tentative goals, and ending the interview. (The case is an amalgamation of a number of cases we have worked with through the years.)

PHONE INFORMATION

The amount of information a therapist possesses before a first interview varies with the treatment setting—for example, mental health clinic, social service agency, or private practice. In some settings a thorough biographical interview is conducted over the phone by an intake worker who gathers information such as the ages of the members of the couple, the number of children, and the names and ages of extended family and who makes this data available to the clinician. At other times, the initial phone contact is brief, supplying only the names and telephone numbers of the prospective clients.

For our purposes, Lynn called the therapist's office to ask for couples counseling. She said she and her husband were having difficulties and would like to speak to someone. She made an appointment for the following week.

GREETING

As the therapist opened the waiting room door, Lynn and her husband Carl sat next to one another quietly talking.

Therapist: Hello, it is nice to meet you. Did you have any trouble finding the office?

After showing the couple the way to the therapist's office, the therapist asks the couple to sit anywhere they feel comfortable. As each spouse chooses his or her seat, the therapist begins what appears to be idle chatter.

Therapist: Did you have a long drive? How did you get my name?

In the greeting stage, the therapist is breaking the ice and welcoming the couple into therapy. Not only does this set a tone of informality, but it also reduces the couple's initial anxiety. In all probability, each member of the couple has rehearsed what he or she is going to say but is now drawing a blank because of anxiety. The "idle" chit-chat eases the couple into the therapist's office and gives them a chance to catch their breaths.

DEFINING THE PURPOSE OF THE FIRST SESSION

One errs if the greeting stage lasts too long. The therapist is the expert, and the couple is there with a problem. A prolonged greeting stage confuses the couple— "When are we going to talk about our problem?"—and inadvertently raises anxiety. Thus, at some point the therapist calls the meeting to order and provides structure by highlighting a statement of purpose:

Therapist: I would like to tell you what we will be doing in this interview. First, I would like to find out some biographical information on your family and then hear from each of you as to why you are here today and what are your expectations. Later I would be happy to share with you my impressions and recommendations. At the end of the session, I will leave time for you to ask me any questions you may have.

Besides structuring the first interview, this statement indicates the give-and-take nature of therapy. The therapist is defining a norm of mutuality and reciprocity and inviting the couple to participate in the therapy process. Each person will be listened to and will be able to ask questions. The therapist will also share observations and impressions and is available for questions. Therapy is a conjoint venture, not something that the therapist will do to the couple. By inviting the couple to participate in the process, a therapeutic norm is being created and a clear message is given: In this encounter, power is shared and mutuality is valued.

Although a more thorough genogram may be constructed in later sessions, initial, brief biographical information helps orient the therapist by placing the couple within a context. For example:

Therapist: How long have the two of you known one another?

How long have you been married?

Any children? Ages?

Any extended family nearby? Family members you might see on a regular basis?

How long have you lived in the area? Any significant moves in the past? Any major illnesses or significant health problems? (particularly probing for caretaker roles or chronic stresses)

Briefly, Lynn and Carl have been married for 4 years. He is 32 years old and she is 31. They had met through mutual friends 6 years earlier, dated for a year, and were engaged for a year before marrying. Their daughter, Jenn, is 18 months old. After a maternity leave, Lynn returned to work 6 months ago. Lynn and Carl relied on neighbors to help provide child care in an emergency, but Lynn's mother, who lived in the area, cared for Jenn most of the time. Carl's parents were retired and lived out of state. All are in good health and Jenn is developing normally.

In gathering the above biographical information, the therapist is also observing nonverbal behavior. For example, Lynn took the initiative in answering these questions. She answered them directly without glancing at Carl. Carl appeared more to be observing than participating at this stage of the interview. His face was expressionless, thus making him difficult to read. His body language, however, communicated a noninvolvement and a wait-and-see attitude.

At this stage of the interview the therapist is already forming initial hypotheses concerning the couple's relationship and potential problems:

1. The couple has been going through two major life transitions with the birth of their daughter and Lynn's return to work. Had they been actively trying to have children? Was Jenn's birth a surprise? How was the decision made for Lynn to return to work? What changes has that brought for them as a couple?
2. The child-care arrangement would throw the couple into close contact with Lynn's family. Is this a supportive involvement? Does the involvement contain any hidden emotional costs?
3. Lynn, at least initially, takes the lead in the couple's interaction and presentation to the therapist while Carl sits seemingly passive. Is this a pattern

that carries over to their other interactions? Does Lynn consistently initiate and Carl react? Is Carl just slow to warm up?

Again, these are initial hypotheses that will be confirmed or negated with further data. Initial hypotheses, however, begin the formulation of the problem identification stages.

Defining the Problem

After briefly gathering biographical information, the therapist moves to the heart of the first interview: the definition of the problem. Defining the problem consists of (1) eliciting individual perspectives, (2) exploring differences in perspectives, (3) moving from blame to collaboration: a search for positives, and (4) introducing a systemic definition of the problem.

Eliciting Individual Perspectives

Although there is a high probability that each spouse will initially blame the other, each person needs the opportunity to state his or her opinion and to be listened to.

Therapist (The comment is directed to both members of the couple, and the therapist observes who responds first.):   I wonder if you would tell me what brings you here today. What were your reasons for calling and what do you hope to gain from our meeting?

Lynn (*does not hesitate or look at Carl*):   Since the baby was born, everything seems to have gone downhill. We barely talk to one another, and when we do it usually results in an argument over one thing or another. We just don't communicate any more.

(Carl stares straight ahead saying nothing.)

Lynn: I feel like I don't get any help around the house and with going back to work I am overwhelmed.

(Carl continues to stare straight ahead.)

Therapist: Carl, I was wondering how you see things.

Carl: She's been really tense since the baby was born, and going back to work has made it worse. But, we need the money and nobody can get by on one paycheck anymore. We tried, but it's just not enough to go around.

Therapist: So, in what ways has your marriage been affected?

Carl: Like I said, Lynn is always tense and on edge.

Therapist: Are you saying that is the reason the two of you are having difficulties at this time?

Carl: Yes.

At this point, an early outline is beginning to form with hints of blame and lineal causality. Lynn feels overwhelmed and disconnected from her husband.

Carl, on the other hand, sees their problem based inside of Lynn: She's tense and on edge. Implied in their presentation is that things would improve if the other person changed.

Rather than support these lineal definitions of their problems, the therapist moves to further explore the couple's patterns.

Therapist: Given how you each see the problem, how have you each tried to solve it?

Lynn: I try to ask him over and over to talk to me and give me a hand, but he either ignores me or tells me he will do it later.

(Carl sits and stares.)

Therapist: Carl?

Carl: All she does is nag and criticize. I help out a lot and we both work hard and by the evening she is too tired for anything.

Although the therapist could pursue either Lynn's or Carl's view of the problem, the therapist makes a choice and asks what they each have tried and how they see things. This accomplishes four objectives:

1. Assessing if the blaming permeates other areas of their marriage,
2. Assessing areas of satisfaction in their marriage that are not affected by the major transitions,
3. Assessing degrees of change in marital areas that have been affected, and
4. Assessing global similarities and differences in their perceptions of the marriage.

Even at this early stage of the interview, however, the central dynamic is readily visible. Each blames the other for the current state of affairs, and each wants the other to change. They have attributed the problems to qualities inside the other person: He is not giving or open, and she is overwhelmed and tense. To belabor these points by asking for further examples may only reinforce the blaming and lineal causality exchanges. Therefore the therapist decides to shift focus to gain leverage in redefining the problem. In doing so, the therapist attempts to change nouns into verbs and static personality traits into patterns of interaction.

Therapist: Lynn, what do you mean when you say the two of you no longer communicate with one another? From what you have described so far, I believe you are talking about your daughter and things about your house. Are there other things you have quit talking about?

Lynn: Well, we don't talk like we used to, about one another.

Therapist: About one another?

Lynn: Yes, we used to talk about what we felt about things and one another. We just don't any more because he is busy working or watching television.

Therapist: Before we get to the reasons, I want to understand what used to happen and what you would like to happen more.

The therapist is continually moving away from static personality traits—he is stubborn; she is demanding—to highlight interactions. Along the same lines, as much as the word *communication* connotes interaction when used in this context, it possesses a static quality. It implies that communication is something you have or you do not. The statement "We lack communication" is a misnomer. A couple is always communicating. For example, a day of silence between a couple speaks volumes. Consequently, if the therapist accepts the definition of the problem as one of communication, then communication has become a static entity that either exists or does not. Instead of placing a definition on the problem, the therapist is introducing the idea of circular causality and mutual responsibility. (Circular causality will be discussed more fully in Chapter 7. But briefly, circular causality assumes that A causes B that causes C that causes or modifies A. Thus, rather than identify a linear cause—A causes B—from a circular causality perspective, members of a couple mutually shape and reinforce one another without a distinguishable beginning or end.)

Up to this point in the interview, Carl has essentially sat silently watching his wife and the therapist discuss Lynn's view of their communication. Now the therapist can either bring Carl into the discussion—"Carl, I wonder how you see your and Lynn's communication?"—or allow him to identify separately what he sees as the problem. Focusing on the communication issue would probably not facilitate Carl's engagement in the assessment process. From Carl's perspective, not only has Lynn continually told him that communication, or more likely his lack of communication, was their problem, but now the therapist also appears to believe it. Moreover, Carl has not had the opportunity to tell his side of the story.

Therapist: Carl, forgive me for speaking so long with Lynn about communication, but I wanted to understand her position. However, I have been doing this long enough to know that there are two sides to every story. So, would you please tell me how you see things between you?

Carl: Like I said earlier, she is tired all the time. I know it is rough with Jenn and working, but I am trying my hardest too! But all Lynn can do is criticize and nag.

Here the therapist has another choice point. He or she could offer a supportive comment, "You sound as though you are beginning to feel unappreciated in this marriage." This comment has several purposes: (1) it establishes connection with the male client in a supportive way without commenting on who is "right" or "wrong," (2) it globally assesses other areas in which he feels unappreciated, and (3) it assesses if he experiences this as a change in the marriage.

If the therapist does not choose the supportive comment, then he or she would proceed as follows. Instead of asking "What are you criticized about?"—a list that would probably imply a set of personality traits—the therapist asks interactional, process questions concerning when the criticism occurs and how he responds.

Therapist: Under what circumstances do you feel criticized?

Carl: She says I don't do enough around the house and that I don't care enough about her and the baby.

Therapist: When does that usually happen?

Carl: At the end of the day when the baby goes to sleep and the house is a little quieter.

Therapist: What do you do when you feel you are being criticized?

Carl: I just turn it off because I know there is no point in getting into it because it will just go on and on.

Therapist: How do you mean it will go on and on?

Carl: Lynn won't give it a rest. She will keep it up and up and almost follow me around the house.

Lynn (*interrupting the dialogue*): What do you mean go on and on and follow you around the house? If I didn't somehow get your attention we would never talk about anything.

Therapist: Excuse me, Lynn, but I want to hear you both out completely. So let me finish with Carl, and then I want to hear what you each have to say about the other's answers.

(Another choice point is presented. Lynn's interruption threatened to ignite a familiar argument between her and Carl. Although such an argument would be instructive in portraying the couple's dynamics to the therapist, Carl still needed to be drawn out and completely heard. If the initial interview regressed to familiar arguments, Carl would rightfully wonder, "What's the purpose of this [therapy]? We could do this at home.")

Therapist: So, Carl, how does a disagreement finally end?

Carl: Well, either she just finally gives up . . .

Therapist: Gives up?

Carl: Yeah, I just don't say anything, and she finally gives up. Or, she pushes me far enough, and I get angry.

Therapist: And after you get angry?

Carl: Well, she gets hurt, and there's a cold chill in the house for a day or so.

Therapist: How does the chill go away?

Carl: Oh, we just kind of forget about it.

In this early exchange the couple's conflict patterns and conflict resolution styles are initially presented. Lynn is the one most likely to identify a problem. Her requests for help are heard by Carl as criticism. He withdraws, leaving Lynn frustrated and in pursuit. Carl either waits her out or reaches a boiling point and explodes. Lynn then pulls away hurt and a chill comes over their home. Worse still, the disagreement is not resolved but accumulates under the carpet until the next time someone trips over it.

Exploring differences

To this point the first interview resembles individual therapy from the context of an observer (the other spouse). Eliciting each spouse's individual perspective provides order to the interview and allows each spouse the time to relate his or her unique perspective. By doing this, the therapist sends a message that each point of view has merit and will be fully appreciated.

Equally important, however, this sequencing also tests the couple's ability to listen to each other. If the spouses are able to listen to one another—one judges this primarily through nonverbal behavior—this is certainly a better prognostic sign than if the observing spouse sits and rolls his or her eyes or stares out the window. Accordingly, constant interruptions are signs of: (1) an inability to listen to the other, (2) explosiveness, or (3) constant simmering tension between the spouses.

To continue with the interview, after each individual perspective is elicited, the therapist opens and encourages a dialogue between the spouses.

Therapist: Well, you have each listened to what the other has to say, and I would like to know what you agree with and what you disagree with.

Although this comment typically elicits a point-counterpoint exchange between the spouses, it is the quality of this exchange that bears attention.

Lynn (*looking directly at the therapist*):   I don't understand how Carl can say those things. The way he paints the picture, I am some kind of witch.

Here, another therapeutic choice point arises. The therapist has asked the couple to comment on one another's definitions of the problem. Lynn begins by speaking about Carl but directs her comments to the therapist. The therapist has a choice either of remaining silent and thus reinforcing the flow of communication from Lynn to therapist or redirecting Lynn's communication toward Carl and thus facilitating an exchange between them.

Several factors might influence the therapist's choice at this point. If the first interview is highly emotionally charged, marked by a state of tension, constant interruptions, and a rising state of frustration, the therapist may wish to defuse the situation by engaging each spouse in one-on-one dialogues, a pattern continuing the norm first established by the therapist. In doing so, the therapist stands ready to block interruptions and quite literally forces the other spouse to listen.

On the other hand, encouraging each spouse to directly talk to the other makes the couple's patterns come alive in the session. Continually redirecting statements provides the observant therapist with a fund of information to use in analyzing communication skills and the interpersonal climate. For example, is the couple able to maintain contact and listen to one another? What are characteristics of the couple's communication skills? Does their frustration and anger completely interfere with their ability to appropriately respond to one another?

Based on the moderate tension level that is present, the therapist responds to Lynn's comment.

Therapist: Lynn, would you please ask Carl your question directly.

Lynn (*now looking at Carl*):   How can you say I am always criticizing you?

Carl: Because that is what it always seems like to me.

Lynn: But how else will I get you to do something? You just put me off and put me off.

When asked to speak directly to one another, each spouse levels more blame and the heat in the room rises. A therapist may decide to let this discussion continue as a means of more fully understanding the couple's patterns and their communication skills. However, to allow the discussion to continue on its own also risks increasing the couple's frustration and anger.

Thus, while the therapist wishes to facilitate the couple's exchange, he or she also attempts to change the quality of the exchange.

Therapist: Is this how the conversation always goes when this issue is discussed?

(Both Lynn and Carl nod their heads.)

Therapist: Well, I would like for the two of you to try something. I would like for you to try to say what you want to say but in a different way.

Lynn: I don't know what you mean.

Therapist: Well, for example, you ask the question of Carl concerning his comments about being criticized. Find out what he means when he says it.

Lynn: OK. Carl, what do you mean you feel criticized?

Therapist (*interrupting*):   Sorry, Lynn, but that's pretty close to what you have said already. Ask it or state it in a different way.

Lynn: I am confused. I don't know what you mean.

Therapist: Carl, can you help her to ask the question in a different way?

Carl: Sure, just come out and ask me, "*When* do you feel criticized?"

Therapist: I like that, Carl. Now go ahead and answer your own question.

The therapist has interrupted the familiar blame pattern between Carl and Lynn and has asked them to respond in a new way. The therapist does not *tell* them how to do it but instead blocks the old patterns and forces the couple to generate new ones.

As a further example, let's reverse the flow of the exchange.

Therapist: Carl, you said Lynn is always tired and overwhelmed and that is when she will criticize you. What do you think it is like to be tired and overwhelmed like Lynn?

Carl: I don't know.

Therapist: Go ahead and give it a try.

Carl: Well, I guess you would feel like it is never going to end. Like you are never going to get ahead of the game.

Therapist: Why don't you check that out with Lynn?

Carl: Is that what it is like?

Lynn: Yes.

In addition to interrupting the familiar blame patterns, the therapist is asking Carl to: (1) clarify (which entails listening) and (2) empathize with what Lynn is feeling. This affirmation is something Lynn has been wanting from Carl, some recognition of what it is like for her. Also, asking one member of the couple to empathize with the other opens up the possibility of viewing the problem from another's perspective. This may stimulate an early recognition within the couple that there are two sides to every story.

A Shift from Blame to Collaboration

By the time the couple enters the therapist's office, their difficulties may appear insurmountable. Problems dominate their life together. In turn, the couple has lost perspective on what brought them together in the first place—their strengths as a couple. Thus, after listening and exploring the couple's problems, the therapist then shifts gears with a twofold purpose: (1) to uncover the couple's strengths and (2) to change the focus from blame or lineal causality to collaboration or circular causality. Before redefining the problem within a circular perspective, the therapist sets the stage for this shift by identifying the strengths of the relationship.

Recognizing the strengths in the relationship changes the emotional climate of the session—establishes a base on which to strengthen the fundamentals of the relationship. If early strengths can't be identified, this has diagnostic significance. The marriage may not have a stable foundation, and the early attraction that brought the partners together was fleeting and superficial.

Therapist: Well, I think I have at least a beginning understanding of how each of you views your problems and how you attempt to manage them. To balance out the picture, however, I would like to know what you do well together. For example, why were you initially attracted to the other person and how did the two of you decide to get married?

(Both spouses look at one another, each hesitant to go first. Finally, after a brief silence, Lynn begins to speak.)

Lynn: We met through mutual friends. We were introduced at a party at their apartment and soon afterwards we started to date.

(Lynn sticks to the basic facts, not wanting to risk exposing any feelings that Carl might reject.)

Therapist: How did you decide to go out with Carl in the first place?

Lynn: Well, he was very quiet and shy but also was sweet and considerate. Also, I felt a physical attraction toward him.

Therapist: In what ways was he sweet and considerate?

Lynn: He would call me a lot. He would listen to me.

Therapist (*moving Carl into the discussion*):   Carl, what about for you? Why did you ask Lynn out?

Carl: Lynn had a glow about her. She knew everyone at the party, and it seemed like she got along with everybody. She was fun to be with and also pretty sexy.

At this point the therapist continues to explore the couple's early attractions to one another. Not only is this valuable assessment data but, therapeutically, the negative blaming mood of the interview has shifted into the positive aspects of their relationship. This results in a change in the interview's tone. Each spouse is no longer in a defensive stance expecting to be blamed by the other. Instead, each person is hearing positive things said about him- or herself that he or she has not heard in a long time.

After exploring the initial attractions and early dating relationships, the therapist pursues the couple's decision to get married, but, more specifically, what each hoped for in the marriage. The therapist explores the initial marital expectations.

Therapist: After you decided to get married and in the weeks and months leading up to the marriage, what did each of you hope or believe you were gaining by marrying the other person. For example, were you gaining a friend, a partner, someone who will be with you in the ups and downs? Carl, how about you going first this time?

(By asking Carl to go first, the therapist is further disrupting the couple's established patterns. The initiative was now placed on Carl's shoulders.)

Carl: A wife and potential mother for our children.

Therapist: OK, but I guess I am asking something more specific and unique to you. In marrying Lynn how would your life be different?

Carl: She would be there for me. She would create a home.

Therapist: You also mentioned fun and sexy.

Carl: Yeah, that too.

Therapist: Those sound like great additions to your life. Lynn?

Lynn: A partner . . . someone with whom I could share things. Also, he seemed so stable and secure.

Therapist: The stability and security would add something to your life?

Lynn: Yes, I was tired of the dating rat race. I thought Carl was someone I could build a life with.

By developing the positive themes in the marriage, the therapist is creating a richer picture of the relationship. Yes, this is a couple with problems, but it is also a couple with strengths—a point the couple themselves may have forgotten. Moreover, focusing on the negatives alone in the first interview projects a distorted view of the couple's relationship and defines the therapy process as "fixing" the problems, which to this point means changing the other person. Instead, the positives facilitate a redefinition of the couple's problems and set the stage for a therapeutic process that emphasizes the strengths inherent in their marriage.

A Systemic Definition That Frames Circular Causality

A circular or systemic definition of reciprocal patterns replaces the blaming or linear causality approach that focuses on changing individuals. The couple's strengths and hopes are mobilized both to facilitate engagement in therapy and secure a commitment to the change process that will be difficult for both partners.

The therapist first focuses on their strengths and the similarities of their early expectations. He or she then redefines the problems as a series of patterns within a context of patterns that has developed within the changing relationship. The therapist emphasizes that *both* will need to invest in working on changing and strengthening the relationship.

Therapist: It seems to me that as a couple the two of you have lost your way. You both appear to want similar things from one another: someone to build a life with, someone to share with. Also, you each saw the other person as adding something very positive to your life, but, unfortunately, those hopes and desires have been recently lost. Instead, some painful patterns have evolved between you. Lynn, you feel as if you must continually pursue Carl, which cannot be very satisfying to you. Carl, you pull away to avoid the hurt you feel in Lynn's comments. You have turned into two warring camps, guarded against one another.

It seems to me that if these patterns do not change, they will destroy you as a couple. Now, I cannot absolutely promise you that therapy will change your relationship, but if you both are willing to work on these patterns, then there is a chance for you to have the relationship you each hoped for when you got married.

At this point, the decision is up to the couple as to whether or not to proceed with therapy. Neither person has been blamed and the problem has been redefined as the patterns in the relationship. Notice the specific nature of the patterns has not been fleshed out; rather, the therapist is offering another perspective on the marriage—a perspective that builds on the couple's hopes and strengths.

TENTATIVE OUTLINE OF THE THERAPEUTIC PROCESS

It is unrealistic to believe a thorough assessment can take place in a first interview; rather, the initial session begins the therapeutic process by:

1. engaging the couple
2. developing preliminary hypotheses
3. placing the problem within a systemic perspective
4. establishing tentative goals.

The therapist's initial interventions, if successful, have redefined the blame, replaced lineal causality with circular causality, and offered hope to the couple.

In outlining the therapeutic process, the therapist builds on the couple's strengths and desires. On a content level, the spouse's individual wants may appear at odds with one another. Lynn wants Carl to help more with the baby. She would also like more intimacy than they currently have. Carl would like less criticism sent his way and for Lynn to be more like the woman he believed he married. But regardless of the content complaints, both Lynn and Carl have the universal needs of wanting to be heard, respected, cared for, and loved. How can something so simple become so painful?

Therapist: We are coming to the end of the interview and I would like to propose some goals for future meetings. First, I would like to explore further how you each view your problems. In doing so I may need to gather more family history to help me understand what you each have brought into the marriage. Second, I would like for the two of you to observe your patterns and clarify them for me. I am only going on first impressions, and I could be wrong or could misunderstand the situation. And finally, I would like to know more about your strengths as a couple.

This monologue outlines the next steps in the therapy process. The family of origin is introduced as an important variable that will be considered. Next, the couple are given responsibility to observe their own patterns. This shifts the attention away from changing the individual to viewing the couple's interaction as the problem. Finally, the couple are recognized as having strengths and the therapist hints that these will be important for therapy.

By outlining this process at the end of the first interview, the therapist loosely structures future meetings. This communicates that there is a plan to therapy and addresses the couple's unstated question, "What is this therapy business all about and what will be required of me?"

ENDING THE FIRST INTERVIEW

At the end of the first interview, the couple are offered the opportunity to ask the therapist questions. Offering the couple the opportunity to ask questions communicates the collaborative atmosphere of therapy. Therapy will be a cooperative effort between the therapist and couple and not something a therapist does to the couple.

Specifically, these questions may be procedural or of a personal nature. Procedural questions pertain to the conduct of therapy: How long will therapy last? How often will we have to come? What are the fees? Will my insurance cover the sessions? Personal questions are concerned with the therapist as a person.

Throughout the first interview, the partners are assessing the therapist as much as the therapist is assessing the couple: Can we trust this person? Will this person understand? Will we be judged? The opportunity to ask personal questions, therefore, may address some of the couple's initial concerns about entering therapy with this therapist in particular and it further facilitates the engagement process.

Therapist: Well, I have been asking both of you a variety of questions, and before we end I would like to give you the opportunity to ask me any questions you have. Please, is there anything you would like to ask concerning therapy? Or, anything about myself, my assessment or expectations?

While procedural questions are straightforward requests for information, personal questions explore the future therapeutic relationship. Accordingly, personal questions may take three forms: personal questions concerning the therapist, questions concerning the therapist's competency, and questions regarding the therapist's assessment.

Questions concerning the therapist:
    Are you married?
    How long have you been married?
    Do you have any children?

Questions concerning the therapist's competency:
    How long have you been doing this?
    What is your success rate?

These questions are basically concerned with the therapist's ability to understand and appreciate the couple's lives—"Are you married?"—and the therapist's competence—"How long have you been in practice?" More often than not the answers to these questions are not as important as the way in which the therapist answers. For example, is the therapist defensive? Does the therapist avoid certain questions? Is the therapist open and engaging? Again, the therapist's mannerisms communicate volumes of information to the couple.

It should be noted that we are making a distinction between the first interview and later interviews. During the first session, when the couple are deciding whether or not to begin therapy, questions about the therapist are seen as legitimate requests for information to help the couple make their decision. Later on, however, personal questions of the therapist assume a different quality.

In subsequent sessions, personal questions may reflect a defensive posture or a resistance to change, for example:

Therapist: Carl, I think Lynn is trying to send you a message that for some reason you don't want to hear.

Carl: Well, haven't you ever had a disagreement with your wife? How do you react when you are criticized?

Therapist: I don't think my life is the issue right now, but I do wonder if you just felt criticized by me.

In this exchange, the therapist is staying with the interaction between Lynn and Carl, but Carl is reacting to Lynn's comment by defensively attempting to put the spotlight on the therapist. In the therapist's mind two hypotheses exist— either the interaction between Carl and Lynn was too much for Carl and he needed to withdraw and did so by shifting to the therapist, or Carl felt criticized by the therapist. Choosing the latter hypothesis, the therapist redirects the comment back to Carl and also opens up a dialogue between them.

At this point in therapy, Carl's personal question of the therapist was not a request for information but a defensive maneuver. From the therapist's perspective, understanding the defensive nature of the question is the priority.

The third type of questions asks for an initial diagnosis and prognosis.

Questions concerning the therapist's assessment:
    Have you ever dealt with similar problems?
    What's wrong with us?
    Can this get any better?
    How do people usually handle this stuff?
    Should we stay married?

These questions can reflect several themes, such as the couple's anxiety about their relationship and an appeal for the therapist to blame someone.

Carl: Somebody's got to be right and somebody's got to be wrong, so who do you think is right and who is wrong?

Therapist: Honestly, as I said earlier, I don't view it that way. You have both evolved the patterns in your marriage and it will take both of you to change them. But, as I reflect on your question, I wonder why it is important to you that someone be right and someone be wrong.

Here, the therapist responds to Carl's question of blame by highlighting a circular causality perspective and he or she also explores Carl's need to establish blame. Finally, the therapist concludes the first interview by placing the responsibility and decision for continuing therapy on the couple.

Therapist: At this point we have a decision to make. If you would like we can schedule the next appointment, or if you want to go away and think about it, that is fine also. You could call me at any time and we could make the next appointment.

If the members of a couple are highly motivated and they were comfortable with the first interview, each partner tends to quickly look to the other and through eyes and movement of the head they decide to make another appointment. However, in offering the couple the option of postponing the decision, the therapist further underlines the couple's responsibility for beginning change. Also, the therapist is allowing room for the couple to "save face" by letting them think about it without making a commitment one way or another. And finally, diagnostically, the reluctant member of the couple quickly seizes this opportunity.

Carl: Well, I think we should discuss this and then call you back.
    (A silence fills the room and Carl and Lynn stare at one another.)
Carl: We will call you back.

Carl is voicing his reluctance to begin therapy. In many ways this is to be expected because his pattern is to withdraw when threatened. Moreover, although Lynn had been the initiator in the early part of the interview and Carl was silent when it came to making a decision, Carl exerted a form of power by postponing another appointment. One can only imagine what their drive home will be like. Will Lynn raise her objections to Carl's decision to postpone making another appointment? Will Lynn sit in seething silence?

Gender Process Issues in the First Interview

The structural sequence of the first interview outlines the interview's logical progression and highlights the movement from mutual blame to collaboration. Underlying this sequence, however, are the subtle issues of gender. Specifically, men and women frequently approach therapy in very different ways.

MEN ENTERING THERAPY

Conventional therapeutic wisdom says that men are notoriously resistant to psychotherapy. They come only at their spouses' request. They are the empty chair in family therapy sessions as the wife/mother sits with the children in your office. It's the woman saying to you, "I know he should be here, but he won't come." There are even articles that instruct therapists on ways to involve the resistant male (Doherty, 1981; Gaines, 1981; Kaslow, 1981).

In analyzing this phenomenon, we find that the literature on men in therapy highlights the negative impact of the masculine gender role on psychological distress and help-seeking behavior (Gordon & Allen, 1990; Levant, 1990; Meth & Pasick, 1990; Osherson & Krugman, 1990; Scher, 1990). The masculine gender role is blamed for a potpourri of behaviors in men: overwhelming need to control others, fear of dependency, homophobia, inability to commit to a relationship, fear of vulnerability, inability to express emotion.

Psychotherapy involves exploring thoughts and feelings within a therapeutic relationship that builds in rapport and trust. The therapist, at least initially, is in a one-up position as the expert in charge of the proceedings. Because the client's thoughts and feelings are the concern, self-disclosure is primarily a one-way street: I, the therapist, will ask the most detailed and personal questions of you, but you cannot ask the same questions of me. Given the one-down position and the "work" of therapy, a man's suspicion and reluctance to engage in therapy is understandable. It is antithetical to the way most men operate in the world (Scher, 1990).

In light of the influence of gender roles on men's view of psychotherapy, Levant (1990) identified inhibitions for men seeking therapy: (1) difficulty admitting the existence of a problem, (2) difficulty asking for help, (3) difficulty identifying and processing emotional states, and (4) fear of intimacy.

If men are to be autonomous and strong, admitting the existence of a problem, even to oneself, is a personal competency failure. The answer to the question "Why can't a man ask for directions when he is lost?" is very simple—he is never lost! Denial works quite effectively for many men, especially if it protects their need for competency. In our case presentation, Carl is quite clear that the problem resides inside Lynn. He is merely reacting to a wife who is overwhelmed and highly critical.

Likewise, asking for help is akin to public humiliation. "I should be able to control and solve my own problems," says a voice in the man's head. "Who is this therapist to tell me what is wrong and what to do!" For the male, well trained in assessing a situation's power hierarchy, the role of a client is an uncomfortable, one-down position.

The heart of most therapy approaches is identifying and processing emotional states—a distinctly feminine role endeavor. "What are you feeling? How did that make you feel? What did you feel then?" are questions that are anathema to most men. The skill of assessing one's and another's feelings is not fostered in masculine socialization and is frequently devalued in the workplace. "Don't let them get you down and never let them know what you're thinking or feeling."

This deficit or undeveloped skill in men is blatantly exposed in the therapist's office. An "I don't know" or "nothing" reply most often follows the above feeling questions. Worse yet, in the therapeutic context, a man risks feeling inadequate—"Why don't you know what you feel?—and being labeled the problem—"You need to be more sensitive."

Finally, therapy occurs within the context of an intimate, dependent relationship. According to Gilligan's (1982) thesis that masculinity is defined through separation and femininity is defined through attachment, therapy could be seen as a direct threat to a man's sense of masculinity.

Considering the traditional male gender role, its limited applications to intimate relationships, and the perception that therapy is a feminine endeavor, it is no wonder that men view therapy with suspicion. Consequently, when a man does enter therapy it may be (1) because of the absolute insistence of someone or something else—that is, an employer, the court, or a loved one; (2) to help or change another family member—"I am here because my wife has a problem"; or (3) because the pain he feels overwhelms any gender-role inhibitions. Carl agreed to come to a first interview only at Lynn's insistence. Although the marriage was painful to Carl, his defenses kept those feelings at bay.

In therapy, the gender roles of each client and the therapist will exert the greatest influence in the initial assessment and engagement phase. For men, the initial concerns in a therapeutic situation take two forms: (1) who is in charge and (2) what is expected of me. Thus, issues of power and status are addressed right away. This initially may be subtle as the man sits back, observes, and waits for the therapist to act first. Or, it may be more overt, such as challenging questions from the male client, "Do we really have to get into all of this, because what does it have to do with why we are here?" Overall, an initial test of the therapist's expertise and control of the session is to be expected. Although this behavior may be defined as resistance, it may also be seen as an expression of the male gender role in a new situation (Scher, 1990).

More than 40 years of combined clinical experience have shown us that male clients are more likely to read the diplomas on your wall than are female clients. They will ask more frequently about your training and degrees. This is their way of assimilating vital information concerning status and power positions. He will use this information to either (1) collude in power sharing with the therapist or (2) distance himself from the formal, professional authority. A man will concede his status reluctantly, and it won't happen simply because of a degree on the wall.

Couples therapy not only heightens the initial status testing phase, but it is also fertile ground for competition between the therapist and the male partner. Remember, in couples therapy the man's mate is an audience to his interactions with the therapist: "I will demonstrate how clever I am and that I know more than the therapist." For example, a man with a strong, logical disposition is more than happy to engage the therapist in mental games and in the process attempt to control the flow of the session. Or, the insecure man may need to attempt to intimidate the therapist with veiled anger, "Is this *really* necessary?" Although frequently a form of resistance, competition with the male therapist is also a natural outgrowth of the male role.

WOMEN ENTERING THERAPY

Women voluntarily enter a therapeutic relationship for two main reasons. The first pertains to questions concerning their feminine self-concept. Because most women are unable to consciously acknowledge desires outside of traditional feminine scripts, therapy is often a painful look inward and backward to examine the sources of their unhappiness (Lerner, 1988). Many of these women are likely to seek a female therapist and often request that she be a feminist. They then anticipate exploration of what it means to be a female in our society and consideration of cultural and sociological influences on feminine identity formation and social roles.

The second reason women enter therapy is because of relationship issues. Often women seek therapy after a relationship has ended or to improve and enrich those relationships in which they are currently involved.

It is usually the woman who initiates couples therapy. This initiation fits within her role as keeper of the relationship's emotional fires. In addition, women are accustomed to analyzing and talking about their relationships. Because women are more willing to perceive a therapist as trustworthy and have higher expectations for therapy (Campbell & Johnson, 1991), they frequently serve as a "scout" for the couple, initiating the contact, interviewing the therapist, and presenting the problems. Thus, upon entering therapy, women often assume responsibility for defining the problem, giving examples, and explaining why the problems are occurring.

Sensitive to her mate's emotional state, the female partner usually takes great care to ensure that her male partner will feel comfortable with the therapist's gender, personality, and interpersonal style. To achieve this goal, the woman may request a male therapist to elicit a "man's point of view." This is often the case when the couple see the problems residing in their inability to communicate. Her unarticulated hope may be that a male therapist who is an expert in communication and interpersonal relationships will show her man how to communicate with her. This is a trap male therapists must be wary of falling into.

If she believes her husband feels comfortable with women, she may request a female therapist. Her unarticulated hope here is that her worldview and emotional needs will be confirmed. She may perceive this arrangement as more egalitarian and comfortable for her, but rarely will she insist on this arrangement if it will decrease her husband's participation in the therapeutic process. In the reverse situation, because women are accustomed to in egalitarian relationships with males and easily follow leaders and "experts" (Lerner, 1988), the female partner is generally just as comfortable working with a male therapist.

Finally, if a woman has already decided to end the relationship, she often will initiate therapy with the goal that someone else will take care of her husband after she is gone. In doing so, she lessens her own guilt and she hopes her husband will gain insight into his role in the failed relationship. Still functioning in the emotional caretaker's role, the woman hopes the therapeutic relationship will ease his unhappiness and potential loneliness—the therapist is covertly asked to take care of him.

Summary

The first interview begins the process of engagement and assessment. The couple enter the first session with a fair amount of anxiety, unsure of what to expect. Each may expect to be blamed by the other and each fears the therapist may also blame them. The therapist's task is to avoid the blaming based in lineal causality while engaging each member of the couple, defining the couple's problems, and establishing tentative goals.

To accomplish this the therapist avoids static definitions of the problems—"We don't communicate" or "He or she is insensitive"—and instead focuses on the couple's patterns. The problems, therefore, assume the more fluid quality of patterns. Problems are not defined as residing within one person but instead are seen to occur through interactions.

In doing this, the therapist is promoting several therapeutic norms. First, no one will be blamed in the therapy sessions. Second, we are all in this together. It takes two people to create dysfunctional patterns, and it will take two people to develop healthy ones. And finally, no one will be coerced to do anything in the sessions. Each member of the couple decides whether or not to work in solving these dysfunctional patterns.

Assessment:
The Influence of the Past

Sometimes the fluid waters of therapy flow smoothly, other times they are rough, and occasionally they are dangerous. In order for a therapist to navigate through them effectively, he or she needs a map. These maps are perspectives formulated through the marriage of theory and in-depth clinical experience. In contrast to empirical studies that may be replicated and either supported or challenged, a clinical theory's validity lies in the eye of the beholder. For some, psychoanalytic theory is the truth. For others, family systems theory has the answers. Inevitably, therapists gravitate—perhaps because of training, supervision, workshops, reading, or experience—toward one or several theoretical positions or, when asked, will say they are eclectic.

Because of our interest in gender influences, we will not review the various models of marital and family therapy. (This is done in a number of excellent texts, such as Gurman & Kniskern, 1991; Hanna & Brown, 1995; and Nichols & Schwartz, 1991.) Instead, the following two chapters introduce several concepts drawn from the clinical literature that are directly applicable to couples therapy and that will be addressed in later chapters on treatment. This framework is presented for its clinical utility and the map it provides for assessment and intervention.

Because couples present problematic behavior that has roots in the respective families of origin and is maintained through current interactions, the therapist's map conceptualizes past and present influences. To assist the reader, the influence of the families of origin may be understood through object relations theory and Bowen's extended family systems theory. In the next chapter, current interactions are understood through general systems theory and attribution theory. The influence of gender in conceptualizing couples therapy is addressed by highlighting feminist critiques of family therapy concepts and by examining the impact of gender roles in shaping the family of origin influence.

Influence of the Past: Role of Family of Origin

When two people become a couple, two families also merge—a point often missed by the couple themselves. Each partner brings a family legacy into the new relationship. The legacy may be overt, like family traditions and responsibilities, or it may be a covert, unconscious influence. Overt legacies are visible to both partners and are available for negotiation. For example, where and how to spend holidays begins to be negotiated early on. Each member of the couple will be influenced by his or her family of origin and his or her respective obligations and traditions. Covert legacies, however, may blind each partner to his or her own actions and motivations.

The following sections review two theoretical positions that have a great deal to say about the role of the family of origin in couples therapy: object relations theory and Bowen's extended family systems theory.

OBJECT RELATIONS THEORY

Object relations theory grew out of psychoanalytic theory. (The term *object* refers to early relationships with significant others, chiefly our family of origin.) Object relations theory accepts the primacy of maternal and early relationships in strongly influencing the development of a child and hypothesizes that we internalize these early relationships which then unconsciously affect our adult relationships. This is accomplished through the key processes of splitting and projective identification.

As a dependent, helpless baby we rely on the care of others. Our most basic needs are met first by our mothers and then by our fathers, brothers and sisters, grandparents, or other primary caretakers. However, because no caretaker can fully respond to all of a baby's needs instantly and satisfactorily, frustration is an inevitable part of growing up. But the primitive mind of a baby cannot differentiate the frustration from the mother. Higher cognitive skills are needed to view the mother as loving but unable to satisfy every need, every moment.

In order to manage this contradiction in the baby's world, objects (significant others) are divided into all-good or all-bad categories. This splitting of good and bad into distinct categories serves defensive purposes. For example, it would be anxiety producing, if not overwhelming, for the baby to view the mother as bad—"If my mother is bad, then my very existence is threatened." As a defense against such anxiety, the baby splits good and bad, projecting all-good onto the mother and repressing her "bad" aspects. Mother is transformed and idealized into an all-good object, never to be tarnished by bad attributes—"Don't ever say anything bad about my mother! She is a saint!" The bad qualities, however, are repressed and according to psychoanalytic theory will push for expression in some other form.

Unfortunately, the greater the ambivalence or rejection the child may feel in these significant relationships, the more the bad aspects must be repressed.

Sometimes, the bad aspects may be internalized into one's sense of self—"My mother is a saint, but I am a screwup." However, as a type of defense mechanism, the bad aspects may also be projected onto a contemporary relationship. That is, a selected person is seen as possessing the negative qualities repressed from early childhood.

For example, a stern, controlling father is split into all-good and all-bad. As an adult, your client may describe his or her father as very loving and giving but uses the spouse as the recipient of the negative projections, viewing him or her as cold and controlling. Sitting in your office, the accused spouse may turn to you and say, "It doesn't matter what I say or do, she always tells me I am cold and indifferent."

Or, as the therapist you may note the narrow, negative views each spouse presents of the other. Every time you attempt to point out other more positive aspects of the spouse's behavior, your comments are brushed aside. As a rule of thumb, the more ambivalence that remains from the earlier relationships, the greater and more defensive the splitting is in the present, increasing the likelihood of projection coloring each spouse's view of the other.

Object relations theory can be applied to couples therapy in many ways. Perhaps, when we fall in love, we are projecting all-good qualities onto our mate. He or she is the person who will fill our unmet needs. The mate is idealized and an illusion is created with our own mirrors. Not long into the relationship, disillusionment sets in—our mate is not perfect. He will not meet all my needs. She will not make me feel wonderful and lovable. At this point the first serious arguments may occur. Although the arguments may be about specific, concrete issues—for example, going to the in-laws' for a holiday—the underlying agenda is the disillusionment that has begun to set in.

Partners with a fair amount of personal maturity come to accept the good with the bad. Their partner is human! However, the greater the splitting that occurred in early relationships, the more difficult it may be for someone to accept the shortcomings in another or to give up the fantasy of what the mate should be. Hurt and anger result as the infantile needs are unrecognized and unattended.

Object relations theory also explains the repetitive, recycling, dysfunctional patterns in which each member of the couple appears to collude. For example, he fears engulfment based on his own enmeshed relationship with his mother. As a result, he is emotionally withdrawn from his wife. She, sensing his rejection, attempts to close the emotional gap. He then accuses her of suffocating him, she feels rejected, and a painful fight ensues.

In a variation of a theme, her father was cold and distant. She thought her husband was a prince who would love her in ways her father never did. He says she is always criticizing him and that he cannot do anything right in her eyes. He then pulls away, which only serves to fulfill her unconscious fear and prophecy, leaving her depressed, angry, and rejected.

As a map, object relations theory is invaluable in understanding repetitive, dysfunctional patterns in couples—patterns highly resistant to change because they are fueled by unconscious motivations. Framo's (1981) work exemplifies the application of object relations theory to couples therapy.

Building on object relations theory, Framo (1981) believed that each member of the couple carries perceptual, emotional distortions of early relationships from his or her respective families of origin. Problems evolve as each partner projects unrealistic expectations on the other and engages in negative projections—at times the partner should be all-good and loving while at other times the partner epitomizes past hurts. Therefore, couples fight over (1) unconscious, unresolved issues with members of the family of origin projected into the current relationship and (2) the unacknowledged parts of themselves that they identify in one another.

Accordingly, within Framo's model, positive change occurs when partners acknowledge the legacy of their family of origin and when they acknowledge that their complaints about their partners reflect, to a large degree, unresolved issues from childhood. The goal of couples therapy is to challenge these distortions and provide insight into the family of origin legacy.

For a more complete summary of object relations theory and its application to couples therapy see Scharff and Scharff (1987) and Slipp (1984). (Slipp's book details the evolution of object relations theory from traditional psychoanalytic thought.)

BOWEN'S EXTENDED FAMILY SYSTEMS THEORY

Influenced by evolutionary theory, Bowen's (1976, 1978; Kerr & Bowen, 1988) most basic premise is that humans evolved a cognitive capacity that can overrule and control our more primitive, emotional reactive system. However, more often than not, reactive emotional processes override our cognitive controls and that hampers our ability to effectively problem-solve. When this occurs life becomes a series of emotional reactions to events around us, while a buildup of strongly charged events threaten to overwhelm us.

The powerful emotional systems of our families of origin act as a whirlpool to draw us back into the family dramas. These dramas evoke emotional responses at the expense of effective, cognitive problem solving. When it comes to our family of origin and its legacy, we may lead with our hearts and not with our heads.

While Bowen's theory is elaborate and intricate, three key concepts resurface again and again when working with couples: (1) differentiation, (2) triangles, and (3) influence of birth order.

Differentiation

Differentiation has evolved into two different yet similar conceptual processes. First, differentiation refers to the capacity to distinguish or separate while still integrating cognitive and emotional functioning. For example, when faced with a stressful event—perhaps an argument with our partner—we may first react emotionally with hurt or anger or fear. Although this may be a legitimate initial response, if we expect to resolve the conflict we will need to think it through—"Did he really mean what he said or was he just angry too? We have got to talk and understand what happened or this could go on for days."

This does not mean cognition should dominate and that we should become "Spocklike" but that our intellects give us a choice over our emotions—"I am so hurt, I just want to pack my things and get out of here but that would not solve anything." Within Bowen's model, the greater our capacity to differentiate our emotional and cognitive responses, the more effectively we problem-solve and the more effectively we address our stress.

Differentiation also refers to our ability to separate while still being connected to our family of origin's emotional system. As mentioned above, the family of origin may serve as a strong emotional whirlpool that at any given time could pull us into the emotional currents of family dramas. For instance, in families with a poor level of differentiation between emotional and cognitive functions, as one family member is upset, emotional ripples spread throughout the family. Family members may take sides or become angry with each other. The family is awash in turmoil and often operates from one emotional crisis to another. Differentiation is the level of one's ability to step back from the whirlpool, assess what one can and cannot do to remedy the situation, and then *choose* the appropriate course of action.

Differentiation does not imply a cold, intellectual approach in dealing with one's family but rather emphasizes the ability to *choose alternative courses of behavior.* At times we may choose to emotionally jump right into the family currents, or we may choose to not get involved and to detach ourselves from the conflict. We may have the full range of emotional reactions, but our actions are tempered by our cognitive, rational processes and our ability to maintain self-enhancing boundaries between ourself and the family system. (In psychodynamic terms, think of the difference between primary and secondary processes or between the id and the ego.)

Although not constructed as an empirical measuring instrument, Bowen's Differentiation of Self Scale is a continuum from 0 to 100 degrees of differentiation. The scale functions as a clinical assessment tool that may also guide intervention. For example, people whose scores fall between 0 and 24 are considered highly undifferentiated from their families of origin. Their sense of self and who they are are directly tied to the family of origin. The family's values and attitudes are their values and attitudes. They lack a sense of an independent self. In times of stress, because of their poor differentiation of emotional and cognitive functioning, they are quickly drawn into the family drama.

Individuals between 25 and 49 degrees of differentiation have achieved greater differentiation than the first group, but they still may be drawn quickly back into the family of origin's emotional system. By and large, they are able to separate the emotional and cognitive reactions and this allows them to function fairly well. They possess a sense of self distinct from their family of origin. They may hold opinions different from their families. However, in times of stress, particularly those involving the family, their level of differentiation may drop. Emotional reactions may overwhelm cognitive functioning and they find themselves quickly back in the whirlpool.

Moving further up the scale, people who fall between 50 and 74 possess a good sense of self separate from their families. Cognitive functioning holds a superior position in relation to emotional functioning. Their opinions and beliefs may be quite different from their family of origin and may reflect an evolution of personal thought. They possess an ability to step back from family turmoil and choose the level of involvement. They may care deeply about the family members but that does not mean they have to jump right in at the earliest sign of conflict—"That's an issue between my brother and my mother; I am not getting involved in that one."

Finally, those who fall between 75 and 100 are the highest group on the scale and the most adaptive. Again, for Bowen, the greater one is able to differentiate emotional and cognitive functioning, the better one is able to effectively problem-solve. Life is not a roller coaster of emotional ups and downs but is a series of rational choices in problem resolution.

Bowen hypothesizes that we seek out as friends and lovers people who mirror our personal level of differentiation. Thus, the lower the level of differentiation the couple possesses, the greater the need to bind the anxiety accumulated that they and their families experience.

From an outsider's perspective, a couple's ongoing conflict may appear quite dysfunctional and destructive; however, inside the couple the conflict binds the undifferentiated anxiety. It is as if the personal anxiety each person experiences becomes too much and must be acted out. Fighting serves as a steam valve for the buildup of pressure. Consequently, the continuing rounds of arguments serve a functional purpose for each partner as the argument gives vent to anxiety.

Moreover, the couple's conflict contains secondary gains. Each partner not only acts out his or her anxiety but can blame the other for the problems—"If he or she would just . . . then we would be happy"—thus sparing him- or herself any responsibility for the problems.

Triangles

The concept of triangles is one of the most useful ideas at a couples therapist's disposal. Not only does it enable one to discern family dynamics, but it also serves to conceptualize interactions between the couple and the therapist. It is the basic building block of emotional interpersonal systems.

Briefly, a dyadic relationship is a tenuously balanced emotional system. Ideally, the partners are able to resolve their conflicts between themselves. However, because of each member's level of differentiation, emotional issues may overwhelm the couple's ability to effectively problem-solve, placing tremendous stress on the dyad. In this turmoil and as a means of siphoning off the stress, one or both members of the couple may reach out to a third person. The third person may be a friend, a relative, or one of their children. In the absence or unavailability of a third person, either member of the couple may turn to other distractions—for example, food, alcohol, or work.

Given this dynamic, the most damaging scenario is when a child is triangled into the marital conflict. Each parent may seek an ally in the child and will invest time and energy into that relationship. Although this overinvolved parent-child relationship successfully serves as a distraction and siphons stress from the marital relationship, it stunts the emotional growth of the child. The child may be privy to information inappropriate for the child's age—"Your father is having an affair"—or may be asked to perform a spousal function—"Your mother is impossible to deal with; I need someone to talk to." Either possibility triangles the child into the marital conflict and lowers the child's level of differentiation.

Obviously, the more members in a family, the more potential triangles. One triangle leads to another, which leads to a series of interlocking triangles. For example, marital conflict overwhelms a couple. The mother invests herself in her relationship with her daughter, placing the father in the outside position of the triangle. The father then invests himself through sports with his son. The brother and sister form triangles with each parent. The brother is jealous of his sister's relationship with their mother; the sister resents the lack of attention she receives from their father. The brother and sister then fight like cats and dogs and no one understands why.

Imagine also the therapeutic context. A couple enters your office by definition highly charged emotionally. The therapist is a readily available and potential third member of the triangle. Sensing this, both partners tell their side of the story seeking alliance with the therapist. Not only is energy invested in this effort, but each partner is quick to see signs that the therapist is taking the other person's side. In this highly charged atmosphere, the couple dyad seeks to triangle the therapist into the emotional turmoil (see discussion of the imbalanced gender triangle in chapter 4).

Influence of Birth Order

Endorsing Toman's (1961) work on the effects of birth order on personality, Bowen believed that sibling position greatly influences the degree of a person's differentiation. Within Toman's framework, birth order determines seniority and juniority rights as well as exposes one to male and female differences.

For example, firstborns usually carry the family mantle for achievement. They are also at some point placed in charge and give orders to younger siblings— "Watch your brothers and sisters while I go to the store." Younger siblings are accustomed to being the baby of the family with little responsibilities. They are typically told what to do and have to make few decisions for themselves.

Brothers and sisters also learn about the opposite sex from one another. They learn about cooperation, competition, and conflict resolution with the opposite sex. Moreover, the brothers' and sisters' friends serve as other opportunities for learning.

The influence of birth order and sibling relationships shapes hypotheses when working with couples. For example, when a youngest daughter marries an older brother, both may be comfortable with seniority issues. He is used to being in control, and she is used to following the lead of an older sibling. Or, two babies of their respective families marry one another and each wants the other to make the decisions.

Following this model, the worst, and therefore potentially the most conflictual, relationship would be an oldest sister with younger sisters marrying an oldest brother with younger brothers. For this couple, not only would control be an issue but each would have difficulty understanding the opposite sex's perspective.

Again, the model does not predict 100% accurately, and it would be misleading to base an assessment on birth order alone; still it does generate useful clinical hypotheses to guide the initial stages of assessment.

FEMINIST CRITIQUE OF BOWEN'S THEORY

Recent feminist critiques of family therapy argue that current models are based on the value system of the American family of the '40s and '50s (Walters, Carter, Papp, & Silverstein, 1988). As such, the models support traditional gender roles and fail to take into account the differential in power and status between men and women in the larger social systems in which families are embedded (Luepnitz, 1988; Walsh & Scheinkman, 1989). Moreover, no systems formulation can be gender free:

> Formulations that purport to be gender-free or "neutral" are in fact sexist because they reproduce the social pretense that there is equality between men and women. Women, in fact, are disadvantaged in our society, and a failure to acknowledge this fact doubly disadvantages them. Second, all interventions need to take gender into account by recognizing the different socialization processes of women and men, with special attention to the way in which these socialization processes disadvantage women. We need to recognize that each gender hears different meaning in the same clinical intervention and accordingly feels either blamed or supported by an identical therapeutic stance. (Walters et al., 1988, p. 17)

Looking again at several family therapy concepts expands the above point. For example, Bowen's concept of differentiation of self values a person's capacity to differentiate or separate from others. Although a Bowenian therapist would argue that a highly differentiated individual may *choose* to become emotionally involved with others, the emphasis again is on maintaining emotional distance and the value of cognitive over emotional processes.

But, some feminist authors maintain that Bowen originally viewed differentiation as a process that achieved a sense of self *in relation to others in the family* and therefore is consistent with a feminist framework that views the development of self as one in relation to others (McGoldrick et al., 1989). Bowen, however, did not employ such language and his words are thus left to interpretation.

The feminist critique of Bowen is on two general levels. The first level is his narrow focus on the maternal lineage. He excluded a focus on the male and he assumed that women overinvest in their children. This assumption connotes that closeness and investment in a relationship are correlated with pathology. The second level of critique is based on the assertive-directive role of the therapist as coach. This role often modulates the expression of feelings and can inadvertently give the message that the maintenance and expression of strong feelings is a negative phenomenon. This is particularly relevant in couples therapy where a woman may struggle with the strong expression of anger at her mate.

The differentiated individual possesses the ability to step back from the relationship when emotionality threatens to overload the system. Sanctioning emotional distance and making it a *requirement* of an integrated adult is a criticism often leveled at theories that endorse a male model of mental health whereby independence, autonomy, and rationality are valued.

Theories so grounded often fail to emphasize the inherent biases in gender-role assumptions and fail to recognize that behavior occurs within broader societal guidelines. This myopic view leads to the assumption by both clients and therapists that assigned gender roles are not interactive or negotiable in a relationship, but that men and women are inherently different. This thinking can easily assign gender-specific qualities such as autonomy and separateness to men (healthy) and connectedness and dependency to women (pathological).

Several authors who place a greater value on connectedness (McGoldrick et al., 1989; Walsh & Scheinkman, 1989) point out that many clients, particularly men, need assistance in expressing emotion and developing more intimate relationships. This is a trend reversal (from differentiation) not addressed in Bowen's theory.

SUMMARY

A couple represents the blending of two families of origin. As such, each partner enters the relationship with a personal family of origin legacy. Often, knowingly or unknowingly, these personal legacies are stirred in the couple's intimate relationship.

The personal legacy may involve projecting the family of origin dynamics onto the partner. When this happens, the partner is responded to more like a figure from the past than as a unique individual. Likewise, the partner may unknowingly play out the assigned role. Thus, what a couple presents to a therapist may be the blending of two family of origin dramas in one play.

The family of origin also determines the degree of differentiation. Free-floating anxiety may manifest itself in marital conflict, the dysfunction of one spouse— for example, alcoholism—or the impairment of one or more children. In these cases, effective problem solving is sacrificed to emotionality. Anxiety and crisis become a way of life. The couple presents the therapist with a series of problems all fueled by the couple's basic level of undifferentiation and unresolved family of origin issues.

On closer examination, the concept of differentiation is influenced by gender roles. From a feminist perspective, one must analyze the concept of differentiation by gender expectations and roles. The degree of differentiation that is comfortable for women may certainly differ from that which is comfortable for men. In the development of self, women often value early family relationships and wish to maintain connection. In a feminist framework, the development of empathy is both an affective and cognitive function. Therefore, one can be highly *involved* in the family of origin, yet also *differentiated from* the pull of the system. (For an elaboration of this thesis see Jordan, Surrey, & Kaplan, 1991).

When assessing differentiation of self issues in couples several gender-related variables become important:

1. The goodness of fit in the degree of (dis)satisfaction and (dis)connection inherent in these relationships. A woman may be highly connected to her

family of origin and find that quite satisfying, whereas a man may be disconnected from his family and may find that comfortable.

2. The reciprocity, or the sense of mutually satisfying interactions in these relationships. What are the qualities of the interactions with the families of origin? Are they mutually satisfying? Conflictual? Neutral?
3. Or, are relationships maintained out of guilt and obligation? What is the basis of the connections with the families of origin? Love? Enjoyment? Obligation? Guilt?

In terms of the couple's relationship, the key is each partner's awareness of his or her relationship with his or her family of origin and the role the family of origin plays in his or her life. (For a reference on marital therapy based on Bowen's model, please see Guerin, Fay, Burden, & Kautto, 1987.)

Family of Origin Issues: Assessment

In assessing family of origin issues, the therapist first constructs the couple's genogram and explores potentially unresolved issues from childhood. Next, each partner's level of differentiation is assessed, paying particular attention to his or her role in the family projection process. Then the significant triangles within the extended family systems are identified. Finally, family of origin gender roles and the couple's goodness of fit pertaining to traditional versus egalitarian roles serve as guides to current difficulties.

GENOGRAM

Besides graphically portraying multiple generations of a couple's family tree, a genogram is a nonthreatening way of opening up family of origin issues (McGoldrick & Greson, 1985). When done as part of an initial evaluation, constructing a genogram is a fact-finding task: How many siblings do you have? How old are your parents and where do they live? Have any significant changes occurred in your family? These seemingly innocuous questions concerning demographic material open the door to further exploring the family relationships. To illustrate, we refer back to Lynn and Carl.

Figure 6.1 is Lynn's and Carl's genogram and illustrates the relationships based on the couple's self-report and the therapist's observations. To summarize:

Early Extended Family History

Lynn's parents were divorced when she was 11 years old. She remembers little about her father before the divorce, describing him as never at home. Following the divorce, Lynn's father moved out of state and Lynn had little contact with him during her teenage years. He died 2 years before her marriage to Carl. She went to her father's funeral out of obligation and reported experiencing little grief, but she did feel regret for not really knowing him.

Lynn remembered the divorce as very upsetting, but her most vivid memories were of the tight bond she formed with her mother and younger sister during

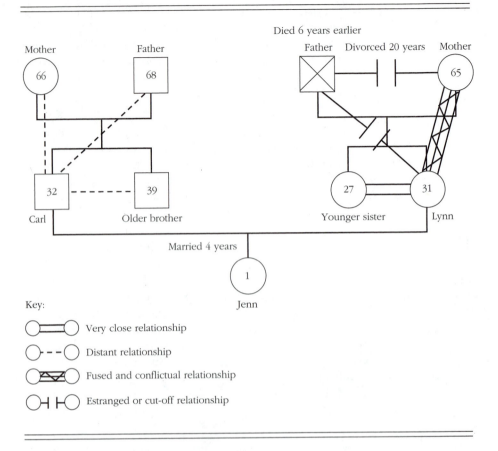

FIGURE 6.1   Three-Generation Genogram

that difficult time. Because of the divorce, Lynn's mother began working full-time to try to meet the financial pressures. Lynn, in turn, became the little mother around the house, helping out where she could and taking care of her younger sister. Although she acknowledged the difficulties of those years, Lynn also spoke with pride of the family's ability to survive. Because of the early burdens placed on her, she felt she had to grow up fast but valued her own sense of maturity.

Carl, on the other hand, was the younger of two brothers and described his upbringing as stable and consistent. His parents had been married for 40 years and, until he left home, he lived in the same house his entire life. He experienced an uneventful childhood in which his father went to work and his mother stayed at home. Carl described his father as quiet and his mother as reserved. Because his brother was 7 years older, Carl alluded to little inter-action between them. As he put it, "We were just too far apart in age. I would be starting a stage and my brother would be ending it. We were never in the same school together."

Current Extended Family Relationships

Although she remained close to her younger sister who was single and lived in the same town, Lynn described an ambivalent relationship with her mother. As Lynn entered her early 20s, she began to establish her own life outside of the family. This created strains between Lynn and her mother. Although fully established in her job, Lynn's mother's social circle was quite small. She talked to a few neighbors and she would have lunch with some people at work, but she didn't have any really close friends outside of the family. As Lynn reported her mother saying, "My girls are who I care about." Through persistent effort Lynn had established a life outside of the family, but she would still at times feel guilty concerning her mother. As Lynn stated, "Even when I was out having a good time, my mother would still be in a corner of my mind."

Recently, the birth of the baby threw Lynn and her mother back together. Lynn's mother had been an invaluable help following the birth of Jenn, providing an extra pair of hands. While grateful for her mother's help, Lynn also felt her mother's "advice" intrusive. Lynn's mother was ever willing to offer an opinion, as the voice of experience. More often than not, Lynn would bite her tongue and smile politely. But sometimes, after a sleepless night nursing a baby with an ear infection, Lynn would snap back at her mother by basically saying, "Keep your opinions to yourself," to which her mother would say nothing and would withdraw with a hurt expression.

To compound matters, Lynn had recently returned to work and her mother, who now worked part-time, would pick up Jenn at her child care and bring her home. Often, when Lynn would arrive home, her mother would want to discuss the problems with Jenn's child care—an issue that provoked Lynn's guilt over working.

Following Carl's father's retirement 4 years earlier, Carl's parents had moved out of state. Because of the distance, Carl saw them about two times a year, and those visits usually involved a holiday or special events. Carl mentioned in passing that whenever he called his parents his father would say hello, ask how things were, and turn the phone over to Carl's mother.

Carl's older brother was married and lived about 60 miles away. Although there were occasional phone calls between them, the brothers would primarily get together when their parents visited.

Family of Origin Assessment

The family of origin may influence an individual and thus the couple in a number of ways. In conceptualizing these influences, Gerson, Hoffman, Sauls, and Utrici (1993) refer to family of origin frames of reference. That is to say, we carry certain perspectives from our family of origin that color our present relationships. It is as if we view our present intimate relationships through the family of origin lenses. Specifically, they identify six frames or lenses:

1. *Coping frame*—We learn our initial anxiety coping styles from our families of origin. Lynn adapted to the upheaval of her parents' divorce by assuming increasing responsibilities. Carl learned that withdrawal was the best strategy

when faced with interpersonal stress. In their marriage these two frames created what Guerin et al. (1987) refer to as an overfunctioner and underfunctioner dynamic. Lynn would characteristically assume the responsibilities in her marriage. She would see what needed to be done and act accordingly. Because he was the baby in his own family and because his mother did not work outside of the home, Carl was accustomed to someone else assuming the initiative and responsibilities. In fact, this was one of the reasons he was drawn to Lynn; she appeared so competent.

2. *Modeling frame*—Children absorb all manner of behavior from simple observation. Lynn's mother struggled to financially survive. Carl saw his father retreat into the newspaper and television and saw his mother perform all the traditional female gender roles.

3. *Role frame*—Lynn's role in her family of origin was the older, competent sister. She put her own needs in the background to focus instead on what others or the family needed. Little was demanded of Carl as the baby in the family. He was expected to do well in school and stay out of trouble.

4. *Definition frame*—This is the family of origin's ability to define reality. For Lynn, life was a struggle to overcome obstacles. Men were unreliable, and the best one could do is look after oneself. For Carl, routine is security. Women took care of men and conflict is best avoided.

5. *Reversal frame*—Because of what she saw her mother go through, Lynn promised herself to never be in that position. Consequently, her marital difficulties cut her to the core. The prospect of divorce terrified Lynn. Carl, on the other hand, saw little from his family of origin that he would do differently. Lacking any other perspective, Carl viewed the distance he saw between his parents as normal.

6. *Loyalty frame*—Lynn's sense of responsibility to her family of origin continued into her adulthood. She was still protective of her younger sister, but her loyalty and responsibility to her mother had become increasingly stressful. Although describing himself as loyal to his family, Carl felt no need to initiate regular contact with his parents or brother.

In terms of the overall influence of the families of origin on Lynn and Carl's marriage, the absence of fathers is particularly noticeable. Lynn reported few memories of her father, whereas Carl described a distant, aloof father. Neither volunteered many details nor descriptions of their fathers. One wonders if Lynn hoped that Carl would be a father figure to her—a male in her life on whom she could rely and trust; a man who would be a gentle, caring father to her daughter. But counterbalancing these hopes was a reality that said men do not stick around. Lynn's dilemma was how to fully trust Carl but still protect her vulnerability.

Carl's father was physically present but emotionally absent. Although his father never said it, Carl believed he was loved because his father worked hard for the family. The most Carl could learn from his father is that men are reserved and worked to support their families. Moreover, the formal relationship between his parents provided Carl with few guidelines for intimate relationships. Carl, however, saw Lynn as competent, strong, and someone who would take care of things. Consequently, Lynn's request for equality and, in particular, intimacy in their marriage frightened Carl.

Levels of Differentiation

According to Bowen's (1976) Differentiation of Self Scale, both Lynn and Carl fell between 25 and 49 degrees of differentiation. Both partners were capable of separating their emotional and cognitive reactions; however, in times of stress the emotional would frequently overwhelm the cognitive.

The demands of working and child care and the responsibilities to her mother and sister were increasingly overwhelming Lynn. When that happened she would lash out at Carl for his lack of support and snap at her mother to mind her own business. She would later regret these outbursts but still felt justified in her reactions.

Carl, on the other hand, reacted to stress by pulling inward. On the surface he would appear to be in cognitive control with his calm demeanor and logical thought, but his intellectualizations masked a thin veneer covering and containing his emotions.

Significant Triangles

The genogram highlighted several significant triangles operating within the extended families:

1. The central triangle in the family conflict involves Lynn, Carl, and their baby, Jenn. Only 1 year old, Jenn served as the third point of the nuclear family triangle by providing a focus for Lynn and Carl's disagreements. Arguments about child care and helping with the baby were much more frequent than discussions about their marriage. In fact, since Jenn's birth, the marriage had taken a backseat to the demands of an infant. Clearly, Lynn's resentments concerning Carl's lack of support were overt, but Carl's resentments were not initially voiced. One wonders if he resents Lynn's focus on the baby. Did he feel misplaced after Jenn was born?

2. The next central triangle involves Lynn, her mother, and Jenn. Jenn's birth had thrown Lynn back into daily contact with her mother. Previously, a few phone calls a week was the extent of it. Now, Lynn and her mother were brought together around the issue of motherhood. This circumstance may involve some role confusion for Lynn, because she now relates to her own mother as both a daughter and a mother of a daughter.

3. One is left to speculate on the possible triangles involving Carl and his parents. He was guarded and circumscribed in describing his relationship with them. At best, he portrayed a formal and distant relationship pattern.

GENDER ROLES SHAPING THE FAMILY OF ORIGIN INFLUENCE

Wamboldt and Reiss (1989) reviewed 12 longitudinal studies of marital success/failure that tapped two birth cohorts: individuals born in the 1910s and 1920s who married during the Great Depression and World War II and baby boomers born in the 1950s. Personality characteristics—for example, neuroticism, impulsivity, and sociability/shyness—were a moderately strong predictor of marital success or failure, accounting for between 25% and 50% of the variance. Interaction measures—for example, communication and ability to resolve conflict—accounted for 35% to 65% of the variance. The authors concluded that the ability to manage interpersonal conflict and the accompanying negative emotions are vital to relationship success, but that is not the entire story.

Gender differences were noticeable in both cohorts. Specifically, women who maintained a positive relationship with their own mothers rated their marriages as more satisfying. In contrast, a man's closeness to his own mother was not as important during the early years of marriage, but a close mother-son relationship was associated with marital difficulties later in the marriage. Also, men and women who were closer to their fathers rated their relationship satisfaction higher.

Wamboldt and Reiss (1989) argued that these findings supported the hypothesis that the influence of our families of origin persists into later life and is associated with success or failure of relationships. However, these findings are correlational and, as such, do not tell us how or in what ways the family of origin influences adult relationships. It remains for future research studies to determine causality.

Furthermore, the reasons for the identified gender differences are equally speculative. Wamboldt and Reiss (1989) hypothesized:

> Women, as "relationship specialists," appear more finely attuned to the subtleties of communication within their intimate relationships and tend to persist in their attempts to resolve areas of relationship conflict, whereas men (at least those in distressed relationships) are more likely to withdraw in the face of high intensity and/or persistent conflict. (p. 321)

To test their hypothesis, Wamboldt and Reiss (1989) examined 16 premarital couples who described themselves as "seriously attached or engaged" in a 1-year longitudinal study. Their findings showed correlations between the females' families of origin and relationship satisfaction. Specifically, high expressiveness (the amount and quality of interactions) in the woman's family of origin was associated with greater relationship satisfaction, whereas high conflict in the woman's family of origin led to a decrease in relationship satisfaction for the man. Finally, low expressiveness and high control in the male's family of origin were associated with lower satisfaction for both men and women.

The results of the study lend support to the woman-as-relationship-specialist hypothesis, because it was the women's families of origin experiences that were most associated with relationship satisfaction. If a woman rated her family of origin high in interaction and expressiveness, then she was more likely to rate her current relationship positively. The researchers hypothesize that a highly rated family of origin implies that the woman has learned necessary relationship-building skills. High conflict in the woman's family of origin offers the woman little modeling in building positive relationships.

What is missing in this study is data measuring *how* high ratings in expressiveness and interaction affect the male's rating of his current relationship. Without a control group and comparison between genders, we cannot accurately state that gender is the intervening variable between family of origin interactions and current marital satisfaction. Therefore, the above findings, although interesting, must be cautiously evaluated.

Returning to our case, because of her parents' divorce early in her life and her adoption of caretaking responsibilities, Lynn witnessed little modeling of male-female relationships. Currently, Lynn experiences pangs of guilt and doubt in her relationship with Carl. The relationship is not going well and she often obsesses on how she can make it better. To compound matters, Lynn's relationship with her mother is still conflictual.

Again, gender roles may influence this relationship. Walters et al. (1988) argue that the conflict between mothers and daughters is a consequence of women living together in a male-dominated society. That is to say, the struggle inherent for women living in a male-dominated society is to turn it inward into a struggle between mother and daughter in which each blames the other for what is wrong in their lives.

At another level, Lynn's and her mother's difficulties over the baby flow naturally in a confluence of gender roles in which women are relationship and child oriented. Jenn's birth signaled a significant and overlapping area of concern for Lynn and her mother. It is within this area that Lynn and her mother have their most heated disagreements. Although one could step back and call Lynn "overprotective" and her mother "intrusive," these labels overlook the influence of gender roles that each woman is attempting to fulfill.

Carl, on the other hand, appears disengaged from his family of origin. He describes his relationship with his parents as polite and formal. However, as he describes his family of origin, particularly issues of control and criticism, the therapist suspects that the emotional distance is a self-imposed defense. Although unable to articulate his own vision of the marriage he wants, Carl wishes for something different from his parents.

From an individual diagnostic perspective, Carl could be labeled "retentive" and "emotionally uninvolved." But he too is fulfilling his gender role by working and providing for his family. His range of emotional expressiveness is no different from his father, brother, or the men he sees around him. As a result, he is genuinely confused and hurt by Lynn's criticisms.

Goodness of Fit: Traditional Versus Egalitarian Roles

Lynn's initial complaint that Carl does not help with child care and household responsibilities would appear to reflect a stereotypical conflict between traditional and egalitarian roles. Although appealing in its simplicity, the traditional–egalitarian dichotomy does not fully capture the subtleties of the goodness of fit assessment.

Lynn identified with her mother's Italian heritage. Family obligations and responsibilities are important to Lynn. From her mother, Lynn learned to place family loyalty above peers and friends.

Italian families reflect traditional gender roles, with the father as the head and the mother as the heart of the family (Rotunno & McGoldrick, 1982). Lynn, however, has few memories of her father and remembers growing up with her mother and sister where everyone had equal roles. Everyone would share in household duties and provide emotional support for one another. As she grew older, Lynn shared decision making with her mother. Although she identified with her Italian heritage, Lynn entered her marriage expecting egalitarian roles.

Carl, on the other hand, was third-generation Irish. His mother dominated the family life, while his father was on the periphery. McGoldrick (1982) observed that in Irish families feelings are characteristically repressed and disagreements result in a buildup of resentments. In this atmosphere, traditional Irish husbands primarily avoid their wives. Carl remembered few disagreements between his parents and described his father as quiet.

When asked, Carl endorsed egalitarian roles, but he lacked models to draw on. In principle, he believed men and women were equal, but when it came to concrete tasks, Carl fell back on traditionally defined roles. Although not opposed to taking care of the baby, he took little initiative in the area and saw it as Lynn's prerogative.

Thus, both Lynn and Carl brought mixed expectations regarding gender roles into the marriage. Lynn wanted Carl to assume more responsibility around the home but by equally sharing all the tasks, not by fulfilling a traditional role. Carl endorsed egalitarian roles, but his model was of a dominant mother and peripheral father. He had no difficulty letting Lynn run the home but passive-aggressively ignored her requests when he was asked to perform tasks he was not comfortable with. His underinvolvement reflected his Irish heritage (McGoldrick, Preto, Hines, & Lee, 1991).

Overall, the goodness of fit was moderate. Both Lynn and Carl, in principle, believed in equality, but in practicality their behavior mirrored traditional gender roles with regards to household responsibilities. It was within this area that the presenting problem was framed.

SUMMARY

Family of origin influences are best assessed in the process of creating a thorough genogram. However, both internal and external constraints may limit the time available to complete the task. For example, although the genogram provides invaluable information to the therapist, the couple may become confused by the therapist's line of questioning. If they have entered therapy with specific communication problems, why then is the therapist spending so much time on the families of origin? Complicating matters, the therapist's probing questions may be touching sensitive areas that result in a couple's increasing defensiveness.

External time constraints on therapy required by agency or managed care protocols may also limit the amount of time spent on constructing a thorough genogram. Presenting complaints may demand that a therapist spend less time on past relationships and more time on resolving the specific reasons for referral.

The impact of the family of origin may also be viewed through gender lenses and the goodness of fit. Despite endorsing egalitarian roles on an abstract level, in the concrete tasks of day-to-day life, both Lynn and Carl fell back on their family of origin models and cultural gender roles. Lynn automatically assumed full responsibility for Jenn while Carl readily acquiesced. As the demands of working outside the home and full responsibility for Jenn began to take their toll on Lynn, she reached out to Carl. Carl, however, heard criticism because he felt he was an equal partner in the relationship. He tried to help Lynn out when she asked but that was precisely the problem from Lynn's perspective: She had to ask!

Conclusion

Sitting with a couple in therapy, it is not difficult to picture both families of origin also present. Their impact may be conscious or unconscious and may fuel the couple's resentments and disappointments.

Object relations and Bowen's extended family systems theories offer a means of conceptualizing the family of origin influence in the couple's presenting problem. Each partner may carry family of origin legacies into the relationship that underlie the presenting problems. The couple's level of differentiation also hints at the free-floating anxiety present in the relationship. The cyclical ups and downs in the relationship are understood as a means of binding this anxiety.

For assessment purposes, a genogram helps to place the couple within a broader extended family context, one highlighting ethnic and cultural influences. Embedded within the broader context are forces shaping the couple's goodness of fit along the traditional–egalitarian dimension. As we have seen with Lynn and Carl, the goodness of fit is both a combination of espoused values and concrete behavior. Even when both partners endorse egalitarian values, they are still left with the task of building egalitarian roles, usually without the benefit of role models from their respective families of origin.

Acknowledging the power of family of origin legacies, when two people become a couple they begin to build their own history of patterns. The couple presents to the therapist current patterns of behavior that have become problematic. Thus, the therapist needs a means of conceptualizing current patterns and assessing their maintenance and influence on the relationship. The next chapter is devoted to understanding and assessing these issues.

CHAPTER SEVEN

Influence of the Present: Current Patterns

Although each member of a couple carries into the relationship his or her family of origin legacy, the couple also creates a history together shaped by past and present interactions. One way of conceptualizing current interactions is through general systems theory (Bertalanffy, 1968). Although the concept of systems theory may mean different things to different therapists, certain underlying principles are universally acknowledged. Next we will highlight several basic principles to guide assessment and intervention with couples.

First, therapists look for the attributions that often underly a couple's behavior. As mentioned earlier, attributions reflect the cognitive meanings attached to one's own behavior and the behavior of one's partner. On closer analysis, many of the problematic patterns couples present to a therapist are maintained and reinforced by negative attributions concerning the partner and the relationship.

Next, the patterns of reciprocity are assessed. Are the individual roles complementary? What does each partner do that is valued by the other? Are both partners satisfied with their reciprocity equilibrium? What would each partner like to change?

A couple's developmental stage and the environmental stresses currently affecting the partners also must be assessed. Each stage of development presents its own unique challenges, and environmental stresses may hamper mastery of those challenges.

Overriding all of the above issues is the couple's level of motivation. Partners may have overt or covert reasons for initiating therapy and may have different levels of commitment to the relationship.

General Systems Theory

Although object relations theory and Bowen's extended family systems theory enable us to conceptualize the role of the family of origin in current couple functioning, each theory emphasizes individual intrapsychic phenomena. That is to say, what goes on within each member of the couple shapes the interaction.

General systems theory, however, moves to the next level of analysis and views the couple as a system embedded within larger systems. In the analysis, the couple is viewed as an entity in and of itself, a system defined by its interactions. From this perspective, current interactions become the focal point of our assessment and intervention.

Systems theory operates like a telescope; we choose the level of the system on which we wish to focus. As mentioned in Chapter 2, the influence of gender on a couple is embedded within families of origin, communities, and society. The therapist then chooses which level of the system to address. A couple is also a system embedded within extended families, cultural and ethnic systems, and the larger society. What is the system and what is a subsystem depends upon our level of focus. For example, a couple may be considered a subsystem of two extended family subsystems of two ethnic systems. The labels *system* and *subsystem* are less important than the recognition that systems and subsystems are mutually influential.

Two key concepts that will be a basis for discussion later in the book are lineal versus circular causality and boundaries.

LINEAL VERSUS CIRCULAR CAUSALITY

A complains that B is emotionally aloof. B says that A wants to spend all their time together and that he or she feels suffocated. A replies that if he or she did not pursue B then they would not have a relationship. B argues that he or she would be closer to A if he or she was less dependent and possessive. At this point the couple turns to the therapist and asks who is right and who is wrong.

Lineal causality assumes a linear, sequential cause-and-effect relationship: A causes B causes C causes D. From this perspective, a therapist is left with three possible causes and avenues for intervention into A's and B's problems: (1) B is fearful of intimacy and this must be addressed in therapy; (2) A is overly dependent and these needs will be the focus of therapy; or (3) both A and B collude in avoiding intimacy, using their arguments to maintain the distance between them.

In contrast, a circular systems perspective assumes there is no single and direct cause of an action or behavior. Behavior is a result of circular feedback loops operating within the system. That is to say, behavior does not occur in isolated sequential patterns, but every action within a system influences multiple reactions that influence further reactions. Or, in other words, members of a couple mutually influence each other.

From a circular systems viewpoint, A and B are caught in a cyclical, dysfunctional pattern. B pulls away as A seeks closeness. A attempts to close the expanding emotional gap by pursuing B. B feels suffocated and responds with further disengagement. A becomes angry and criticizes B. B becomes angry in return. Although not satisfactory, the argument is, at least, from A's point of view, some type of contact. B hates to argue and begins to distance again, thus reigniting the cycle.

Where lineal casuality attempts to identify causes—who has the problem?—circular casuality focuses on patterns. In the above case, nobody's right and nobody's wrong. They have simply evolved a pattern in their relationship that is mutually dissatisfying. Both have created it, both maintain it, and both will need to change it.

BOUNDARIES

Boundaries refer to the emotional barriers that protect and enhance the integrity of subsystems. Individuals may be considered subsystems of a couple system and the couple may be a subsystem of two extended families. Boundaries are the rules that define patterns of interaction between subsystems, rules that may be overt or covert.

For example, during the initial phase of a relationship, each member of a couple assumes that he or she will spend all available free time with the other. (Covert Rule: If we are a couple, then we spend all our time together.) Sometimes, the first arguments are over boundaries—"What do you mean you want to go out with your friends on Friday night?" Sometimes, establishing boundaries that define a couple as a new subsystem distinct from the two families of origin is the first task for the newly married couple. How much time do we spend with each family? At whose house do we spend Thanksgiving? Do we need to see your parents each week?

Boundaries run along a dimension from enmeshed or diffused to disengaged or rigid. For example, a couple's boundaries may be enmeshed with one of the families of origin. The couple cannot make a decision without factoring in the family of origin's opinion. Loyalty and responsibility to the family of origin may outweigh commitment to the couple relationship.

In contrast, subsystems rigidly separated from one another reflect disengaged boundaries. There is little interaction between the subsystems and any that does occur is perfunctory and stilted—"We live near my family but we never see them, and when we do it is usually at holidays for a few hours."

Both enmeshed and disengaged boundaries hamper a couple's growth. Enmeshed boundaries sacrifice belonging at the expense of individuality. In these cases, the partner or the families of origin are considered before individual needs. In a strongly enmeshed couple, individual needs are frequently repressed because expressing them might jeopardize relationships—"What do you mean you are not coming for Thanksgiving?"

On the other hand, disengaged boundaries maximize individuality at the expense of connnectedness. The partners lead basically separate lives seeking connections outside the relationship. Members of a disengaged couple treat one another as porcupines—if you get too close, you will get pricked.

General systems theory, as applied to psychotherapy, is not without its own gender biases. Inherent in general systems theory, and particularly as it constructs family theory, is the tendency toward "beta bias" (Hare-Mustin, 1989). This term, adopted from the language of empirical research, connotes the theory's tendency to ignore differences when, in fact, they do exist (a Type 2 error in hypothesis testing). Systems theory implies equality in the relationship of one part of the system to another part, which might not be the case.

For example, two very important differences within families and couples are *not addressed* in systems thinking. The first is a structural (hierarchical) component in which men, within the systemic perspective, have a higher status than women. This is the concept of male authority and the male's role as "head of the household." Inherent in this status differential is a power differential. When clinicians encourage a negotiating or bargaining exchange between members of a couple, it is often with the underlying assumption that equality exists within the relationship. A gender-sensitive clinician understands that women often begin negotiations from a more subordinate position within the couple.

The second difference overlooked in systems theory is the influence of gender roles in shaping behavior. For example, as discussed earlier, men and women do differ in their communication patterns and their expression of marital roles. Particularly in traditional relationships, instrumental (task-oriented) roles are often performed by the male and expressive (emotionally oriented) roles are often performed by the female. Men and women are mutually shaping their interactions but within the context of their respective gender roles. Systems theory does not address the differences in these roles nor does it address power imbalances within the couple system.

The concept of boundaries emphasizing a separateness between family members and subsystems also contains gender biases. Boundaries define the closeness and distance in relationships and fail to recognize a different feminine understanding of relatedness (Walters et al., 1988). For example, violating a boundary to increase closeness may be labeled "intrusive" or "controlling" rather than "caring."

The concept of circular causality may also be scrutinized. If both members of a couple play a part in creating the problems, then where and how much does individual responsibility enter the picture? For example, in a spouse abuse situation in which the husband physically abuses the wife, circular causality argues that the woman is also contributing to the abusive pattern. She fuels the violent episodes as much as the husband. From this perspective, her subordinate role is reinforced as she begins to wonder, "What did I do to set him off?"

Despite its shortcomings regarding gender roles, systems perspective sheds light on current, ongoing couple interactions. The problems the couple presents are not isolated arguments but disagreements embedded within a system of patterns, patterns governed by rules and role prescriptions. Furthermore, a couple is viewed as an entity in and of itself attempting to maintain stability but also adapting to change.

As a footnote, in the field of marriage and family therapy, the term *systems theory* means different things to different people. In this text it is used as a generic term that refers to a way of thinking about clinical issues, particularly with respect to: (1) circular versus lineal causality, (2) viewing a couple as a system within a larger extended family, and (3) a framework for viewing gender inequalities and differences within the larger societal system. Overall, systems theory provides guidelines for understanding current patterns of interaction and for viewing a couple not as a sum total of two individuals but as an entity in and of itself. For every intimate dyad, there are two partners and a third entity called their relationship.

Current Interactions: Identifying Patterns

The therapist is confronted with the challenge of identifying and changing current interactions. In assessing these patterns, the therapist first views the couple from a systems perspective and then begins to sequence the patterns. While doing so, the therapist explores attributions that underlie these patterns and the couple's patterns of reciprocity.

SYSTEMS PERSPECTIVE

Lynn, Carl, and Jenn may be seen as a subsystem embedded within their family of origin systems and a broader environmental context. This environment contains current cultural mores, work roles, and societal and gender expectations. Although it maintains contact with each larger system, the marriage of Lynn and Carl creates a new subsystem.

A subsystem's integrity as a unit is maintained by its boundaries that interface with the two larger systems. For example, the boundary with Lynn's side of the family is slightly enmeshed. Although able to make decisions on her own and able to allow her nuclear family to take precedence over her extended family, Lynn still feels a powerful obligation to her mother and sister. This obligation can on any given occasion draw her back into arguments with her mother and stimulate a desire to protect her younger sister. The pull of these obligations frequently places Lynn in the middle of the two systems. At times she is faced with conflicting demands and finds it difficult to establish priorities.

In contrast, the boundary with Carl's extended family is more disengaged. Carl's contact with his family is more formal and infrequent. He does not turn to his extended family to meet his emotional needs, such as support and affiliation, and thus he expects Lynn to meet most of those needs. For example, an underlying issue briefly alluded to in the first interview was Carl's jealousy of Jenn. Jenn's birth shifted Lynn's attention from Carl and left him feeling rejected and alone. Although at this initial phase of therapy he would vehemently deny such feelings, Carl's withdrawal behavior increased in both frequency and intensity following Jenn's birth.

Jenn's birth also upset the couple's reciprocity equilibrium. Before their daughter's birth, Lynn and Carl had established patterns that were traditional and mutually comfortable. Both worked and Lynn assumed the majority of housework with Carl periodically helping out. Lynn did not mind this arrangement because she arrived home before Carl and felt she was doing what she was accustomed to. Of course Jenn's birth changed all that. The couple was now faced with establishing a new homeostasis—new patterns that better fit the realities and increased demands of the family.

Unfortunately, their capacity to manage change was limited by their poor problem-solving skills and an inability to evolve new behavior. When faced with the demands for change, the couple responded with more of the same old patterns (first-order change). Carl, in particular, clung to the old patterns, leaving Lynn to assume more and more responsibilities.

In assessing current interactions, the therapist (1) sequences the patterns, (2) identifies pursuer-distancer patterns, and (3) explores the reciprocity disequilibrium.

SEQUENCING THE PATTERNS

The therapist should be active in delineating the patterns via lineal and circular questions. For example:

Therapist: Which of the two of you is most likely to identify and bring up what you see as problems?

(Lynn and Carl quickly glance at one another and Lynn speaks.)

Lynn: Well, I don't know if you could say I bring up problems, but I am the one most likely to point out what needs to be done.

(Lynn is sensitive to Carl's complaint that she is critical and is reluctant to endorse the therapist's question.)

Therapist: Sorry, that's not what I meant. Who is most likely to point out what needs to be done around the house?

Lynn: Well, then that would definitely be me.

Therapist (*using this as a starting point to begin to sequence the patterns*):   When do you bring those things up?

Lynn: Usually after the baby has gone to sleep and I am doing some laundry.

Therapist: How do you point things out?

Lynn: What do you mean?

Therapist: For example, how do you approach Carl when you want some help?

Lynn: I tell him I need some help.

Therapist: What happens next?

Lynn: He usually does not respond and I ask him again.

Therapist: And then what happens?

Notice that in this line of questioning the basic themes are *who, when,* and *what.* These questions detail the behavioral sequence of the couple's interactions: who initiates, when does the person initiate, what is the other person's response, and what additional responses does that response elicit. Although the questions appear lineal in nature, when they are sequenced progressively they identify circular patterns of interaction.

A particular pattern emerged from the above questions. To summarize:

- Lynn is the spouse most likely to identify a problem.
- For example, Lynn would feel overwhelmed and ask for Carl's help.
- Carl either does not immediately respond or says he will get to it.

- Lynn grows frustrated and asks again.
- Carl hears her requests as criticism and he withdraws.
- Lynn senses his withdrawal and pursues the issue.
- Carl withdraws further.
- At this point two outcomes are possible: (1) Lynn gives up, quits pursuing this particular issue, and a subsequent chill comes over the relationship; or (2) Lynn pursues past Carl's tolerance threshold and he angrily criticizes Lynn, forcing her to withdraw.

As a means of discerning the prevalence of this pattern, the therapist explores another theme.

Therapist: Lynn, you also mentioned that you did not feel the two of you were as close as you once were. I was wondering what you meant by that?

Lynn: We used to be able to talk, to spend time together.

Therapist: What stops that from occurring now?

Lynn: Well, there does not seem to be much time any more.

Therapist: But, when you do want time together how do you go about getting it?

Lynn: I usually complain to Carl about the lack of time together.

Therapist: Does that usually work?

Lynn: He never seems interested anymore.

(Here, the therapist is at another choice point. To continue encouraging Lynn to speak to this issue risks a litany of complaints that would only force Carl into further withdrawal. But, to let the issue drop would close the door on the central question of intimacy in the couple's marriage. Keeping the theme but shifting the focus, the therapist explores Carl's view of closeness.)

Therapist: Carl, what do you do when you want time with Lynn?

Carl: She is always tired or too busy with the baby.

Therapist *(avoiding the detour of blaming Lynn)*:   That may be, but still, when you want time together, what do you do?"

Carl: I usually just wait for Lynn to approach me.

Although the theme of intimacy is being explored, the identified pattern is repeated. Lynn initiates and Carl waits.

(The therapist is at another choice point. He or she could pursue with Carl his choice to remain passive when trying to get what he wants—for example, closeness with Lynn. This would further assess Carl's degree of passivity and his expectations of Lynn. The other alternative is to drop this line of questioning here without further pursuit. Stopping here offends neither partner and subtly underscores how much Lynn is expected to pursue.)

PURSUER-DISTANCER PATTERNS

Fogarty (1976) first described the "pursuer-distancer" dynamic among couples. Briefly, he observed that as one member of a couple pursues emotional contact with his or her partner, that partner will distance from the contact via watching television, working late, and so on. Furthermore, partners alternate pursuing and distancing in different areas. For example, the husband may withdraw emotionally but pursue sexual contact.

Fogarty (1976) hypothesized that the pursuer is attempting to fill his or her own inner emptiness. Consequently, he advised therapists to "never pursue a distancer" but instead explore the pursuer's motivations. As for the distancer, he assumed that once the distancer is no longer pursued then he or she will move back toward the partner.

Guerin, Fay, Burden, and Kautto (1987) describe the pursuer-distancer patterns as personal operating styles. That is, each person possesses an affinity for one style or the other. They believe a personal operating style is determined by the individual's constitutional temperament, which is also shaped by the family of origin and the marital relationship. For example, a person with a pursuer operating style desires relationship time, comfortably expresses personal thoughts and feelings, is open to the environment, and has a fast personal rhythm (a person who moves through life at the extremes of high speed and dead stop). In contrast, a person with a distancing operating style values alone time, avoids the expression of personal thoughts and feelings, is selective in attending to the environment, and has a more deliberate pattern of energy and decision making.

The two operating styles may be complementary to one another in times of low stress:

> In a low-stress environment, when the spouses are functioning fairly well, the pursuer's energy and intense emotionality toward the relationship provide a counterpoint to the distancer's cool, logical steadiness. The impatience of the pursuer provides impetus, and the reliability of the distancer provides staying power to accomplish the shared tasks of the relationship. The emotional personalism of the pursuer fills a perceived lack in the distancer's life, and the distancer's calm reasonableness is a reassuring check on the pursuer's impulsiveness. (Guerin et al., 1987, p. 46)

In times of high stress, however, the styles become conflicting polarities. The pursuer seeks comfort in emotional contact, whereas the distancer needs to move away from the conflict.

Instead of assuming emotional personalism, we view the pursuer-distancer styles not as aspects of an individual's personality but as behaviors that either spouse may evidence dependent upon the issue and context. For example, Figure 7.1 portrays three possible pursuer-distancer behavioral patterns.

Pattern 1 represents a classic unidirectional pursuer-distancer pattern. Person A is most likely to initiate contact with Person B. B in response distances from A. A eventually gives up pursuit and B no longer withdraws. Notice, the initial emotional distance between them is maintained throughout the interaction.

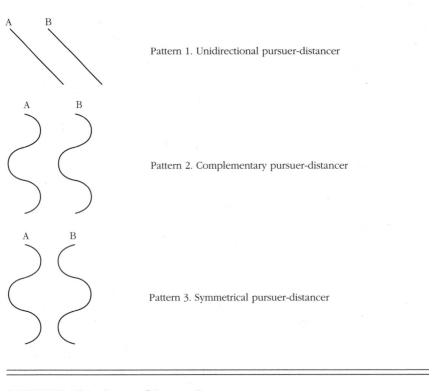

A   B

Pattern 1. Unidirectional pursuer-distancer

A   B

Pattern 2. Complementary pursuer-distancer

A   B

Pattern 3. Symmetrical pursuer-distancer

F I G U R E   7.1   Pursuer-Distancer Patterns

In Pattern 2 there is a bidirectional or complementary pursuer-distancer pattern. A and B pursue and distance in parallel. The emotional gap between them is maintained but through reciprocal actions. Thus, at any given time, if A stops and begins to withdraw from B, B will begin to pursue A and vice versa.

In Patterns 1 and 2, partners establish an emotional distance between them. This distance may vary for every couple. One couple may spend all their time together, and another couple will have few common interests. Despite the differences in emotional distance, both couples may describe themselves as "close." Thus, the pursuer-distancer patterns described above maintain the unconsciously agreed to distance.

Pattern 3, however, represents symmetrical pursuer-distancer behavior—that is, both partners distance and pursue in approximately the same rhythms. With this pattern, a couple may experience intense closeness but also stilted distance.

When viewed as behavioral patterns and not inherent personality characteristics, we are able to discriminate finer subtleties in the couple's relationship. A couple may evidence all three patterns dependent upon the issue and context. For example, a discussion concerning in-laws may resemble Pattern 1 whereby nothing is ever fully addressed or resolved. It is as if the couple have agreed to not confront one another directly on the issue. Pattern 2 may characterize a couple's sexual relationship. At any given time one spouse may be pursuing sexual contact while the other pulls away. Or, in Pattern 3, we see a couple's roller coaster ride of intimacy. Their periods of intimacy may mirror the movement of an accordion—an intense intimate relationship followed by periods of emotional distance.

Moreover, seen as behavioral patterns, either member of the couple may be pursuing or distancing in any given context. As an evolving process, a marriage or an intimate relationship is never static or complete. Distance and pursuing reflect a couple's attempt to form a close relationship while maintaining individuality—an ever changing process.

From a clinical perspective, the concern is the impact of the pattern on the relationship, not that the patterns are occurring. For example, a rigidity of roles bodes poorly for a relationship. If one member of the couple is always pursuing and the other always distancing, not only does the couple's intimacy level suffer, but the couple's ability to effectively problem-solve is greatly diminished—for example, every time the pursuer brings up an emotional issue, the distancer withdraws. Furthermore, the pursuer's frustration with his or her attempts at intimacy will increase and slowly extinguish any flames of love.

Unfortunately, Pattern 1 characterized Lynn and Carl's relationship. As discussed above, Lynn would more than likely initiate and pursue contact with Carl. Carl's chief response was first to ignore or minimize Lynn's request and then to withdraw as Lynn continued to pursue. After 3 years of marriage, their roles and patterns were increasingly rigidified. As is characteristic of the unidirectional pursuer-distancer pattern, Lynn's increasing frustration was the motivation and impetus for counseling.

Given this dynamic, the therapist would commit a misstep if he or she let the evaluation phase of treatment be dominated by Lynn's complaints concerning Carl. In fact, if this occurred, the therapist would be colluding in continuing the dysfunctional pursuer-distancer pattern. That is, by not directing the conversation, the therapist would encourage a familiar pattern in Lynn and Carl's relationship: Lynn pursuing and Carl distancing.

Worse yet, a therapist could follow Lynn's cues and attempt to pursue Carl. Carl, at least in the initial stage of therapy, would distance himself from the therapist's pursuit. Although this would validate Lynn's complaint, Carl's resistance to therapy would grow. Consequently, the therapist's art lies in the ability to address the salient issues without reinforcing the dysfunctional pursuer-distancer pattern.

GENDER INFLUENCES ON PURSUER-DISTANCER PATTERNS

Guerin et al. (1987) described pursuers as seeking emotional closeness through an expression of personal affect and thought, while distancers may seek alone time and avoid emotional expression. If our clinical couple (Lynn and Carl) were to stay within prescribed gender roles, the pursuer would be a woman and the distancer would be a man. However, empirical evidence broadens our understanding of the pursuer-distancer pattern.

In a series of empirical studies, Christensen and his colleagues (Christensen & Heavey, 1990; Heavey, Layne, & Christensen, 1993) examined what they refer to as a demand/withdraw pattern in marital interaction. In concrete terms, one spouse attempts to engage in problem-solving discussion (usually the wife), frequently employing pressure and demands, while the other spouse (the husband) avoids or withdraws from the interaction. Their findings supported three hypotheses: (1) once brought to the couple's attention, couples can agree on the presence of this pattern in their relationship; (2) the frequency of the demand/withdraw interaction is highly associated with marital dissatisfaction for women because in marriages wives consistently want more changes in the relationship than do husbands; and (3) women tend to assume the demanding role whereas men tend to assume the withdrawing role during a couple's conflict.

The researchers offer two explanations for the gender difference findings. First, from an individual perspective, personality differences based on physiological and socializing influences exist between men and women that lead women to pursue and men to withdraw. Second, from a structural perspective, because men possess greater power—for example, status, control of resources—in a male-female relationship, they have no interest in changing this status quo. Withdrawal, therefore, is a means of maintaining it. Women, on the other hand, engage in pursuit and confrontation as their means of challenging the system.

The researchers hypothesize that the more couples mirror gender-stereotyped roles in their relationships, the greater the risk that their conflict will become polarized and rigid over time—the woman continually pursues and the man withdraws. Furthermore, this polarization of roles makes it increasingly difficult for them to resolve their conflicts and, thus, bodes poorly for marital satisfaction or viability.

The data also highlight an interesting gender-reversal pattern that is dependent upon the context. That is, when a husband identified an issue for discussion, both husbands and wives were equally likely to demand or withdraw during the discussion. When the issue was identified by the wife, the wife-demand/husband-withdraw pattern was significantly more likely to occur.

The gender-reversal pattern often raises initial anxiety in both spouses, but it is inversely related to increased marital satisfaction for wives. That is to say, women (although initially anxious when their mate raises troublesome issues) appreciate their partner's concern. Specifically, a husband's demandingness was predictive of longitudinal increase in wives' marital satisfaction. The researchers offer three possible explanations for these findings: (1) the husbands' demandingness avoids the polarization of gender-stereotyped roles (or, in other words, the gender-reversal pattern inhibits the development of rigid roles leading to dysfunctional patterns); (2) wives may react favorably to husbands' demandingness because it reflects engagement over withdrawal in the relationship; and (3) women may be more willing to change to improve the relationship.

The researchers view this finding as support for their societal-structural interpretation of the woman-demand/man-withdraw pattern. Men withdraw to maintain the status quo and avoid any changes that would diminish their power; they do not withdraw because of inherent gender differences. Women demand and pursue because they have more need to change areas in the relationship and not because they inherently seek contact.

Standard clinical wisdom, from a systems perspective, suggests one never pursues a distancer. The underlying assumption is that members of a couple establish an emotional distance or comfort zone between them and that this distance is constantly maintained. Therefore, as the pursuer stops pursuing, the distancer will no longer need to withdraw. In fact, the distancer will reverse direction to restore the comfort zone. This comfort zone varies for each couple (see Pattern 2 in Figure 7.1).

But as mentioned above, Fogarty (1976) advised that instead of also pursuing the distancer, the therapist should focus on the pursuer's needs to pursue. The reasoning is that when the pursuer quits pursuing the distancer will reverse direction and seek contact. Although couched within extended family systems theory, this description of the pursuer-distancer dynamic describes lineal causality: The distancer distances because the pursuer pursues.

Assuming the gender bias in the pursuer-distancer dynamic in couples, to be true therapists would more frequently instruct women to quit pursuing their mates, which would again place the burden of changing the relationship on the woman. She is to change and not pursue her emotional needs in the hopes that her mate will pursue her.

Suffice it to say there are no guarantees that the therapist's insight will result in the desired rebalance of the comfort zone. The man may reverse direction and pursue his mate, or he may just as likely feel reinforced and vindicated in his current distancing position. The status quo has been maintained and his wife has quit pressuring him.

Walters et al. (1988) argued that this clinical intervention may result in the woman feeling ashamed of her need for closeness. Therefore her sense of isolation is inadvertently reinforced by the therapist.

The above research findings, however, offer another possibility. Instead of asking the woman to quit pursuing, the man is encouraged to also assume responsibility for the relationship by identifying changes he wishes. A therapist is more likely to engage a gender-stereotyped couple if the focus of change is on the withdrawing spouse's unexpressed wants. For example, instead of focusing on Lynn's pursuit, Carl would be drawn into the therapeutic session by stating what he wants to be changed in the relationship (see later section on reciprocity).

In conclusion, the pursuer-distancer dynamic is highly dependent upon the context. For example, the husband may be the pursuer and the wife the distancer concerning sexual issues, while the wife pursues and the husband withdraws from verbal intimacy. The woman may pursue issues regarding the children. The man may pursue issues concerning the in-laws. Thus, for many cases, it is not a simple matter of one spouse pursuing another but rather a context-dependent theme—who pursues and who distances, when, concerning what issues, and under what circumstances?

Attributions: Maintaining and Reinforcing Behavior

An emerging area of research on couples and an area with direct clinical relevance is the role of attributions in shaping interactions (Baucom & Epstein, 1990; Bradbury & Fincham, 1990; Miller & Bradbury, 1995). Attributions are the cognitive meanings attached to the partner and one's own behavior. Research studies strongly suggest that attributions are directly related to behavior and play a prominent role in modifying marital satisfaction (Bradbury & Fincham, 1990). For example, one partner forgets to call home at a given time that he said he or she would. The partner waiting patiently at home for the phone call may form one of several attributions:

1. "My partner must be very busy and forgot to call."
2. "I wonder if we were clear with one another on the time to call."
3. "I bet something happened; my partner would never not call."
4. "Well nothing new, my partner is terrible about keeping track of time."
5. "Well, there is another example of my partner's inconsiderateness."

Notice that each of these attributions would be correlated with an emotional response and would lead to behavior associated with emotional response. If I attribute my partner's behavior to an outside event—"He probably had too much work to do"—then I will be solicitous when he does call. On the other hand, if I believe this is another example of his inconsideration, I may sulk, withdraw, or get angry. Attributions, therefore, are the link between cognition and behavior.

Attributions may be categorized along several dimensions (Bradbury & Fincham, 1990):

1. (*Intentional versus unintentional*) Did the partner intentionally forget to call?
2. (*Negative versus positive motivation*) "He forgot to call because he is self-ish and does not care about me." Or, "I know he is working hard to bring in more money."
3. (*Free choice or outside coercion*) "He stayed late because he wanted to" as opposed to "he stayed late because the boss made him and he had no choice."
4. (*Awareness of consequences or lack of awareness*) "He knows I am worried and will call when he gets the first chance"; or, "He does not even realize how this drives me crazy."
5. (*Acknowledgment of wrongfulness versus no such acknowledgment*) "I am sorry for not calling; I know you were worried."
6. (*Capacity to have done otherwise*) "He had no alternative but to stay late."

Distress and nondistress couples differ greatly on these dimensions. Holzworth-Munroe and Jacobson (1985) divided attributions into distress-maintaining attributes for a partner's negative behavior (voluntary, intentional behavior done with negative intent reflecting global personality traits—for example, selfish, mean, cold) and relationship-enhancing attributes (negative behavior was specific to the situation, due to outside circumstances, and unintentional). Distressed couples employed more distress-maintaining attributions and nondistressed spouses were more likely to make relationship-enhancing attributions.

Once negative attributions permeate the relationship, even positive behavior is cast in a new light. In nondistressed couples positive events were seen as further evidence of the partner's good will, while the impact of the partner's negative behavior was minimized by relationship-enhancing attributions—"I know he would never hurt me intentionally." In contrast, distressed couples minimize positive attributions as an aberration, while the partner's negative behavior further maintains and reinforces the negative view of the partner (Bradbury & Fincham, 1990).

Moreover, couples' attributions assume a reciprocal quality. Spouses who attributed higher levels of negative intent to their partner's actions were more likely to respond with their own negative behavior. Furthermore, a wife reciprocating her husband's negative behavior was related to the degree she viewed his behavior as selfishly motivated and worthy of blame. In contrast, nondistressed spouses made similar attributions for self and partners actions—"We both love one another and would never intentionally hurt the other" (Lavin, 1987).

Surprisingly, attributions research has identified gender differences. Specifically, attributions and behavior are more strongly associated for wives than husbands (Miller & Bradbury, 1995). That is to say, in heterosexual couples, when a woman views the man in a negative light and sees him as responsible for the difficulties in the relationship, she is more likely to reciprocate in kind with her own negative behavior than is the man.

Because this has been a recent and consistent finding in marital attribution research, reasons for this gender difference are purely speculative at this stage. However, in light of our earlier discussions on the psychology of men and women, perhaps women are more attuned to relationship nuances, continually evaluating the relationship, forming attributions, and acting on those judgments compared to men. Men, on the other hand, may pay little attention to the same nuances and perceive fewer slights.

Also, the importance and value placed by women on maintaining the relationship make them more sensitive and responsive to the quality of the relationship when compared to men. Thus, a woman's attributions are more likely to be directly reflected in behavior.

By the time a couple enters therapy, a complete set of attributions has been created. The conflict and unhappiness has been going on for a period of time, and each member of the couple possesses a full list of attributions to explain what has occurred. Each partner describes and provides evidence for how the other acts with negative intent, could have acted differently but did not because of ingrained personality traits, and deserves to be blamed for the couple's problems. Accompanying these attributions are self-attributions depicting oneself as trying one's best but the victim of the other's selfish concerns and lack of love.

In recent years the role of cognition and attributions in psychotherapy has gained increased interest. For instance, Hudson and O'Hanlon (1991) speak of rewriting couples' stories. That is, from a narrative and constructionist perspective, couples create stories (attributions) concerning their relationships. These stories give meaning to the relationship while maintaining and reinforcing behavior. The brief therapy of Hudson and O'Hanlon (1991) emphasizes changing behavior by changing the meanings (attributions).

Employing Bradbury and Fincham's (1990) categorization as a guideline, a therapist is in a position to assess the attributions underlying the couple's current interactions.

Therapist: Lynn, you said when you ask Carl for help you get little response. Why do you think that is?

(This reflective question encourages Lynn's interpretation. If the therapist asked Lynn a lineal question such as, "Why does Carl act that way?" Lynn could answer by blaming herself: "I don't think I ask in the right way." Or, she could answer by blaming Carl directly: "He doesn't care." More open-ended and less specific questions allow more possibility to uncover the couple's attributions.)

Lynn: Sometimes I think Carl does not want to hear me. He would rather keep doing what he is doing and not be bothered. (*intentional with negative motivation*)

Therapist: From your perspective, why doesn't he want to hear you?

Lynn: I sometimes wonder if he cares enough. (*negative motivation*)

Therapist: Cares about who or what?

Lynn: Cares about me and how I feel.

Therapist: Why would he not care about how you feel?

Lynn: Because he can be insensitive and cares only about himself. (*lack of awareness and does not acknowledge wrongfulness*)

Therapist: Does that apply to Jenn, too? (*Therapist is exploring the generalizability of Lynn's attributions.*)

Lynn: I know he loves Jenn. (*positive motivation*)

Therapist: How do you know?

Lynn: The way he holds her and talks to her. (*free choice*)

Therapist: Do you point it out to him when he does not listen?

Lynn: Yes, but it only starts an argument and he accuses me of criticizing him. (*lack of awareness and negative intent*)

Lynn's perspective: Carl does not listen to her or chooses not to listen to her because he does not care enough about her and because he is selfish. Moreover, he does not acknowledge he is wrong or that he hurts her. Although based in her experience in the marriage, Lynn's attribution for her unhappiness in the marriage is Carl's intentional insensitivity to her and his selfish personality. She, on the other hand, is doing her best to keep this marriage and family together, but it is an uphill struggle because of Carl's personality.

In the next step of assessment, Carl would be asked similar questions to ascertain the attributions or stories he has created to explain the current state of his marriage. Briefly, he sees himself as a victim of Lynn's constant demands. She has not been pleased with anything since the baby arrived. Carl thinks his best course is to avoid raising any problem because it would only result in an argument. He believes he honestly does help around the house but that Lynn is never satisfied because she is too perfectionistic.

(Please note: Once behavior is attributed to ingrained personality traits, it is an easy step to blaming the respective families of origin for shaping these objectionable traits—"You are just like your mother!")

After exploring each of the spouse's attributions, the therapist explores the rigidity or intractability of the attributions by asking each spouse to comment on what the other has said.

Therapist: Carl, Lynn wonders if you care about her. How would you respond to this question of hers?

Carl: I don't know what she means by that. I would not have married her if I did not care about her. That is just another way she criticizes me. (*intentional*)

(The therapist is at a choice point. Carl could be directed to speak to Lynn and ask her to clarify what she means by caring. Or, the therapist can further pursue Carl's definition of caring.)

In choosing between the two, the therapist closely observes Carl. If he exhibits curiosity or any openness to Lynn's perceptions, the therapist may decide to test this openness by requesting that Carl ask what Lynn means by caring. However, pursuing the interaction between the couple runs the risk of repeating the cycles of blame.

(Sensing Carl's closed defensive posture, the therapist addresses the attribution patterns.)

Therapist: That may be, but how does Lynn know you do care for her?

Carl: Well, I work hard to support the family, and I have given up things to care for the baby.

Therapist: Why do you think she misses seeing those things?

Carl: She only sees negative things. (*intentional, free choice, and capacity to do otherwise*)

For assessment purposes, Lynn would also be asked similar questions. By asking each partner to comment on the other's attributions, the therapist gains an appreciation of the couple's repetitive, cyclical blaming patterns resulting from their attributions and assumptions of the partner's personality characteristics.

Why should Lynn approach Carl with other than demands because he will not hear her to begin with? Why should Carl do anything caring for Lynn when all he is receiving is criticism? Both partners feel similarly unappreciated, unacknowledged, and overworked.

Again, the therapist is at a choice point. The underlying themes of being unappreciated, unacknowledged, overworked, and misunderstood stand paramount between the couple. The therapist may encapsulate and summarize these themes to highlight the observation that both partners share in the marital dissatisfaction. This encourages the "both in the same boat phenom-enon," which can (1) promote a feeling of mutuality, (2) "normalize" the experi-ence at a developmental stage in the family life cycle—offering hope, (3) further test the degree of inherent resentment and anger.

Therapist: It sounds to me like you *both* feel unappreciated and misunderstood in this relationship. Lynn, you feel overworked and isolated from the man you love. Carl, you feel constantly criticized and belittled for your efforts to support your family. However, you both state that this is a change from your early marriage. At some point, in some way your marriage became imbalanced. This kind of imbalance often occurs when a couple become a family and unexpected burdens and changes take place. It would be interesting to ex-plore how this came about in your family.

The couple's response to this type of hope-enhancing summation is diagnos-tic. The best case is that they mutually agree that the marriage has changed and accept the therapist's offer of hope. Or one or both may further retreat into their blaming behaviors, seeing the therapist as a Pollyanna who doesn't take their problems seriously. Since the couple's reaction cannot accurately be predicted, the therapist must use his or her own clinical judgment whether to provide a hopeful comment at this stage in the assessment.

The topic of attributions will be revisited in the next chapter which discusses the change process. At this point in the assessment, the couple's attributions illustrate the strength and rigidity of their views and the potential pitfalls for their therapist. For example, even though the marriage is relatively young, Lynn and Carl are polarized along their own rigid lines. Consequently, both may initially be highly resistant to changing their attributions and will likely attempt to persuade the therapist as to the correctness of their respective visions.

To compound matters, when each was asked about his or her decision to have a child, both Lynn and Carl viewed their decision differently.

Lynn: We both talked about having children one day but Carl kept putting it off.

Carl: I wanted us to have more money in the bank before we started a family.

Therapist: So, how did the two of you make this decision?

Lynn: We just decided if it happens it happens.

Therapist: Carl?

Carl: I got tired of arguing about it.

Lynn: Carl would have never been ready to have a child.

Carl: I told you I was worried about the finances, but you wanted what you wanted.

Thus, even with this important decision, Lynn and Carl disagree and attribute separate meanings to the event. For Lynn, Carl was never going to be ready and the only way they would have children is if she actively pursued it. For Carl, Lynn did not consider anything else except what she wanted. Unfortunately, both sets of attributions hint at underlying resentments each feels toward the other. These resentments will surface later in therapy.

Summary

Current interactions come alive in your office and depict the patterns that maintain and, in some cases, comprise a couple's problems. Generally, systems theory offers a means of conceptualizing a couple as an entity in and of itself embedded within larger systems. Whereas a lineal definition of a couple's problems is typically presented—"If only he or she would change, then we would have a better relationship"—the concept of circular causality frees a therapist from this line of thinking, focusing instead on reciprocal and circular patterns of interaction. From this new vantage point, the therapist proposes changing the pattern of interactions rather than changing individuals.

Likewise, the couple's patterns of interaction are usually reinforced and maintained by individually held attributions, attributions that justify and predict the patterns of interaction. Because research data strongly suggest that attributions influence marital satisfaction rather than vice versa and that changing attributions may play a prominent role in modifying marital behavior (Bradbury & Fincham, 1990), cognitive-behavioral interventions offer another tool for changing dysfunctional marital patterns.

Reciprocity

As detailed in Chapter 4, reciprocity refers to the exchange balance couples evolve. The exchange equilibrium is based on the values each partner ascribes to specific behavior. For example, although Lynn would rather stay home with her baby for several years, she must work to meet the financial pressures. She accepts this, but what upsets her is that Carl still assumes she will also manage household chores. For Lynn, the relationship is greatly imbalanced. Carl, on the other hand, believes he is shouldering most of the financial burden but is receiving little emotional support from his wife. From Carl's perspective, Lynn has become completely absorbed in the baby. He also believes the relationship is imbalanced.

Assessing the reciprocity equilibrium is a three-step process. First, individual perspectives are explored. Each partner was initially attracted to the other for a variety of reasons. Although those reasons may be foggy memories by the time the couple enters therapy, the early attractions hint at what each mate hoped to receive from the other.

Therapist: What attracted you to your partner?

What did you hope you were getting when you decided to get married?

What did you value in the relationship at that time?

Second, the relative value attached to specific behavior is identified. Partners rarely define to one another what they value in each other. Further still, they may have no idea what their partners value in them. Making these covert values overt illuminates new perspectives for the couple.

Therapist: Lynn, what do you do that Carl values?

Carl, what does Lynn do that you value?

Therapist (*eliciting feedback from each partner as means of underlining misperceptions*):   I was wondering, were either one of you surprised by what the other said?

And finally, the roadblocks to balancing the equilibrium are highlighted.

Therapist: It would appear that you each value something from the other and that you each offer something of value. What do wish there was more of in your relationship?

Therapist (*after each partner has spoken*):   Given what you want more of in your relationship, what stops this from occurring?

At this point of the interview, the partners' response to this question is quite diagnostic. If they respond with the familiar blaming sequence, then one assumes the blaming attributes are strongly entrenched in the relationship, foreshadowing a poor prognosis. If, however, the blaming does not reignite and the partners' emotional tone softens, then one assumes each partner is listening to the other and is still emotionally open to the other.

Although exploring the reciprocity equilibrium is part of the assessment process, it also is a therapeutic intervention. Simply asking what each partner values in the other and what each believes the other values in him or her makes covert assumptions overt. The couple are then in a position to at least understand that there are differences in their perceptions and to potentially correct the misunderstandings.

Developmental and Environmental Stresses

DEVELOPMENTAL STRESSES

Just as individuals develop over time, marriages also evolve. Certainly, a marriage of 4 years differs from a marriage of 10 years, which differs from a marriage of 20 or 30 years. Financial pressures ebb and flow. Children are born, are raised, and leave the family. A couple's definition of intimacy changes with time. Sexual energy may become richer and deepen or may become nonexistent. Although couples enter therapy with problems they find difficult to manage, their conflicts are nested within a developmental stage. Each stage provides a different context for problem identification.

From the social constructivist perspective, couples at Lynn and Carl's stage face two interrelated tasks: (1) defining their heritage and (2) defining a new relationship identity as a couple (Wambolt & Reiss, 1989). In defining their heritage, couples establish themselves in relationship to the individual family of origin. What are the impacts of each family of origin? To whose family will we be closer? Whose family will be the most problematic? What qualities of that family do I want in my current relationship, and what qualities do I wish to exclude?

The process of defining one's heritage implies that we attach cognitive meanings to our family of origin experiences—that is, what do I think of myself now because of my experiences in my family? In defining a new relationship, two individuals become a couple. The questions that define a relationship identity involve some of the following: Who are we as a couple? What are our relationships with our in-laws? What do we believe in? What are our goals? How do our goals compare with those of the previous generation?

The elements of ethnicity and "Americanization" may play a greater part in these definitions for couples with a strong ethnic background. Great tension can exist within families as children of first-generation Americans adopt behavior and standards that seem anathema to those of immigrant families.

These processes evolve through consensus building. Two individuals become a couple not when they say "I do" but as the above concepts are negotiated and agreed to. Thus, where past studies define interactional variables by measures of conflict and ability for conflict resolution, the social contructivist position emphasizes consensus building and the capacity for the two members of a couple to develop shared meanings or shared attributions. For example, the relationship identity reflects a congruency of attributes—how you see me is how I see myself. Consequently, the greater the incongruence between the two sets of attributes, the greater the potential for conflict.

Therefore, the basis of their current problems is twofold: (1) Neither Lynn nor Carl possesses a clear view of the relationship they want to build. They struggle with their relationship identity. They each have a vague idea of the desired relationship, but their inability to negotiate their differences impedes consensus building. (2) Their attributions are incongruent. When they describe themselves and each other, it appears as if they are describing two people who have never met.

ENVIRONMENTAL STRESSES

Lynn had worked from the beginning of their marriage. She hoped to stay home longer with her baby, but needing to ease the family financial pressure, she returned to work when Jenn was 8 months old. Carl worked in sales; therefore a significant amount of his income was based on commissions. Because of the uncertain nature of Carl's income, Lynn felt she needed to have a job with predictable income. However, while Lynn's job provided relief financially, it forced changes in the couple's lifestyle in terms of time spent together, day-care arrangements, and household chores.

Developmentally, marital satisfaction tends to decline for single- and dual-earner couples during the stage of pre-school-aged children when there are maximum child-care demands. Parents as compared to nonparents report more work-family pressure because of difficulty in modifying work schedules to accommodate family needs (Lewis & Cooper, 1987). In addition, mothers report much more work-family pressure than fathers, but both spouses report dissatisfaction with their partners' contributions to domestic roles (Lewis & Cooper, 1987). It is hypothesized that the higher levels of distress in women may reflect an unbalanced division of labor in the family, the women's tendency to experience a broader range of affective intensity, or both (Barnett, Brennan, Raudenbush, & Marshall, 1994).

The research findings mirrored the complaints Lynn and Carl brought into therapy. Carl felt he was as equally committed to the family as was Lynn. Nevertheless, in the day-to-day routines of running a household, Lynn assumed the burden of chores and reported the most distress. Carl felt he was hustling to make as much money as possible, and he helped out whenever he could. Unfortunately, the couple's inability to reconcile these domestic issues, in addition to the environmental stresses, was close to pulling their marriage apart.

Motivation for Therapy

While assessing the above dimensions—(1) family of origin and goodness of fit issues, (2) current patterns of interaction, (3) attributions reinforcing and maintaining those patterns, (4) the reciprocity equilibrium, and (5) developmental and environmental stresses—the question of motivation floats through the assessment phase of therapy. Why is the couple seeking therapy at this time? Who is most motivated to begin therapy? How resistant is the other spouse to begin therapy?

Couples seek therapy for a variety of reasons. Some reasons are clear, and others remain hidden agendas that influence the therapeutic process. Individual partners may possess overt and covert motivations for seeking therapy. Unconscious motivations may further complicate the clinical picture. Finally, individuals and couples vary in the degree to which they are committed to the relationship. The following sections list and discuss a variety of motivations for couples seeking therapy.

OVERT AND COMMITTED

These couples enter therapy with both partners motivated and committed to the relationship. They have identified problems and wish to make the relationship stronger.

OVERT AND UNCOMMITTED

These couples have typically been in difficulty for a long time. In fact, they may have previously been in couples therapy. Although they may disagree about the causes of their conflicts, they agree they have relationship problems. Because of the chronicity of their difficulties, one or both members of the couple may be at best ambivalent and at worst uncommitted to the relationship. They stay together for a variety of reasons—for example, children, finances, religion—but a tenuous balance characterizes the fragile relationship.

These couples seek therapy when the scale tips and creates an imbalance in the relationship. For example, environmental stresses may force the couple to interact with one another more than usual, and these interactions heighten the conflict. Although the couple may make little progress on their presenting problems, the therapy sessions serve as a steam valve to relieve mounting pressure in the relationship.

This type of couple usually stays in therapy until the pressure subsides—for example, when environmental pressures lessen—and then terminates. However, one can expect these couples to recontact the therapist at some later point when future imbalances occur.

COVERT AND COMMITTED

Many times couples enter therapy committed to their relationship but genuinely confused over their continuing conflicts and distance. They love one another and want the relationship to work out but fear their differences may be too great.

While their commitment is clear, the reasons for their conflicts remain covert. For example, one or both partners may have unresolved family of origin issues that carry into the current relationship. Or, the couple may have developed dysfunctional problem-solving styles.

A therapist may be invaluable to these couples by uncovering the family of origin influences, by identifying the current dysfunctional patterns, or by doing both. From a motivational perspective, each partner's commitment to the relationship is the foundation from which to explore unresolved issues and to develop more satisfying interactions—for example, negotiation and problem-solving skills.

COVERT AND UNCOMMITTED

These are the most difficult cases for a couples therapist. Not only are one or both partners not committed to the relationship, but their reasons are nested in hidden agendas that may be conscious or unconscious.

For example, one or both partners may have decided to end the relationship but lingering guilt stops them. Couples therapy, therefore, offers a face-saving means toward separation or divorce, because following a failed attempt at therapy, they can say to friends and family, "Well, we tried everything. We even went to counseling but that did not help either."

A variation of the same theme is that one partner has secretly decided to end the relationship but has not clearly told the other. Therapy, therefore, offers a convenient and safe forum to request a separation. Of course, this does not occur until after several sessions of evidence gathering to further support the separation decision.

Another hidden agenda in many of these cases is a desire for the therapist to take care of the deserted ex-partner. This pattern is common in couples in which one spouse is depressed and possibly suicidal. The spouse who wants to leave hopes that the therapist will provide a "safe harbor" to ward off a major depression or suicide attempt.

Another common pattern is for one or both partners to have an extramarital affair or affairs. The affairs may be a way for the person to explore the possibilities of leaving the relationship or a means of avoiding the intimacy of a monogamous relationship. Regardless, the affairs are the hidden agendas in therapy. A therapist may have a vague notion that he or she does not possess all the facts concerning the case but is continually frustrated in attempts to uncover more. In these situations, one or both partners appear intent on keeping the therapy sessions on very superficial levels.

Returning to Lynn and Carl, although they had been experiencing difficult times and Lynn was the prime motivator for seeking therapy, both were committed to the relationship. Neither had talked of separation or divorce, and both dearly loved their new daughter. Still, at times, their repetitive arguments seemed hopeless. The therapist's task, therefore, was to assist the couple in understanding and changing the relationship so it could become more satisfying.

Planning Interventions: Individual Versus Couples Therapy

Following the assessment phase of treatment, the therapist and the couple must collaborate to set the goals of therapy. The therapist must also decide on the structure and sequence of the interventions.

Whether to employ individual sessions and to what degree is a challenge for any couples therapist. The decision is frequently based on the therapist's theoretical model and the couple's presenting problems. For example, a pure systems therapist who emphasizes current interactions and seeks to affect those patterns immediately would rarely consider individual therapy sessions. On the other hand, a therapist believing in the power of the family of origin to influence current relationships may recommend individual therapy to first address the family of origin issues before beginning conjoint couples therapy.

Braverman (1993), for example, argued that although systems theory is useful in understanding the reciprocity of current relationships, it is not sufficient to understand individual dynamics, particularly childhood issues that diminish an individual's ability to form intimate adult relationships. To address these concerns, Braverman (1993) recommends individual over couples therapy in the following situations:

1. A couple has benefited from couples therapy, but one partner felt the need to further work on him- or herself.
2. Couples therapy cannot progress because of the individual pathology of one partner.

3. One spouse evidences unresolved and ambivalent attachment to his or her family of origin.

4. Volatile couples in which conjoint sessions have resulted in more conflict and turmoil and not less.

While Braverman's guidelines are helpful, the literature does not offer one clear set of guidelines. Instead, a therapist weighs each couple on a case-by-case basis. To stimulate the reader's own criterion development, we offer the following guidelines based upon our own assessment criteria:

Couples therapy is indicated when:

1. Both partners are motivated for change and there is an absence of individual pathology or severely conflicted relationships with the families of origin.

2. One member of the couple is strongly motivated for change, the other member is ambivalent, and there is an absence of individual pathology.

3. One or both partners are ambivalent about beginning therapy but agree to a trial period—for example, a set number of sessions followed by a reevaluation of progress.

4. Partners define themselves as committed to the relationship but acknowledge the severity of their difficulties and possess at least an initial awareness of the families of origin influences.

Individual therapy may proceed or supplant couples therapy when:

1. Both partners are uncommitted or ambivalent about the relationship and need to first clarify their individual positions.

2. Individual psychopathology strongly interferes with the establishment of intimacy—for example, active alcoholism, sociopathy, major depressive episode.

3. Emotional or physical abuse characterizes the relationship.

Although the above lists are not inclusive and other criteria may already have occurred to the reader, liabilities exist for each choice. For example, to begin couples therapy without a sense of each partner's motivation risks a negative experience for all parties, including the therapist. These sessions drag on and on with little continuity or progress. It soon becomes evident that one or both members of the couple have no desire to change or are biding their time before they leave the relationship. There is usually little honest self-disclosure. These cases frequently end with the couple telling their friends, "We tried therapy and it did not help."

Individual therapy preceding or supplanting couples therapy also involves liabilities. For example, the partner not participating in individual therapy may become jealous of the therapist-partner relationship. The individual sessions inadvertently become a source of tension in the couple. Moreover, individual therapy may be so successful that therapy has now created further problems in the couple relationship because the partner in therapy begins to change in ways the nonparticipating spouse finds threatening.

Because Lynn and Carl were committed to the relationship and at least Lynn was highly motivated for change, the therapist recommended conjoint couples sessions. Although family of origin issues were certainly prominent in the case assessment, the therapist believed that these issues, addressed in conjoint sessions, would facilitate the development of a couple's identity and underline the existence of a new family beginning with the birth of Jenn.

Case Assessment Summary

Both Lynn's and Carl's families of origin provide a context for their presenting complaints. Because of her parents' divorce and her role as the oldest daughter, Lynn became the parentified child at an early age. Possessing a highly developed sense of responsibility, Lynn cared for her younger sister and served as a confidant for her mother. Lynn's image of her father was sketchy. Although she had dated different men from her late teens until her marriage to Carl, Lynn viewed men's reliability with suspicion. Although she loved Carl, Lynn questioned his responsibility and therefore found it difficult to let herself rely too extensively on him. An underlying doubt is that he too would let her down and would not be there when she needed him.

Carl's portrayal of his family of origin left more questions than answers. He described a traditional family pattern in which his father worked outside the home and his mother worked within it. Women took care of home and family. Although he described his family in the blandest of terms, the therapist noted the absence of emotional contact. Carl saw his parents one or two times a year and reported little contact with his older brother. When pushed on this issue, Carl admitted his mother controlled the family and that his father basically went along with what she wanted. In Carl's view, women can be competent and strong but also intrusive and engulfing. Although he was drawn to Lynn's personality strength and admired all she coped with in her life, he feared she would try to control him. Unwilling to confront her directly, Carl would fall into passive-aggressive behavior that further fueled Lynn's fear of his irresponsibility and led to her increased criticism of his behavior.

At the time of referral, the birth of their daughter threw Lynn and Carl into a developing crisis. Financial and child-care stresses exacerbated the couple's fears for the future. Lynn felt abandoned by Carl and complete responsibility for Jenn. Carl felt neglected by Lynn and engulfed by her attempts to control him. In addition, child-care responsibilities threw Lynn back into an enmeshed, ambivalent relationship with her mother, thus adding to the couple's stresses.

Although the family of origin dynamics and developmental stresses provide a background context for the couple's complaints, current, repetitive, dysfunctional behavioral patterns were evidenced in the sessions. For example, of the two of them, Lynn was the most likely to identify problems and issues. Lynn would then pursue Carl and attempt to engage him. Because he "heard" Lynn's pursuit as criticism, Carl would withdraw. Carl's withdrawal heightened Lynn's fear of abandonment, so she pursued more forcefully. Lynn would drop her pursuit only after all efforts had resulted in failure. She would then also withdraw from the relationship to protect herself from the hurt she felt.

A variation of the theme occurred when Lynn pursued past Carl's tolerance threshold. At this point Carl would angrily criticize Lynn and force her withdrawal. When Lynn withdrew, Carl did not pursue. Unfortunately, not only did these patterns fail to resolve the couple's issues, but they added more bricks in the walls of resentment and frustration.

By the time of referral, the couple had reduced the combination of stressors to personalized attributional complaints. For Lynn, Carl was irresponsible, uncaring, and selfish. For Carl, Lynn was tense, overwhelmed, and critical. Each partner would quickly blame these attributes for the problems in the marriage.

The dysfunctional problem-solving patterns and personalized attributes distorted the reciprocity equilibrium. Instead of a positive reciprocity pattern—"I will do for you and you will do for me"—a negative reciprocity existed—"I am not going to do for you until you do something for me." Both partners felt overworked, underappreciated and undervalued.

Fortunately, both Lynn and Carl were strongly committed to their relationship, but the commitment was being eroded by their chronic conflicts. It was at this point that they sought couples therapy.

Summary—Assessment Tree

As a means of summarizing the assessment process, we offer the following assessment tree.

I.   Family of origin issues
   A.   Are there significant events in either partner's history that would be strongly influencing their current relationship—for example, parents' divorce, death of parent, previous marriage, past significant relationships, adoptions, foster parents?
   B.   What was learned from the respective families of origin?
        What were the coping styles?
        What models or roles were evident, particularly gender roles?
        What motivations strongly influenced family of origin—for example, life is a struggle, it is important to maximize security?
        What characteristics of their parents' marriages would the spouses wish to re-create or avoid?
        What was the family of origin's definition of loyalty and closeness? (Cultural and ethnic issues can greatly affect this area.)
   C.   What is each partner's level of differentiation?
   D.   What is the quality of current family of origin relationships?
   E.   Are there any current and past significant triangles?

    F. What is the goodness of fit of the cultural roles?

       Identification of respective ethnic identities.

       Place each partner along the traditional–egalitarian gender role dimension.

II.   Identifying current dysfunctional patterns

    A. Define the problematic behavior in terms of concrete behavioral sequences.

       How does each partner mutually influence the other in these patterns?

    B. Define the pursuer-distancer patterns.

       Which pattern characterizes the couple: unidirectional, complementary, symmetrical?

       Are the patterns rigid or flexible? Is one person always the pursuer while the other distances?

       Do the roles change dependent upon the topic discussed?

III. Attributions

    A. What attributions has each partner constructed for him- or herself and his or her partner—for example, intentional versus unintentional, negative versus positive motivation, free choice versus outside coercion, awareness of consequences versus lack of awareness, acknowledgment of wrongfulness versus no such acknowledgment, and capacity to have done otherwise?

    B. How rigid or inflexible are the attributions?

    C. What type of responses are justified by these attributions—for example, "Well, if he does not care, then I do not care either."

IV. Reciprocity equilibrium

    A. What attracted each partner to the other? What qualities?

    B. What behavior is currently valued?

    C. What blocks receiving and giving to one another?

V.   Developmental stresses

    A. The couple is at what stage of development?

    B. What issues face them at this stage?

    C. How are they addressing those issues?

VI. Environmental stresses

    A. What environmental strains exist for the couple—for example, health, financial, job insecurity, child care?

    B. How has the couple addressed these strains?

VII. Motivation

    A. Why is the couple seeking therapy at this time?

    B. What are the overt or covert individual motives for seeking therapy at this time?

       Overt and committed?

       Overt and uncommitted?

       Covert and committed?

       Covert and uncommitted?

    C. What does each partner hope to achieve in therapy?

CHAPTER EIGHT

Process of Change

The couples therapist is an agent of change. Change, however, may occur in many ways. Change results from the persistent efforts of the therapist and couple in working toward agreed upon goals. Or, change may occur in serendipitous ways—for example, the car breaks down on the way to the therapy session and the couple engage in new behavior to manage the situation. Change may also result because of or in spite of the therapist's brilliant intervention.

Definitions of change also vary. Change may be defined as making the unconscious conscious, reworking family of origin agendas, rebalancing the system, developing new behavioral patterns, altering cognitions or attributions, or negotiating environmental pressures in a different way.

Because of our focus on gender influences in couples therapy, it is beyond the scope of this book to discuss the diverse conceptualizations of change as each one flows from a given theoretical model. (This is accomplished much more thoroughly in other reference books—for example, Gurman and Kniskern, 1991, and Nichols and Schwartz, 1991.)

We have chosen to focus on current interactions and the attributions maintaining and underlying a couple's behavioral patterns. We do not wish to minimize the powerful forces of the respective families of origin. Placing individual partners within the context of their families of origin broadens our understanding of current interactions. Although the families of origin influences are embedded within the current interactions, the connection between the two is not necessarily a component to change. Consequently, teaching the individual partners about the power of their families of origin is not a direct goal of our interventions. Instead, we take a more social constructivist, solution-focused approach (this will be detailed in the following sections). Overall, the following discussion builds on the material presented in the earlier chapters to highlight current interactions, cognitions maintaining those interactions, improving the goodness of fit by negotiating reciprocity, and the influence of gender roles on the therapeutic process.

Before offering specific steps, two concepts provide a framework for our discussion of change: (1) time constraints and (2) first- second-order change. The impact of time constraints on the therapist is seen in the current debate between problem and solution approaches to couples therapy. First- and second-order interventions offer a sequential pattern to change.

Time Constraints: Solution Versus Problem Approach

Clinicians find themselves in a rapidly changing health care environment. For the foreseeable future, managed care will strongly influence the practice of psychotherapy. As a result, a premium is placed on the clinician's ability to provide effective, measurable, and brief therapy. A trip to the local bookstore will reveal many recently published books on psychotherapy with "brief" or "short term" in the title. Even though one may bemoan this dramatic shift in health care delivery in which insurance companies, instead of the clinician, dictate the length of treatment, it is increasingly a fact of life—in most cases, clinicians are limited in the number of couples therapy sessions they have available. Most couples' financial resources are similarly limited, and as consumers they may desire the most expedient form of treatment. The question, therefore, is one of balancing time and effectiveness.

Theories of psychotherapy evolve with their proponents heralding the value of each. If there were one tried-and-true method, then there would be one book to follow. Instead, a potpourri of books, theories, and workshops awaits the couples therapist. Sometimes new models develop out of an existing theory; sometimes a new model offers a radical departure from the established path. But, as Nichols and Schwartz (1991) caution, therapists err when they believe that their models (theories) are describing and identifying "real" family interactions, instead of acknowledging that their theories are just that—"theories" (a coherent group of propositions used as explanations).

For example, the concept of differentiation is a useful clinical theory that provides a conceptual model to guide assessment and intervention. However, it is just a concept that we use to label behavior we have observed. Or, in other words, differentiation provides therapists with a socially constructed means to categorize behavior. From a different theoretical position, the same behavior could be labeled or categorized in a different way (for example, a behaviorist would use a concept such as mutually reinforcing behavioral patterns). Thus, to say someone is "undifferentiated" is a utilitarian, shorthand, clinical category, not an identification of "real" attributes.

The demythizing of family therapy theories is further bolstered by the constructivist perspective (Efran, Lukens, & Lukens, 1990; Goolishian & Anderson, 1987, 1990; Keeney & Ross, 1985). Briefly, from the constructivist vantage point, the therapist and each partner bring particular assumptions about the "problem" into therapy. For example, the therapist may view Lynn's and Carl's problems as unresolved issues from their respective families of origin, while Lynn "sees" Carl as rejecting and Carl "sees" Lynn as critical. What is the truth? Does each person possess a kernel of it? Does the therapist, as an expert, possess the truth? The constructivist position would argue that none of the above is true;

rather, in the process of therapy, Lynn, Carl, and the therapist will coconstruct the definition, meaning, and solutions to the problems.

From the constructivist perspective, the ways in which the therapist conceptualizes the couple's problems determines the therapeutic process: who is seen, what questions are asked, how the data are analyzed, what goals are set, what techniques are employed, and how the outcome is evaluated. Thus, the construction of problems focuses and drives the treatment sessions.

Moreover, reality is not objective fact but rather an agreed-to consensus among a group of individuals or an individual belief about oneself in the world. This is not to deny the occurrence of real factual events that we have experienced in our lives, but the constructivist position is more concerned with the meaning we have attributed to those events. For example, a client may say, "I am an adult child of an alcoholic." Objectively this implies that one or both parents were identified as alcoholics and this could be verified by others as a real fact. However, what that phrase *means* to a person varies from individual to individual. For one person, the phrase explains a series of broken relationships. For another, it means he or she is overresponsible and overcompensates. Therefore, facts are not disputed, but the meanings we attribute to those facts are.

In therapy, each individual member of the couple, and sometimes even therapists, confuse meanings and facts. Lynn does more housework than Carl (fact). Does this mean Lynn is fulfilling her gender role (meaning)? Does this mean Carl is lazy and does not appreciate Lynn (meaning)? Or, does it mean Lynn is an overcompensating daughter from a dysfunctional family (meaning)? Likewise, Carl is less expressive emotionally than Lynn (fact). Does this mean he is emotionally blunted and unable to express feelings (meaning)? Does this mean he is cut off from his feelings (meaning)? Does this mean he is a victim of his gender role (meaning)?

The answers to these questions evolve during the course of therapy. But more important, *how* they are answered may determine the success or failure of therapy. To illustrate, Lynn may agree that she is an overcompensating daughter from a dysfunctional family. This then becomes a focus of therapy whereby her overcompensating patterns are identified, understood, and changed. Or, the therapist and Lynn may agree that Carl is "out of touch" with his feelings and that he needs to "reconnect emotionally" if the couple's relationship is to improve. Lynn and the therapist then proceed to attempt to change Carl. Of course, another possibility is that one or both members of the couple reject the therapist's definition of the problem, whereupon therapy will bog down or, worse yet, the couple will unilaterally terminate therapy, agreeing that the therapist has more problems than they do.

Reversing the logic, if problems are thus constructed, then solutions are also coconstructed between the couple and therapist. But more important, solutions may be far easier to construct than problems. As mentioned above, each member of the couple and the therapist may possess his or her definition and meaning of the problem. These various meanings can block change when they assume a rigid, static quality. Each person maintains his or her meanings, attempting to persuade the other to see the same meanings, thus negating any possibility of change.

DeShazer (1994), a leading proponent of a brief therapy approach, argued that a therapist errs first in accepting the client's definition of the problem and in making that the focus of treatment—for example, Carl is unemotional, let's make him more emotional. Instead, deShazer (1994) initiated change by reversing the field/ground and focusing on "nonemotional" aspects of the couple's relationship. How does Carl express affection and caring? When are there moments when he is spontaneously emotional? The quest then is to identify when he is spontaneously affectionate and to expand that particular range of behaviors.

This is similar to an approach first articulated by Watzlawick, Weakland, and Fisch (1974) and formalized into brief therapy principles by Fisch, Weakland, and Segal (1982). Their theory is that the defined problem is not the problem but that the attempted solutions are what have created and maintained the problem. Let's use Lynn and Carl to illustrate this rather convoluted framework. For example, Lynn views Carl as unemotional. She criticizes him for his inability to express emotion. Carl does not say, "Thank you for pointing out the deficiencies in my personality." Instead, he becomes defensive and expresses less emotionally than before. The downward spiral of their relationship escalates. Thus, Lynn's solution to her problem only increases Carl's withdrawal from her and confirms his view of the problem—Lynn is tense and critical.

Specifically applied to couples therapy, Hudson's and O'Hanlon's (1991) brief treatment model is influenced by constructivist views and focused on solutions as opposed to explanations of a couple's problems. Hudson and O'Hanlon intervene to change couples' interactional patterns, particularly via meaning and action, rather than attempt to uncover or learn the origin of the patterns. For Hudson and O'Hanlon (1991), facts are aspects of the situation that everyone agrees to, and stories are meanings and interpretations we give to those facts.

Friedman (1993) referred to the solution-focused approach as "possibility" therapy. That is, in contrast to the problem-oriented approach, the solution-focused framework:

1. views therapy as a cooperative/collaborative process,
2. avoids elaborate theoretical explanations for the couple's behavior,
3. seeks solutions by accentuating the couple's resources and competencies rather than the couple's deficits and limitations,
4. is future-oriented and avoids become stagnant by useless attempts to change the past,
5. offers new perspectives or views of the problem, and
6. helps couples reach their goals and not the imposed goals of the therapist.

Much of a therapist's training and coursework are concerned with the theoretical explanations for people's behavior. Psychodynamic theory offers rich insights into the individual psyche. Object relations theory vividly portrays the unconscious projections from parent to child. Bowen's family systems theory explains the transmission of anxiety and undifferentiation from generation to generation. All of these theories, although providing valuable insights into the nature and roots of a couple's interactions, are still deficiency oriented and rooted in the past—what is wrong and what are its roots?

A solution-focused approach may present a radical shift for a therapist. The solution-oriented therapist works to empower a couple by building on the partners' strengths and creativity. The problems couples present may be maintained and reinforced by poor solutions or are narrative "stories" that each partner tells to him- or herself and to others. Therefore, based within a constructivist framework, new solutions may be coconstructed and a couple's story may be rewritten.

We are not advocating one approach versus another or arguing the effectiveness of one over another; that is left for future research to determine. Rather, each approach uses time and symptom definition differently. For example, thoroughly exploring each partner's family of origin as a means of gaining insight into current dysfunctional patterns takes time. Equally important, it also requires strong motivation on the clients' part. The members of a couple must "see" the benefits of exploring the past if they are to embark down that road.

This is not to say that family of origin issues are ignored by briefer forms of treatment—these issues are evident in the first interview. Instead, it is a matter of what one does with the material when it surfaces in the course of therapy and what emphasis to place on it. Again, a predetermined number of sessions and limited time may influence the decision more than a preferred theoretical perspective.

Finally, just as time constraints influence the assessment process (see Chapters 6 and 7), time may dictate the type of change desired in couples therapy.

Sequence of Change: First and Second Order

Sometimes change occurs because a person does less or more of a particular behavior. For example, one may hypothesize that the less Lynn pursues Carl, the less he will withdraw. Or, the more Carl helps around the house, the less Lynn will feel overwhelmed and, therefore, the less she will criticize him. Building on these hypotheses, the therapist would attempt to increase or decrease existing behavioral patterns.

This is referred to as first-order change (Watzlawick et al., 1974). The structure or the rules governing the couple's relationship are not challenged; rather, change is sought through existing patterns. The goals would be to increase Carl's participation in household chores and decrease Lynn's criticisms. Please note, however, the lineal explanation to the couple's problems: If each partner would only do less or more of certain behaviors (quantitative changes), then the problems would be greatly ameliorated.

Although at times these seem like merely commonsense solutions to problems, first-order interventions may be quite helpful for many couples. The therapist may suggest something that has not occurred to the couple or, as a result of the therapist's encouragement and prompting, each member of the couple may perform more or less of a behavior and hence may greatly enhance the quality of the relationship.

Many couples, however, enter therapy having already tried the commonsense solutions and are locked in a battle over who should change or who should change first. Lynn and Carl fall into this group. Their commonsense solutions have failed, resulting in an increase in tension, frustration, and dissatisfaction. Asking Lynn to stop pursuing and Carl to help more around the house would probably fail. As a couple they each believed they had made such attempts and that the partner had not reciprocated.

Second-order change is not quantitative but qualitative shifts (Watzlawick et al., 1974). The structure and rules governing the couple are altered as new patterns emerge to replace the dysfunctional ones. Implied in the concept of second-order change is a recognition of circular causality. It is a view that the couple's existing patterns continually cycle because they are fueled by the structure or rules governing the relationship.

For example, Lynn's role as emotional caretaker in the relationship is shaped and reinforced by her gender role and her role in her family of origin. Because of Carl's lack of responsiveness, Lynn is anxious and fearful that she is failing in her role. Fulfilling his gender and family of origin roles, Carl works hard to support his family and values emotional distance. He believes Lynn's criticisms are unjustified and that Lynn does not accept or appreciate his need for alone time. Within this context, each feels justified in his or her position, and each position fuels the couple's circular, dysfunctional pattern.

As a logical sequence, first-order change may be the commonsense solutions the couple has tried on their own. In reviewing the attempted solutions, the therapist may offer additional commonsense advice that has not occurred to the partners. In some cases, this is enough to implement the desired change. In other situations, however, second-order interventions are required, interventions that challenge the basic rules and norms of the relationship.

Summary of Treatment Approach: Sequential Solution

Each therapist, although most will call him- or herself eclectic, evolves a model of change. It may be based in a particular theory or on the beliefs of a supervisor or it may be the result of training, workshops attended, and personal experience. Being aware of and being guided by one's conceptualization of change provides a consistency to therapeutic approach, a consistency that maintains one's equilibrium when the inevitable impasses of couples therapy occur.

Clinical theory—for example, Bowen's theory, behavioristic models, or general systems theory—provides a means of conceptualizing a couple's behavior. In turn, change occurs within the theory's logic. For example, from a behavioristic perspective, if behavior is shaped by reinforcement, then to change a couple's behavior one needs to change the reinforcement patterns. Likewise, if a couple's patterns reflect the legacy of the families of origin, then family history assumes primary importance.

The following sections detail a series of interventions with Lynn and Carl. An underlying bias in these interventions is the influence of constructionism and solution-focused approach. We have chosen this perspective because it provides a context for the discussion of gender in terms of the goodness of fit and reciprocity and views couples therapy as a collaborative effort.

For example, viewing gender as social constructivism, it is a logical step to employ a constructivistic perspective when implementing change. Carl, for example, is not seen as someone with intimacy problems. Instead, he may be reflecting the masculine role. Lynn, on the other hand, is not critical and hostile but is instead a woman fighting for her family's emotional connections. Reframing their arguments as characteristic gender-role patterns minimizes the mutual blaming and offers new opportunities for change.

Before reframing, however, the therapist assists the partners in understanding their goodness of fit in terms of traditional and egalitarian gender roles. Each partner brings to the relationship his or her definition of male/female, husband/wife, or lover/lover role expectations. These expectations combine cultural, ethnic, and family of origin influences. Change begins to occur when partners relinquish personalized attributions—she is emotional, he is aloof—and view the partner as someone struggling with and carrying out socialized gender roles.

In making these covert expectations overt, the therapist enables the partners to evaluate their expectations of themselves and of one another. In doing so, reciprocity improves as each partner more clearly identifies what he or she values. The concept of reciprocity is also based in solutions. The questions are: What do you want more or less of? What do you want to do more or less of? Again, what it is you want and how to get it is the focal point, not what's wrong with the other person. Moreover, making these covert expectations overt increases the possibility of successful negotiations. At the very least, each partner is clearer as to what they want and what they are willing to give.

From the constructivist argument, if Lynn and Carl have learned their roles via society and family of origin, then new behaviors may also be acquired. Furthermore, within the therapeutic context, the therapist and couple coconstruct the definition, meaning, and solutions to the couple's "problems." The therapist and couple are not, therefore, in opposition to one another, with the therapist identifying or teaching the partners about their problems. Instead, the therapist and couple form a collaborating treatment alliance that minimizes resistance to change.

A solution focus also builds on the strengths of the relationship. A couple may complain of communication problems, but at certain times with some issues they communicate well. For example, couples may function and communicate well as parents but flounder in the intimacy of their own relationship. From a solution-focused initiative, rather than focus on communication problems of intimacy, the question is what stops their successful communication patterns as parents from transferring to other areas of the relationship or how can they learn to transfer their communication skills from one area to another?

Sequential refers to an orderly progression of the levels of intervention. Following the assessment phase of treatment, first-order change interventions are initially tried. These interventions are designed to increase the partners' awareness of their goodness of fit and to improve communication skills that will enable the couple to more successfully improve their patterns of reciprocity.

For example, Lynn and Carl may be struggling to effectively communicate with one another. Their struggle may be due to poor communication skills or to a misunderstanding of what the other is trying to say. Along with their misunder-standings, they may also be unaware of their expectations of one another. Placing their behavior within the context of family of origin and gender-role expectations may increase their awareness of the difficulties and lead to new appreciation of one another's communication styles. Accordingly, with increased communication skills and an increased awareness of one another's roles, Lynn and Carl would be in a position to better balance their reciprocity equilibrium.

Unfortunately, many couples who seek therapy have tried to negotiate their differences but to no avail. The basic rules in their relationships allow their circular arguments and dysfunctional patterns to continue. A basic inequality in the woman's role may lead to chronic disappointment and frustration for her. Or, coming from argumentative families of origins, both partners may studiously repress and avoid conflict. Although their relationship is free of overt conflict, the partners suffer from an inability to successfully address differences of opinions and thus to effectively problem-solve.

Consequently, second-order interventions are attempted after first-order initiatives have failed. Second-order interventions challenge the basic rules of the relationship so that the stalemate may be broken and more successful reciprocity negotiations may take place.

Case Presentation: Steps Toward Change

FIRST ORDER FIRST

First-order change interventions assume that the partners are motivated and committed to the relationship but are struggling because of their communication patterns or a lack of awareness of individual needs. To address these concerns, in the treatment sessions the therapist focuses on improving communication skills, exploring the goodness of fit, and negotiating reciprocity. As a means of furthering these goals, homework assignments facilitate and reinforce change patterns.

Communication and Negotiation Skills

By focusing on communication and negotiation skills, the therapist assumes that one of the root causes for the couple's problems is poorly developed skills. These poorly developed skills may reflect patterns from the respective family of origin, patterns that the couple have evolved during their relationship, or both. Regardless of the origin, old, faulty patterns may be identified and new behavior may be learned in therapy that will improve the couple's problem-solving ability. The therapist monitors the couple's communication in the sessions and pushes the couple to compromise.

Steps in this process include (1) identifying what solutions have been tried, (2) structuring and monitoring the communication process, and, when needed (3) articulating difficult or unexpressed emotions.

Identifying previous solutions.   Following the assessment of the problematic patterns, a simple, straightforward question is:

Therapist: How have you tried to change your relationship?

Lynn: I have tried to talk to Carl, but I cannot get through. He just won't listen. If he would just help out with the house and baby, then everything would be better.

Carl: I told her I am trying, but she never recognizes the things I do.

Therapist: You are each telling me more about the other person than what you have tried as individuals or as a couple to improve things. Please tell me specifically what you have tried.

Moving away from the partners' blaming descriptions of one another, the therapist pushes for detailed descriptions of what has been tried. In doing so, not only are failed solutions identified, but each partner becomes aware of what the other has attempted.

At the very least, having identified previous solutions, the therapist is alerted to what not to suggest. Moreover, the therapist is in the position of discovering how or why the couple's solutions did not work.

Lynn: I felt Carl and I needed more time together after Jenn was born. So, I offered to arrange a baby-sitter so that we could go out.

Therapist: Did the two of you go out?

Lynn: Once or twice but not very often. We usually just stayed home with the baby.

Therapist: That sounds like a good idea for just the two of you to go out occasionally. Why did you not go out more often?

Structuring communication.   The therapist employs a number of techniques to actively structure communication. For example, the therapist may focus specifically on listening skills.

Therapist: Carl, we just heard what Lynn would like from you. She, however, frequently wonders if you have heard her. Would you please look at her and tell her what you just heard her say?

Asking a partner to paraphrase what he or she just heard ensures that the message was heard and also opens up a dialogue between the two partners.

Therapist: Lynn, Carl just paraphrased what you said. Was that an accurate summary? Please repeat what he just said.

The therapist may take a more active stance by establishing communication rules for the sessions.

Therapist: In order to improve your communication, I would like for each of you to follow two simple rules: (1) begin sentences with an "I" and (2) turn every question into a statement.

These two rules accomplish several goals. First, beginning each sentence with an "I" minimizes the blame game. Initially, each member of a couple may be more familiar and more comfortable beginning sentences with "you," such as, "You never listen to me" or "You are so selfish." The "you" at the beginning of a sentence signals a blame message and puts the partner on the defensive. Beginning a sentence with "I" fosters self-disclosure and opens the door for new communication patterns.

Second, often a question implies a statement. For example, "Do you want to go to your mother's house for dinner?" may be a legitimate question, or it may imply the speaker's reluctance to visit his or her mother-in-law. Although questions may serve as a means of testing the waters before making a statement or decision, they avoid direct statements and thus blur and confuse communication. A simple diagnostic sign when working with couples is the ratio of questions to statements. The greater number of questions each partner asks of the other, the greater the defensiveness.

Sometimes the most effective technique is to censor interruptions.

Therapist: I don't know if the two of you have noticed, but each one of you frequently interrupts while the other is speaking. Not only does this appear to frustrate the person, but I wonder if you fully hear the other person. With your permission, I will block the interruptions and encourage the speaker to continue.

In summary, to improve a couple's negotiation skills with first-order communication interventions, the therapist: (1) encourages active listening, (2) elicits feedback from each partner by asking the partner to summarize what he or she just heard, (3) facilitates the expression of feelings and thoughts directly and succinctly, (4) requests the use of "I" statements and that questions be turned into statements, and (5) prohibits interruptions and blaming.

Goodness of Fit

After working on and monitoring communication skills, the therapist is in a position to explore the couple's goodness of fit. As discussed earlier, goodness of fit refers to the couple's compatibility along the traditional–egalitarian dimension. This is a three-step process where the partners are made aware of their gender biases and expectations, where they explore how these expectations affect the perception of the other, and where they study how they have attempted to resolve differences in their views.

1. Awareness

Therapist: When we were talking about each of your families of origin, I was wondering what you observed about the roles for men and women.

Therapist: What do you each believe today should be the roles of men and women in a relationship?

2. Consequences of gender beliefs

Therapist: Based on what you believe the roles of men and women should be, what have you come to expect of your mate?

3. Identifying attempted solutions

Therapist: It would appear the two of you differ concerning your beliefs. How does this affect your relationship and how have you tried to resolve it?

Besides increasing the partners' awareness of the hidden gender expectations in their relationship, the therapist is also identifying potential or existing gender inequities. For example, in a couple where the husband endorses traditional gender roles but the wife is pushing for a more egalitarian stance, a therapist can highlight these differences and the consequences.

Therapist (*to the man*):   You believe a woman should take care of the children and the home, but your wife would like to share these responsibilities. How has this difference of opinion affected your relationship? How have you attempted to resolve these differences (*solutions tried*)?

There is, however, a trap in working with traditional couples where the woman desires a more egalitarian relationship. Hearing and sensing the woman's frustration at the inequities, a therapist may inadvertently or intentionally become a champion of her cause. This is particularly true if the therapist shares the same ideology as the woman.

In these scenarios, the therapist acts as an advocate for the woman and finds him- or herself attempting to change the man's point of view. In lineal causality terms, the therapist believes that if the husband shifts his position, then the goodness of fit would improve and the woman will no longer be a victim of male dominance.

Although the therapist believes this is sociopolitically correct, this belief overlooks the reality of the couple. First, the man will not perceive the push for egalitarian relationships as his mate's agenda but he will see it as the therapist's agenda. This will foster a power struggle between the therapist and the man that the man will always win because he can quit coming to therapy and unilaterally terminate the process. Moreover, if the therapist does battle under the banner of equity, the woman may applaud such efforts but will have learned little herself about successfully negotiating change in her relationship.

Instead, the therapist may wish to empower the woman's position, being careful not to act for her. To empower the woman, the therapist may encourage her opinions, validate them, and work with the couple to resolve the differences. Circular causality argues that change will occur as the woman, with the help of the therapist, addresses the inequity and as her mate correspondingly shifts position.

Overall, it is not the therapist's place to advocate one end of the traditional–egalitarian dimension over another. While a therapist may possess strong beliefs about traditional or egalitarian gender roles, his or her job is to increase the partners' awareness of their beliefs and biases and help them accommodate to one another's views.

Reciprocity

Regardless of the partners' positions on the traditional–egalitarian dimension, reciprocity is concerned with equal exchange of value. Again, a logical sequence is to first identify what is valued and then attempt to reset the reciprocity equilibrium.

Therapist: I am curious as to what you each believe the other values from you. What do you believe the other values about you?

After each partner identifies what they believe the other values, the therapist asks for feedback to confirm or modify these beliefs.

Therapist: Well, you each heard what the other has said. In what ways would you modify what he or she said?

By increasing the couple's awareness, the therapist is then in a position to reset the reciprocity equilibrium.

Therapist: I would like to take turns and have each of you tell the other what you would like.

Therapist: Lynn, look at Carl and tell him what help you would like from him.

Therapist: Carl, please tell Lynn what you would like from her.

At this point in therapy, the surface complaints are most readily available, specifically child care and household chores. Using this as a starting point, the therapist focuses on these issues, assuming that if the partners can learn to successfully improve reciprocity in these areas that learning may generalize to other issues—for example, intimacy and family of origin boundaries.

Therapist: Because you each mentioned it, I would like to focus this session on negotiating an agreement surrounding household chores and responsibilities.

Please note that the therapist is not focusing on why the other person is not giving his or her mate what he or she wants. Rather, the therapist is asking what does he or she value and what would he or she like more of?

Homework Assignments

A therapist may take a further stand to facilitate first-order change via homework assignments.

Therapist: Lynn and Carl, I would like to assign you a homework assignment this week. Lynn, over the weekend I would like for you to go out for the afternoon alone or with a friend. Carl will be in charge at home, will take care of any chores, and will watch Jenn.

The homework assignment is designed to force the couple to change the fixed patterns of interaction and explore role reversal. The effect of the homework will serve as the starting point for the next session.

Therapist: I thought we would begin by reviewing what happened last weekend. I am curious. What went well? What did not go so well?

If the homework assignment was successful, then the couple has taken a step forward. If the assignment was unsuccessful, then the therapist explores what interfered and adjusts the next assignment accordingly. For example:

Therapist: Lynn, how did your day off go?

Lynn: Well, the baby was running a bit of a fever and looked like she was coming down with a cold. So I stayed home to take care of her.

Therapist: Did Carl ask you to stay home?

Lynn: No, I just thought I should be there.

Therapist: Did you think Carl could take care of Jenn?

Lynn: I just thought I should be home.

Therapist: Carl, did you want Lynn to stay home?

Carl: Well, I appreciated it.

Therapist: Is there any way for Carl to learn what to do if Jenn is running a temperature? Lynn, what would he need to learn?

Thus, even though the homework assignment was not carried out, there are lessons to be learned. The couple is not blamed for the incomplete assignment (focusing on their problems); rather, the events redirect attention to solutions: What does Carl need to learn so that both he and Lynn will be comfortable with his caring for their daughter?

Summary

Employing first-order change interventions, the therapist serves as the expert guiding and directing the couple into new, more effective and satisfying interactions. By focusing on concrete behavioral patterns, the therapist assumes the couple needs to develop more effective problem-solving skills. Keys to change are the couple's level of motivation to improve the relationship and their willingness to follow the therapist's directions.

Thus, to summarize the steps in first-order change:

1. Identify what solutions have been tried.
2. Clarify gender biases and expectations.
3. Attempt to reset reciprocity equilibrium.

4. Monitor the couple's communication pattern while seeking compromise.
5. Employ homework assignments as a means of offering the couple "real-life" challenges. Most importantly, the success or failure of the homework assignments is viewed as a learning experience to further refine the steps toward change.

As a word of caution, a communication problem is frequently a catchall for more subtle and complex issues. Calling them communication problems is sometimes the only way a couple can conceptualize their issues. For example, a communication problem may actually mean my partner will not do what I ask of him or her. Also, a therapist may observe a couple quite effectively saying what they mean and listening to one another but just not conceding any ground. The couple may not have a communication problem as much as a stubbornness problem.

In the beginning of treatment, however, a conservative approach is to increase the partners' awareness of gender roles, identify what is valued, and develop more effective communication and negotiation skills (first-order change). Again with committed, motivated couples, this approach results in rapid gains. A therapeutic alliance is formed, the couple readily responds to direction, and therapy moves in progressive steps. Working with these couples reaffirms one's career choice as a couples therapist.

Unfortunately, this type of couple represents a minority of any therapist's caseload. Instead, couples are more likely to enter therapy with a host of ingrained, blaming patterns, with hidden agendas forming the foundation of the conflict. This becomes readily apparent after several first-order interventions fail miserably. For example, homework assignments are not done and the couple offer transparent excuses, "We did not have time to do what you suggested." Or, in response to the therapist's suggestions, the couple reply in unison, "We have tried that before and it never worked."

When met with resistance to first-order interventions, the therapist shifts direction and attempts second-order change—a change in the rules of the relationship. The following section outlines several second-order interventions.

IF AT FIRST YOU DON'T SUCCEED: SECOND-ORDER INTERVENTIONS

The foundation of second-order change is challenging the basic rules and norms of the couple's relationship. One would not necessarily employ all of the following interventions. Instead, the therapist would use his or her art to match the intervention with the couple. This can be a trial-and-error process as several interventions are attempted until the appropriate one is found. Also, some interventions make sense in the beginning of therapy whereas others require a stronger therapeutic alliance.

The following is not a cookbook or a how-to listing. Interventions without a conceptual base make little sense. Thus, we will attempt to provide a brief conceptual explanation for each of the interventions.

Challenging the Definition of the Problem

As was mentioned earlier, each member of a couple enters therapy with a unique definition of the problem. Even if they initially agree—for example, "We fight over everything"—a therapist quickly discovers these individual interpretations greatly differ—each partner believes the fights are caused by the other.

Each member of the couple has constructed what he or she believes are the problems and their causes. For example, Lynn takes the initiative in the early stage of treatment by defining the problems and documenting Carl's contribution to them. Carl, in turn, senses criticism and becomes increasingly passive and quiet. After a particularly frustrating weekend and in the heat of the moment, Lynn points out Carl's withdrawn demeanor as evidence for her frustration. She is the victim of Carl's detachment and noncaring. Of course, Carl may now emerge from his defensive stance and offer Lynn's behavior as an example of her negative, critical attitude.

The end result is that the therapist is asked to become a judge. Who is right and who is wrong?

Lynn (*to the therapist*):   How are we supposed to solve our problems when he sits there, silent!

Carl (*to the therapist*):   How am I supposed to respond to her continual criticism?

Therapist (*diplomatically*):   Well, there are always two sides to every story and no one is always right or always wrong. You both just have different points of view.

Despite the therapist's belief that he or she has successfully sidestepped these appeals for alliance, the reality is that the definitions of the problem have not been challenged and instead each of their opposing positions have been affirmed. Although they may be a little annoyed at the therapist's neutrality, the therapist's ambivalent statement offers hope individually to Lynn and Carl that the therapist may still be won over. Consequently, for Lynn and Carl, proving one's position could become the subtext to therapy.

When therapists don't challenge the definition of the problem, they frequently find themselves continually frustrated because of the lack of therapeutic progress. It appears that despite a number of attempted interventions the couple is still stuck in their polar opposite definitions of the problem.

If the therapist accepts either or both partners' definitions of the problem then he or she is operating within the couple's construction of the problems. When the therapist sees the problems the same as the couple, few alternatives are seen, and the therapist becomes as stuck as the couple. For example, please solve the problem on the next page (Figure 8.1):

If you are unable to solve the problem, it is because you are operating within the "perceived" box formed by the nine dots. Attempt to solve the problem now by using the space outside of the perceived box. That is, step outside of the perceived definition of the problem. (see Figure 8.2 for the solution).

Instructions: Please connect all nine dots by drawing four straight lines without taking your pencil off the paper.

F I G U R E   8.1   Nine-Dot Problem

Solving the problem results in an "ah-ha" and laughter. The answer was so obvious once one broke out of the imaginary box.

Returning to Lynn and Carl, the following exchanges present challenges to the couple's definition of the problem.

Therapist: Lynn, how do you know things would improve if Carl helped out more around the house?

Lynn: Well, it would certainly help and I would feel less stress.

Therapist: Would that then change how you react to him?"

Lynn: I would probably be nicer.

Therapist: What do you mean nicer?

Lynn: You know, nicer.

Therapist: I am sorry, I do not know what that means for you and in relation to Carl.

Lynn: Well, I would probably be a little more considerate of him and give him a little more leeway and be less on his back.

Therapist: So, you could be more considerate of him and give him more leeway, once he gives you what you want?

Begin here

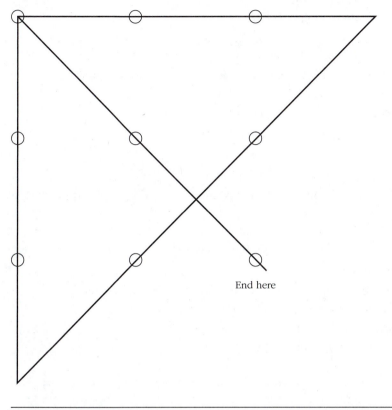

F I G U R E 8.2   Nine-Dot Solution

Lynn: Yes!

Therapist: So you are waiting for Carl to change before you will?

Couples in conflict polarize their positions into retentive stances: "I will do for you after you do for me." Each partner feels completely justified in his or her stance and the relationship becomes a tug-of-war. In the above example, the therapist challenges Lynn's retentive position by exploring the rules to their game.

Shifting to Carl, the therapist challenges his definition of the problem in another way.

Therapist: Carl, you said the difficulties in your marriage are caused by Lynn's anxiety and her criticism of you. Is that correct?

Carl: Yes.

Therapist: Was Lynn this way when you first married her?

Carl: No.

Therapist: So something has happened to her in the meantime?

Carl: I think it was Jenn's birth.

Therapist: How did that change her?

Carl: She assumes so much responsibility. She feels guilty because she has to work and leave Jenn with her mother.

Therapist: So Jenn's birth has had a tremendous impact on Lynn?

Carl: Absolutely!

Therapist: Tell me, how has it changed you?

Carl: Well, I feel the responsibility, too.

Therapist: In what ways?

Carl: Financially. I worry about paying the bills.

Therapist: Because of your responsibility and worry over the bills do you react differently at home?

Carl: No, I don't think so.

Therapist: What then do you do with your worry? .

Carl: I keep it to myself.

Therapist: Is there any reason you would not share it with Lynn?

Carl: I guess there are always too many other things to do.

Therapist: Since we have the opportunity now, please tell her some of your worries over bills and the future.

Notice, Carl's denial is accepted by the therapist, who continues to stay with the issue by exploring alternatives. The therapist uses the opportunity to ask Carl to engage in new behavior: "Will you tell Lynn your worries?" Carl will probably be awkward doing so and may need encouragement from the therapist, but by sharing with Lynn, Carl is engaging in the very behavior Lynn has wanted. Carl's lack of sharing is not identified as a problem he must work on. Instead, the therapist accepts Carl's position but offers and encourages alternative responses.

Challenging the definition of the problem sets the tone for the initial phase of therapy. The therapist is not accepting either party's definition of the problem. Thus, blaming is minimized and the therapist is removed from the position of judging who is right and who is wrong. Furthermore, by challenging the definition of the problem, the therapist and couple begin to explore the hidden rules of the couple's relationship, rules the couple were not aware of and that reinforced the circular causality of their relationship.

In uncovering the rules, the therapist is making the covert overt. In doing so the therapist may encourage or facilitate attempts at alternative behaviors or may simply allow couples to view their patterns from another perspective. Once the patterns are identified the partners are in a better position to decide if they wish to continue them.

Agree to Disagree

In the first blush of love we believe we have found a kindred spirit. We inevitably discover, however, that our lover is different from us in many ways. These differences may complement us as individuals but can also tear us apart as couples when they surface as sources of conflict. For some couples, differences and the subsequent disagreements are intolerable. Disagreements are studiously avoided and conflict issues are swept under the rug. Disagreements are threats to the relationship.

Unless one partner clearly dominates the other, conflicts and disagreements are an inevitable part of a couple's life. The problem is not that couples disagree, rather, it is the partners' style of managing their disagreements that matters. Consequently, learning to disagree fairly is a main ingredient in a couple's relationship.

Neither Lynn nor Carl were comfortable with conflict. Lynn's references to conflict were the guilt-ridden struggles with her mother in which no matter what the outcome, Lynn wondered if she did something wrong. Carl, on the other hand, saw little if any conflict between his parents, and his father's rare show of anger was enough to paralyze Carl.

Lynn's and Carl's avoidance of disagreements was less problematic before their daughter's birth. With more time and energy for one another and without financial and child-care worries, Lynn and Carl were able to avoid threatening disagreements. Lynn, for example, may have disliked having all the responsibility for household chores but she felt like Carl was trying and with time he would help more. As for Carl, without feeling the pressure from Lynn to help out, he paradoxically helped more. Cleaning up after dinner was a leisurely time for them to talk and there was certainly less laundry to do.

In the initial interview, Lynn's and Carl's inability to disagree was striking. While at first glance it would appear to be Carl's fault (lineal causation) because he withdrew from Lynn, on closer evaluation, Lynn would also withdraw when Carl became angry. A rule appeared to exist—a rule to which both Lynn and Carl agreed—that conflict was to be avoided. With this in mind, the therapist proceeded to address this covert rule by asking a series of questions.

Therapist: What happens when the two of you disagree?

Lynn: It's tough to disagree when Carl just pulls away in silence.

Carl: I know it does not matter what I say. So, I say nothing and let her do what she wants.

Again, the couple present the polarity of their perspectives. At this point, the therapist could further pursue the reasons and explanations behind each of their positions but instead attempts to explore the underlying rules.

Therapist: Well, what would happen if the two of you did openly disagree with one another?

Lynn: I don't know.

Carl: I don't know either.

Therapist: I could be wrong, but it appears you both want to avoid any disagreements. I wonder why?

(Silence from Lynn and Carl as they both shift uneasily in their chairs.)

Therapist: Let's take a step back. What did you each observe when your parents disagreed?

Because both Lynn and Carl balked at examining their own fears of disagreement, the therapist stayed with the theme but defused the emotional charge by
first discussing past history. Without going into great detail, the therapist explores each family of origin, looking to tie past patterns into the couple's current
interaction.

Therapist *(in a series of questions)*:   How did your parents disagree with one
another? What was the result of their disagreements? Who was hurt by the
disagreements?

Briefly, Lynn saw disagreements leading to a divorce between her parents. The
absence of conflict in Carl's family hinted at its potential destructiveness. Both admitted that the last thing they each wanted was a marriage full of disagreements.

Therapist: I can understand you both wanting a conflict-free marriage. But, by
now, you both know realistically that is not possible. Disagreements, however, do not have to be destructive. For example, what would be a positive
outcome if the two of you openly disagreed and resolved the disagreement?

Rather than define their avoidance of conflict as a problem, the therapist focuses
on the positive gains in disagreement. Or, in other words, their fear and avoidance of disagreement is their solution to inevitable differences. Unfortunately,
their solution causes and maintains their problem. Viewed from this perspective,
the therapist challenges this covert rule and explores alternatives.

Challenging Attributions

As detailed previously, self-attributions and motives attributed to the partner underlie and reinforce a couple's patterns. Challenging couples' attributions is a
three-step process: (1) making covert attributions overt both on an individual
and couple level, (2) challenging the validity of these perceptions and beliefs,
and (3) asking what is gained by holding on to these attributions.

Personal attributions are more often than not privately held and left unexpressed. These attributions may be vague impressions or half-formed thoughts.
Thus, the first step in challenging attributions is to make these covert processes
overt.

Therapist: Lynn, what stops the two of you from being closer?

Lynn: I think Carl is unable to be very close with someone.

Therapist: When did you start to believe this?

Lynn: About one year after we were married.

Therapist: Did you think this when you were dating and engaged?

Lynn: No.

Therapist: Why didn't you see it at that time?

Lynn: I don't know.

Therapist: Do you think he was unable to be close then?

Lynn: No, we were close.

The therapist is attempting to clearly define Lynn's attribution concerning Carl's ability for closeness and in the process delineate when and how this attribution began to take shape. In delineating the when and how, Carl's inability for closeness is seen less and less as an inherent personality trait and more as a reflection of changes in time and circumstance. The monolithic, intractable personality trait attribution is challenged by the therapist's questions and Lynn's own words.

Therapist: Carl, you said Lynn is constantly criticizing you?

Carl: That's right.

Therapist: Why do you believe she criticizes you?

Carl: She gets overwhelmed by taking care of the baby and working.

Therapist: Sounds like she has a lot to attend to, but why would that result in criticizing you?

Carl: I think she takes it out on me.

Therapist: Why would she do that?

Carl: I don't know.

Therapist: Perhaps you should ask her now why she takes it out on you.

In making Carl's covert attributions overt—"I think she takes it out on me"—the therapist probes further—"Why would she do that?"—and is met with a vague, unspecific answer—"I don't know." Here, the therapist is at a choice point of either pushing Carl to further clarify his answer or involving Lynn in the discussion. Pushing Carl further would likely risk increased defensiveness on his part. Taken at his word, he truly does not know nor has speculated on why Lynn would take out her frustrations on him. Thus, the therapist shifts direction instructing Carl to elicit Lynn's reaction to his attributions. As a result, privately held attributions are made overt on the couple's level.

Having surfaced covert attributions, the validity of these attributions is challenged.

Therapist: Lynn, I am confused. You said you believed Carl lacked the ability to be close with you, but then you said this was not true in the beginning of your relationship. How do you explain the difference?

As mentioned earlier, attributions often assume an all-or-nothing quality with little gray. Lynn sees Carl as flawed in his ability for intimacy. However, as the therapist closely questions the when and how of these attributions, discrepancies appear. By identifying discrepancies, monolithic attributions are challenged.

Therapist (*in a rhetorical question*):   Carl, why would Lynn, who says she wants to be closer to you, criticize you and thus push you away? It does not make sense. What else could she be trying to accomplish?

Finally, the therapist asks each partner what is gained by holding on to their respective attributions.

Therapist: Carl, believing Lynn is a critical person does what to you?

Carl: I don't know what you mean.

Therapist: Well, how does it affect you if you feel criticized?

Carl: I just don't want to be around her.

Therapist: Do you stay away?

Carl: I don't leave the house, but I just try to avoid her.

Therapist: What does it do to you to feel criticized?

Carl: I get angry.

Therapist: Angry?

Carl: Yeah! It feels really unfair.

Therapist: Does Lynn know when you feel this?

Carl: Probably not.

Therapist: Any reason you would not want to tell her?

Carl: It just never occurs to me.

Therapist: So, she doesn't have a clue what she is doing to you?

Carl: I guess not.

Therapist: Now I am really confused. How is she supposed to change in ways you would like?

Here, the therapist pushes to connect Carl's attributions with his behavior. In doing so, the therapist subtly shifts a view of change from the responsibility of the other person to the person holding the attributions. The attributions are then framed as part of the problem.

Therapist: It seems to me that as long as you see Lynn as a critical person taking something out on you, you must stay away from her. Is this what you wish to do? Stay away from her?

Carl: No, I want to stay away only when she is critical.

Therapist: How do you know when she is being critical and when she is requesting help?

Having challenged the critical attribution, the therapist asks Carl to distinguish that from other behaviors. By placing the responsibility for change back on Carl, the therapist hopes to put further cracks in Carl's rigidified view of Lynn and have Carl entertain alternative explanations.

Delineating Boundaries Within Triangles

As discussed earlier, when dyads are unstable and a degree of conflict or tension exists between the members of the dyad, there is a tendency to bring a third party into the conflict, forming a triangle. By involving a third party, each partner has the opportunity to build an alliance or defuse the level of tension. For example, if Carl, rather than directly confronting Lynn, complains to a friend about Lynn's behavior, he may feel a sense of relief at "getting it off his chest." This is further enhanced if the friend is sympathetic and views the situation the same way, "Yeah, she seems real critical to me."

Even though a triangle may reduce intrapersonal tension, it does little to effectively address the issues. If Carl talks only to his friend about Lynn, then there is little possibility of Carl and Lynn resolving their problems. Moreover, Lynn may feel increasingly excluded as Carl avoids confiding in her and is very loquacious with his friend. In all probability, however, Lynn has also formed a triangle with her sister or mother or friends that reduces her inner frustrations.

The simple point is that triangles greatly diminish a couple's capacity to effectively resolve their differences and thus to grow as a couple. Therefore, therapy attempts to identify these conflict-avoiding triangles and to delineate boundaries (as discussed earlier, boundaries are the unwritten rules of social interaction defining interpersonal space) more conducive to effective problem solving and intimacy building.

In delineating interpersonal boundaries, the therapist is asking each partner to define his or her level of involvement with one another and with the third parties. The question posed by the therapist is how involved should I be or do I want to be in this relationship?

The "triangling-in" process may involve extended family members, children, friends, or even therapists. Lynn and Carl present four central triangles: (1) Lynn, Carl, and Jenn; (2) Lynn, Jenn, and Lynn's mother; (3) Lynn, her mother, and her sister; and (4) Carl, his mother, and his father. These triangles play an intimate part in the couple's life.

Therapist (*addressing the Lynn, Carl, and Jenn triangle*): I have noticed that if the two of you are going to argue it usually involves an issue over Jenn.

Lynn: Well, that has been the biggest change in our lives

Therapist: I understand that but I was wondering, if Jenn was not there, what would you fight about?

The therapist explores the partners' capacity to address each of their own interpersonal issues. For example, what themes may be submerged beneath the issue of Jenn? Who will bring up these themes, Lynn or Carl? How does the other partner respond when these subjects are brought up? Or, will the couple deny other issues and resist further exploration.

Carl (*while Lynn sits silently*):   Jenn is really the only issue we keep going around and around about.

Therapist: Is that right, Lynn?

Lynn: Well, that is the issue that brings on the most arguments.

Although the therapist may view the focus on Jenn as a way of avoiding intimate issues between Lynn and Carl, presented with the couple's united front, the therapist is left with little choice than to focus on the Lynn, Carl, and Jenn triangle. Both Lynn and Carl have signaled the therapist that other areas of their relationship may be too threatening at this time but that they would be comfortable discussing the relationship between themselves and their daughter.

Besides serving as a means of avoiding the marital, dyadic conflicts, emotionally charged triangles powerfully shaped in the couple's families of origin continue to strongly affect his or her relationships. More importantly, these previously formed triangles may consciously or unconsciously affect the couple relationship.

Therapist: Lynn, I was wondering about the pros and cons of having your mother provide your day care?

With this question, the therapist begins to explore the Lynn, Lynn's mother, and Jenn triangle. Although the issue between Lynn and her mother is rooted in the past, the therapist chooses a current situation as a means of accessing the triangle.

Lynn (*following a listing of the pros and cons of her mother's help with Jenn*):   Overall, at times it can be very frustrating. My mother vacillates between taking over and telling me how to raise Jenn. She also makes me feel guilty for leaving Jenn to go to work.

Therapist: Is it a familiar theme for your mother to take over but also for you to feel guilty when she does?

Lynn: I think that has always been an issue between us.

Therapist: But now you are the mother. So how do you wish to respond to your mother?

The therapist attempts to empower Lynn and support whatever boundaries Lynn wishes to draw with her mother.

In a variation on a theme, the therapist may constructively bring Carl into Lynn's dilemma, forming a triangle.

Therapist: Lynn, your dilemma with your mother is quite clear. I was wondering, is there any way Carl could be helpful with this issue?

If Carl can help Lynn with this issue, then not only is their relationship strengthened, but a boundary is drawn between Lynn and Carl as a functioning family unit and Lynn's mother as a supportive grandmother to Jenn.

Following her parents' divorce, Lynn assumed much of the child care for her younger sister as her mother began working full time. Lynn's mother found herself relying on Lynn more and more both for her help and as a confidant. Lynn filled the void in the family that her father had left.

Increasingly, Lynn felt these relationships burdensome, particularly after her daughter's birth. There was enough for Lynn to do in taking care of Jenn, working full-time, and trying to run a house without responding to her mother's and sister's needs. Lynn, however, felt guilty about these feelings, which served as a source of tension for her. Although these relationships may be seen as peripheral to the marital dynamics, they did serve as a source of tension and periodic conflict between Lynn and Carl.

Therapist (*addressing the couple*):   I was wondering, how have the relationships changed with Lynn's mother and sister since the birth of Jenn?

Lynn: It's a lot more complicated.

Therapist: How so?

Lynn: I just don't have as much time to talk with them. When I get home from work and my mom is there with Jenn, I don't want to sit and talk the way she does. I would just·like her to leave so that I could start the evening routines.

Therapist: How do you finesse this?

Lynn: I don't. I usually end up talking with her because I feel guilty that she has been with Jenn all day.

By opening up the issue, the therapist is in a position to explore Lynn's extended family triangle and to help her seek more satisfying solutions to her dilemmas.

The last key triangle identified during assessment was Carl's relationship with his parents. In the initial interview, it was not so much what Carl had said but more what he did not say that drew the therapist's attention. For example, Carl had described his parents in nondescript terms. His mother was caring but dominating, and his father was quiet and pacifying. Very little additional information was spontaneously offered. The therapist was left with a vague impression that there was more to these relationships than Carl was either aware of or volunteering.

Therapist: Carl, as opposed to Lynn's upbringing, you had the opportunity to grow up with both of your parents in the house. What did you observe about relationships by watching your parents.

Carl (*somewhat defensively*):   What do you mean?

Therapist: Well, what kind of relationship did they have?

Carl: I don't know. I have not thought about it.

(As was frequently the case, Carl would profess that he drew a blank to many of the therapist's questions. In dealing with Carl, the therapist was frequently in a bind: Do I continue to pursue Carl or back off and leave him alone? To continually question Carl places the therapist in Lynn's role of pursuer and puts Carl in the familiar role of distancer. Still, to not pursue Carl runs the risk of accepting the status quo and Carl's distancing mode of interaction.)

Therapist: I know none of us really thinks too much about our parents' relationship, but it is important because we have learned so much from being around them. For example, now that you are married, do you want a relationship with Lynn just like or different from your parents' relationship?

Because of the importance of the theme and as a means of encouraging Carl to think about relationships, the therapist continues to push the point. Although this approach may alienate Carl from the therapeutic process, he is not being asked about his marital relationship but rather his parents' relationship. The therapist chooses to start outside the marital relationship and work inward toward Carl's relationship with Lynn.

Carl: My parents got along great. They never fought like Lynn and I do.

Therapist: What do you think they do differently than you and Lynn do?

Carl: I don't know. I have not thought about it.

Therapist: That's all right. We have plenty of time to think about it now. So, what do you think they do differently than you and Lynn do?

Paradoxical Choices During Sessions

As identified in the assessment phase of therapy, Lynn and Carl present a classic pursuer-distancer pattern:

- Lynn identifies a problem.
- Carl does not immediately respond.
- Lynn grows frustrated and asks again.
- Carl "hears" her requests as criticism and he withdraws.
- Lynn senses Carl's withdrawal, and she pursues the issue.
- Carl withdraws further.
- Alternative outcomes: (1) Lynn gives up in frustration, quits pursuing, and withdraws herself; or (2) Lynn pursues past Carl's threshold of tolerance, and he angrily criticizes Lynn, forcing her to withdraw.

While clear to the therapist, these patterns have evolved through the couple's history of interaction and repeat with startling consistency. The content of the issue may change—for example, problems with child care, requests for intimacy—but the pursuer-distancer dance is replayed over and over.

Because of its strong repetitive nature, the pursuer-distancer pattern quickly appears in the therapist's office. Any topic may serve to ignite the pattern. At these points, the therapist is in an ideal position to intervene as the partners play out their respective roles. Not only is the therapist making the covert pattern overt, but he or she is also offering the couple alternatives to the repetitive ineffective patterns.

There are several steps to this process: (1) interrupt the dysfunctional sequence, (2) identify the pattern, and (3) provoke alternative responses.

Interrupting the dysfunctional sequence

Lynn: I wish we had the closeness we once had.

Therapist: Would you talk to Carl about your wishes?

Lynn: Carl, I really wish we could be closer. Like it used to be.

Carl: It's pretty difficult when you are always criticizing me.

Lynn: I am not criticizing you. I am trying to get you to help me.

Therapist (*interrupting the dialogue*):   Excuse me, but where will this conversation go now?

Lynn: Nowhere!

Therapist: It is bound to go somewhere.

Lynn: I give up and we just stop talking.

Identifying the pattern

Therapist: Let me try to understand what happens. You [*Lynn*] bring up something and Carl hears it as criticism.

Lynn and Carl: That's right.

Therapist: And then Lynn has a choice. Either she keeps bringing it up or drops it.

Lynn and Carl: That's right.

Therapist: Does this happen frequently between the two of you?

Lynn: All the time.

Carl: I guess so.

Therapist: So what happens after one of these exchanges?

Lynn: I feel completely frustrated and shut out.

Carl: I am a little angry at her criticism.

Therapist: Where does this leave the two of you?

Lynn: Silent and apart.

Once the pattern has been made overt, the therapist is in a position to intervene whenever the pattern surfaces during the sessions.

Provoking alternative responses

Therapist (*following a discussion on the couple's inability to emotionally connect over a weekend and at the first hint that the pursuer-distancer pattern is beginning*):   Lynn, if you keep pursuing Carl about this issue what is he going to do?

Or,

Therapist: Carl, I think this issue is important to Lynn. How are you going to react?

Notice that the therapist is intervening by interrupting the dysfunctional sequence before it concludes at its predictable end point. By interrupting earlier in the sequence, the therapist alerts the couple to the pattern and asks each member what he or she wishes to do next. The therapist does not direct or offer advice but instead presents options:

> What is going to happen next and how do you wish to respond?
> Lynn, do you want to keep pursuing him right now?
> Carl, are you about to pull away right now?
> Carl, would you give Lynn a signal before you pull away?

Thus, choice enters the picture where knee-jerk responses previously existed.

Interventions may take a more paradoxical stance by identifying the pattern and asking the couple to proceed.

Therapist: I think if the two of you continue discussing the problem in this way it will result in mutual frustration. If this is what either of you wants, then please continue.

Or

Lynn, if you want to keep pursuing go ahead, but Carl has that withdrawal look in his eyes.

Or

Carl, if you are hearing criticism right now, you can either check it out or pull away. What are you going to do?

Paradoxical interventions are particularly effective with patterns strongly resistant to change. Although each member of the couple blames the other for the outcome, in truth both partners collude in the repetitive dysfunctional patterns. In the therapy session, this often results in the therapist becoming increasingly active, attempting to change the patterns but inevitably being caught in the pattern web as well. Specifically, the therapist begins to pursue the distancer or encourages the pursuer to quit pursuing. Both of these approaches typically lead to the couple's stereotyped endings. Thus, paradoxical interventions encourage the couple to continue the patterns if they so choose. Ironically, it is difficult for dysfunctional patterns to repeat on demand.

Unable to renew the pattern at the therapist's request, a silence enters the therapist's office. The couple sits confused and may ask the therapist for help. Commonsense advice (first-order change) usually serves only to reignite the patterns. For example:

Therapist: Carl, why don't you tell Lynn when you feel criticized?

Carl: It will not do any good. It will just lead to more arguing because she will not let go of it.

Thus, rather than going around that track one more time, the therapist interrupts the patterned sequence and places the responsibility for change back on the couple.

Therapist (*following a silence in the room*):   If the two of you do not want to continue the pattern, then what alternatives do you have?

Finally, paradoxical interventions also may be used to uncover motives behind the patterns.

Therapist: Lynn, you can go ahead and pursue Carl on this issue, but I bet he can still avoid you. Why do you keep pursuing?

Therapist: Carl, I know it is important for you to keep Lynn at arm's length, but I was wondering why this is so important to you?

Case Summary

Because both Lynn and Carl were committed to the relationship and the presenting problems involved communication issues couched within specific complaints—Lynn wanted Carl to help more around the house and Carl wanted Lynn to stop criticizing him—therapy first focused on improving communication and negotiation skills. Some success was noted within the therapy sessions as long as the therapist took an active hand in structuring the interaction. Specifically, the therapist needed to continually remind the couple to begin each sentence with an "I" instead of a "you" and to turn every question into a statement.

Even with this continual monitoring, there was little evidence that change was taking place outside of the therapist's office. This was most obvious when homework assignments were not carried out. For example, the therapist gave the homework assignment for Lynn and Carl to establish a pattern of child care for the weekends that would give each of them time alone, family time with their daughter, and time alone as a couple. Instead of completing the assignment, the couple returned the following week not only offering excuses—"We did not have any time to talk"—but also accusing the other of the failure. Lynn said she tried to initiate the discussion but Carl was unresponsive. Carl said Lynn proceeded to tell him what to do. It became clear that focusing on communication and negotiating was of limited value.

Moving to more second-order interventions, the therapist challenged the definition of the problem and the individual attributions underlying these definitions. In challenging the individual definitions of the problem, the therapist attempted to eliminate the blame game from the therapeutic equation. Specifically, the other person is not to blame for the unsatisfactory status quo; rather, what am "I" doing that fuels the conflicts? By asking each spouse to go inward to discern his or her fears, emotions, and hopes, the therapist gains access to a wealth of material while avoiding the mutual accusations.

Because the blaming attributions had become such an ingrained pattern in Lynn and Carl's relationship and because homework assignments were ineffective, the therapist found it most helpful to frequently offer paradoxical choices to the couple during the therapy sessions. For example, when Lynn would bring up an issue that might directly raise Carl's defenses the therapist would intervene.

Therapist: Lynn, I know this is an important point you wish to discuss, but I also know that if you continue in this vein, Carl will begin to withdraw to protect himself. If you wish to continue, please go ahead and do so, but realize the consequences.

Lynn: OK, I know he will withdraw, but what am I supposed to do? Keep it all inside?

Therapist: Why don't you figure that out with Carl.

Interrupting the dysfunctional pattern while it was occurring within the therapy session forced the couple to evolve alternatives. The therapist did not tell Lynn what to do but suggested alternatives.

Besides interrupting the dysfunctional patterns, the therapist also sought to establish an overall norm whereby the spouses agree to disagree. This was particularly difficult for Lynn and Carl because neither partner had parental models for the resolution of disagreements, and both feared that open conflict would jeopardize their marriage. To establish this norm, the therapist first explored the couple's fear of conflict and actively fostered disagreement in a safe environment.

In terms of the imbalanced gender triangle, Lynn sought to affiliate with the male therapist. (Please note that we are employing a male therapist as an example to highlight the imbalanced triangle dynamics.) She saw his empathic questions as signs that he understood her position. Still, Lynn was ambivalent regarding having a male therapist. Although she had sought out a male therapist in hopes he would be able to relate to and draw her husband out of his passive-aggressive stance, history taught her to be suspect of males. Worse yet, she feared the therapist would take Carl's side and view her as a domineering woman.

Carl, on the other hand, felt an initial competition with the male therapist. The therapist was easily engaging his wife in conversation, and she seemed to enjoy it. Following his familiar response to threatening situations, Carl withdrew and took a "let's wait and see" approach to therapy. Engaging Carl in the process of therapy without threatening him was one of the therapist's chief dilemmas in treating the couple.

Although some progress was made by focusing more on second-order change techniques, it was limited. There was a sense that the couple had not addressed all the areas of concern and that the conflict over household chores masked deeper issues. Although Lynn and Carl continued to keep regular therapy appointments, the therapist felt an impasse was slowly developing.

Summary

Change within couples therapy is mercurial. It may occur because of or despite the therapist's efforts. It may occur because one or both members of the couple embrace change. It may occur because of events happening outside of the therapy context. It may occur because of a combination of all of the above.

Within the imbalanced therapeutic triangle are three sets of eyes and ears perceiving, perhaps at any given time, three distinct realities. Consequently, the therapist possesses no more of the truth than either member of the couple. Instead, within the therapeutic alliance, all three participants struggle with change. Rather than close the chapter on that amorphous note, we offer a recent study exploring change in couples therapy as viewed by therapists and clients.

CRITICAL INCIDENTS IN COUPLES THERAPY

Choosing therapists with divergent theoretical models (experiential, solution focused, and structural), Wark (1994) asked both the therapists and their couple clients to identify critical change incidents, both positive and negative, that occurred more than once in therapy. The following briefly summarizes the findings:

Positive Critical Incidents as Perceived by Clients

1. *Positive results*—Clients attributed positive outcomes to therapy. For example, subjects reported having learned more about themselves and about communicating in a positive manner as a couple.

2. *The structure of therapy*—Weekly scheduled meetings were mentioned as beneficial in and of themselves. Routinely scheduled sessions focused the partners on their relationship at least once a week. (For some couples, the 1 hour focused on their relationship was far more time than they will spend the rest of the week with one another.)

3. *Therapist's alternative perspectives*—By offering alternative perspectives on the couple's issues, the therapist enlarges the couple's view of their problems. Also, by suggesting alternative means of responding to one another, the therapist expanded the couple's repertoire of behavior.

4. *Nondirective style of the therapist*—By not imposing direction or telling the partners what to do, clients valued "thinking things out for ourselves."

5. *Directive style of the therapist*—While some respondents valued a nondirective approach, others found the therapist's directives helpful.

6. *Focus on the positives*—The therapist was seen as creating a sense of optimism and encouragement and as offering hope where little had been before.

Positive Critical Incidents as Perceived by Therapists

1. *Clients' readiness for change*—Not surprisingly, therapists value motivated clients. One wonders, however, if this is a positive feedback loop whereby the couple is highly motivated, the therapist is more invested and optimistic, the couple is encouraged by the therapist's optimism, and the entire therapy endeavor takes on a mutual, positive tone.

2. *Change techniques*—Techniques are a therapist's bag of tricks. Therapists put great faith in learning and developing new techniques. Again, not surprisingly, the therapists in the study believed their techniques fostered change.

3. *Client-focused attitude*—The therapist valued and encouraged interaction between the members of the couple rather than between the therapist and a partner.

Negative Critical Incidents as Perceived by Clients

1. *No follow-through*—Respondents negatively rated a lack of follow-through during the course of therapy. Topics and issues were not thoroughly developed. More specifically, homework assignments from earlier sessions were not addressed at a later point.

2. *Therapist imposition*—Clients spoke very strongly about feeling misunderstood by their therapist. Some responded that they felt "labeled" by their therapists. Others believed the therapist imposed his or her own judgment and biases on the clients' behavior. And finally, a lack of accurate empathy occurred. Clients disagreed with the therapist's perceptions of them.

3. *No resolution of problems*—The lack of progress toward change became an issue for the clients. It would appear the absence of progress begins to cast a shadow over therapy.

Negative Critical Incidents as Perceived by Therapists

1. *Responsibility for change*—Therapists attributed negative outcomes to their assuming too much responsibility for change. Or, in other words, if the therapist is more invested in change than the clients are, then progress becomes the therapist's issue and not the client's. The therapist assumes the responsibility for change, and the clients resist the therapist imposition.

2. *Insufficient data gathering*—Therapists regretted not accumulating sufficient information from clients. One can only assume that in hindsight, therapists believed the negative outcome could have been avoided if the therapist had been better informed.

A number of observations may be made concerning Wark's (1994) findings. First, different couples may need different things. Some couples respond positively to a highly directive therapist, and others benefit from a nondirective approach. The art to couples therapy is matching intervention styles with the couples' capacity for change.

Second, accurate empathy is a key ingredient in building a therapeutic alliance within which change can occur. This is all the more challenging for a couples therapist who must simultaneously empathize with each gender role without alienating one member of the couple.

A final humbling thought is that therapists may blindly make assumptions concerning their clients' experiences of therapy. The "truth" in couples therapy lies somewhere within three distinct perceptions. Although no one can truly walk in another person's shoes, we can, as therapists, be aware of our own biases and honestly struggle with appreciating and understanding our clients.

Impasse Themes

It is rare for both partners entering therapy to be equally committed to change and to the relationship. One partner may have coerced the other into therapy. One partner may hope to serve as a cotherapist in changing the other person. In another example, the partner may be there to pacify his or her mate. Perhaps one or both partners harbor an ambivalence concerning the relationship. If this is a good relationship, should it be so much work? I am really tired of the fighting! Is my partner going to leave me? Should I leave my partner?

Most of the above issues and questions lie just below the surface in therapy. With positive change, they recede further and further into the background as the partners commit to therapy and the relationship deepens. The therapy sessions may still be difficult at times, but the positive change increases the partners' hope for the relationship.

With other couples, however, these ambivalences cast a shadow over therapy. In these cases after the initial hope for therapy fades, the dysfunctional patterns appear more intractable. The morale of the therapist and couple sinks as few positive gains are achieved. The relationship appears worse than when therapy began. The partners begin to question both the relationship and the merit of continuing therapy. The therapist may also become increasingly frustrated as little therapeutic movement occurs and therapy grinds to an impasse.

What underlies the impasse? Sometimes there are themes indigenous to the process of psychotherapy: transference and countertransference issues. The influence of gender may subtly affect the couple, the therapist, and thus the progress of therapy. At other times there are content themes unique to the couple that impede progress—for example, (1) physical abuse, (2) drug abuse, (3) sexuality and intimacy, and (4) extrarelationship affairs.

These themes may be openly acknowledged by the couple or may serve as conscious or unconscious agendas hidden from the therapist. But, regardless of the nature of the impasse, if therapy is to progress, these impediments must be addressed.

This chapter explores impasse process and content themes. In addressing these themes, specific therapeutic interventions are offered along with a discussion of individual versus couples versus family interventions. Issues unique to treating gay and lesbian couples are also discussed.

Process Themes

TRANSFERENCE AND COUNTERTRANSFERENCE

Although the concepts of transference and countertransference are based in psychoanalytic thought, they are most applicable to couples therapy. In the imbalanced gender triangle, each member of the couple and the therapist carry into therapy the legacy of their respective families of origin. Each possesses a prototype of male-female interaction as well as a reservoir of personal experiences and expectations. Consequently, each participant views the therapeutic process through different colored glasses. Each member of the couple may present different perspectives of the same event while the therapist sees a third side.

More important, each participant projects something of his or her past onto the other members of the therapeutic triangle. Lynn may be a critical mother in Carl's eyes. Lynn sees in Carl the aloof, distant father she vaguely remembers. In the dynamics of their relationship, for Carl, Lynn's critical behavior and, for Lynn, Carl's distancing, frighteningly echo themes from the past. The therapist may see in Carl or Lynn figures from his or her own past. Or, further still, Lynn's and Carl's interpersonal dynamics can resonate with the therapist's own personal relationship history.

The therapist also symbolizes an authority figure. Depending on the gender of the therapist, each partner may transfer feelings from past authority figures— for example, mother, father, grandparent—onto him or her. The therapist may be the good or bad, the judgmental, or the nurturing parent.

Finally, gender shapes and further colors the transference and countertransference forces. In various combinations, the female client may act differently toward and may transfer different feelings onto a female therapist as opposed to a male therapist. The male client may be competitive with a male therapist and seductive with a female therapist. The male therapist may also feel competitive with the male client and protective of the female. The female therapist may view the female client as a victim and may wish to defend her against an oppressive male.

In order to more fully delineate and elaborate on these themes, we will divide transferences and countertransferences into "a priori" mind sets and reactions that have evolved during the course of treatment. (This distinction, in part, is suggested by Shay, 1993.) A priori transference and countertransference reactions refer to the predilections that each participant brings into therapy. However, even though each participant may be predisposed to certain reactions, the actual process of therapy serves to modify or perhaps reinforce a priori assumptions and beliefs.

A priori transference reactions refer to each client's model of whom the therapist will be. These reactions may be based on previous experiences in therapy, the influence of the media, television and movie portrayals of therapists, and the client's personal history in his or her family of origin. These assumptions may be positive whereby the client enters therapy believing the therapist is competent and will be helpful, or these assumptions may be negative whereby the client may be predisposed to reject the therapist.

The following lists a priori transference reactions for each gender:

Female Clients Toward Male Therapists:

1. Positively idealizes the therapist as the man her husband is not.
2. Enacts gender role of compliant female toward male authority figure.
3. In dependent stance, elicits and defers to the therapist's judgment.
4. Seeks therapist's protection.
5. Fears therapist will be aloof, judgmental male.
6. Fears she will not be understood by the therapist and that he will align with her husband.

Male Clients Toward Male Therapists:

1. Devalues therapist.
2. Is competitive with the therapist.
3. Feels sense of shame and feels he will be judged by the therapist.
4. Seeks to establish power hierarchy—that is, who will control whom?
5. Resists dependent position of therapy.

Female Clients Toward Female Therapists:

1. Seeks affiliation—that is, similar experiences of being a woman.
2. Seeks protection and an advocate—that is, someone who will change her mate.
3. Competes in terms of competency as a woman.
4. Competes in terms of partner's attentions.
5. Fears male partner will overpower female therapist.
6. Seeks nurturing from the female therapist.

Male Clients Toward Female Therapists:

1. Seeks to control therapy by testing therapist's strengths.
2. Resists dependent position.
3. May welcome the dependent submission of the little boy to the therapist's role as mother, depending upon the dynamics of his family of origin.
4. May passive-aggressively resist therapist's control and influence.
5. Attempts to charm or seduce the therapist.

The therapist may also enter therapy with a priori countertransference biases. These biases may reflect the dynamics in his or her parents' marriage, sociopolitical beliefs concerning the equality of the sexes, or personal experience.

Female Therapists Toward Couple:

1. Views woman as a victim who needs protection.
2. Views woman as a victim who needs to be empowered.

3. Competes with the man to prove competency.
4. Has difficulty assuming control over powerful male.
5. Has desire to correct the power imbalance in the relationship.

Male Therapists Toward Couple:

1. Competes with the male client.
2. Desires to protect female client.
3. Affiliates with female client.
4. Struggles for control of sessions with powerful male.
5. Desires to correct the power imbalance in the relationship.

In terms of therapeutic impasse, however, it is not the a priori assumptions that bog down therapy but how these reactions are addressed and managed within the actual process of therapy. For example, an impasse is likely to develop when (1) a priori assumptions are fulfilled, (2) a priori assumptions are not addressed or are avoided, and (3) the therapist fails to recognize or relinquish his or her countertransference reactions.

A priori transference assumptions are fulfilled when the therapist's countertransference biases dovetail with the client's presumptions. For example, Lynn hoped the therapist would change Carl, whereas Carl was suspicious of therapy and believed he would be judged and further criticized. A therapist entering the picture could perceive Lynn as the victim of Carl's insensitivity and neglect. Intentionally or unintentionally, an alliance would be created between Lynn and the therapist with the unstated agenda of changing Carl. An impasse is soon created whereby the therapeutic agenda mirrors the marital dynamics: Lynn is a victim and let's change Carl. The impasse grows deeper as the therapist's behavior confirms Carl's initial suspicions and as a response, he passive-aggressively participates in treatment.

Likewise, Carl may be jealous of or may resent the alliance between his wife and the therapist. As Shay (1993) observed, "The very nature of couples therapy, with its emphasis on open communication, expression of affect, and the development of intimacy, may be inherently threatening and humiliating when a male therapist so easily offers that which the woman has unsuccessfully tried to get her man to provide" (p. 96).

Or, what if the therapist views Lynn as a demanding, critical woman? Empathizing and allying with Carl, the therapist minimizes Lynn's complaints and maximizes Carl's contributions to the family. With the therapist as his defender and guardian of the status quo, Carl offers anecdote after anecdote of Lynn's criticism and demanding behavior. The impasse is created when Carl is asked to assume little responsibility for change and Lynn's worst fears are confirmed: She is not being understood or she should not be asking more of Carl. It is her job to care for Jenn and the home.

A priori assumptions are to be expected at the beginning of therapy and their existence is not necessarily problematic. Therapy may even progress without uncovering or addressing these assumptions. However, when an impasse builds, the underlying a priori assumptions may be the culprit.

Therapist: I was wondering. What did you each expect when we began therapy? What did you hope would happen and what did you fear might happen?

As an opening, the above question offers a blank slate on which the couple may write. The therapist is not implying anything or blaming the lack of progress on anyone or anything. Instead, the therapist is attempting to open up the area of a priori assumptions.

Sometimes, however, these assumptions are outside the couple's awareness. In these situations, a therapist may need to address the issue directly by speculating on possible a priori assumptions:

Therapist: Lynn, I have felt that you have wanted me to help change Carl. Is this so?

Therapist: Carl, you have offered evidence time after time of Lynn's critical behavior toward you. Why is it important for you to convince me of this?

Regardless of the means of uncovering the a priori assumptions, once exposed the couple and therapist can connect these assumptions with the lack of change in therapy. Moreover, the therapist can negate the outcome of these assumptions thus facilitating progress. When making the covert agendas overt, the partners' myths of one another are challenged. The therapist is also communicating that he or she will not play the game as the partners have constructed it.

Therapist: Lynn, I believe you would like me to change Carl, but if Carl is going to change it will be because he chooses to and not because of anything you or I do.

Therapist: Carl, I do not see Lynn as the critical person you frequently portray. Instead, I see her, as I see you, as someone struggling to be loved and respected in a relationship.

Finally, the therapist who is blind to countertransference issues creates unnecessary roadblocks in therapy. For example, a therapist may have predilections to rescue or defend perceived victims, to struggle with males for power, to affiliate with females, or to compensate for family of origin relationships by remaking client's relationships into ideal ones.

Of the above methods of countertransference, the therapist's desire to compensate for past dysfunctional relationships is a certain prescription for failure. In these cases, the therapist attempts to remake a couple's relationship along idealized dimensions: "I will help this couple to form the intimate relationship that my own parents never had." Unable to accept the partners' choices for their relationship, the therapist subtly and not so subtly pushes his or her separate agenda. Accordingly, therapeutic progress ceases as the couple feels judged and coerced into directions they do not wish to go.

With Lynn and Carl, the therapist may err by focusing and attempting to build a level of intimacy that the couple may not wish to have nor are capable of at this time. Viewed from a developmental context, Lynn and Carl are both reeling from financial and child-care responsibilities. Their level of intimacy, although not ideal, particularly from Lynn's perspective, had deteriorated rapidly over the past year. For Lynn, Carl simply helping her more around the house would be a sign that he was listening to her and in and of itself a successful treatment outcome.

Likewise, Lynn and Carl would probably terminate prematurely if the therapist attempted to push Carl's capacity for intimacy. Most certainly, the prospects for the marriage would improve if Carl developed a greater capacity for intimacy, and that may come later as he becomes more secure with himself, but at the time of therapy, Carl felt under siege by Lynn's perceived criticisms. In this guarded and defended position, Carl would certainly resist the therapist's intimations that he is emotionally restrictive. Moreover, Carl pulls away from Lynn in response to their conflict. Why should Carl even bother coming to therapy when he feels judged and is pushed into situations where he does not wish to go?

Although it may be nice to believe that therapists are objective, unbiased practitioners, it is naive. How can we be immune to the very thing we treat: relationships? Our hope, however, is to be aware of, as best we can, our own family of origin scripts and gender biases. And when therapy reaches an impasse, the first place to look is within.

Gender Roles in Transference and Countertransference

Each member of a couple enters the relationship with gender role prescriptions. These role prescriptions guide one's own behavior, as well as form the basis of our expectations of our partner. Inherent in these role expectations are the seeds for an impasse in couples therapy.

In a landmark study, Blumstein and Schwartz (1983) investigated American couples (married, cohabiting, gay male, and lesbian) via a national survey involving intensive interviewing. One overwhelming conclusion they drew was that "families are in a significant state of flux, and the uncertainty reverberates throughout society" (p. 35). Part of the reasons for the state of flux is that "couples are trying to grapple with how men and women, how men and men, how women and women, should relate to one another" (p. 45).

An advantage of clearly defined traditional male and female gender roles for a heterosexual couple is the clarity of role boundaries. Each gender is assigned certain responsibilities—you take care of that and I will take care of this. As a result of a clear division of roles, potential conflicts are minimized and the tasks in living together are clearly defined. He will take care of the outside of the house, and she will take care of the inside.

But embedded in traditional gender roles are two major disadvantages. First, stereotypical roles, while providing stability, inhibit change and choice regarding roles and tasks. Personal growth for both members of the couple is sacrificed to maintain the status quo. Equally important, traditional heterosexual gender roles are predicated on male dominance. Thus, although a dominant male role makes for an efficient decision-making process, it comes at great cost to the woman in the relationship (Blumstein & Schwartz, 1983).

We live with rapidly changing social forces redefining what it means to be male and what it means to be female. Many women are equal partners in and at times the sole providers of the family's financial support. Cultural attitudes toward any number of gender issues—for example, male domination, male insensitivity, female submission, women in the workforce—are openly debated. The days of "father knows best" reappear only on television.

But although the challenge to traditional gender roles offers exciting new possibilities, it also harbors uncertainty and resentment. Carl welcomes Lynn's financial support but feels less of a "man" because of it. Moreover, he already feels he does far more with the baby than his father ever did with him. Carl baby-sits and even changes diapers! Lynn, on the other hand, feels guilty leaving her baby. She enjoys her job and secretly likes the break from child-care responsibilities but feels guilty because of these feelings. She sees Carl's behavior as "stupid macho stuff."

Although there are other issues in their relationship, Lynn and Carl reflect the societal confusion and uncertainty over gender roles. Unable to view their conflicts as embedded within the more global issue of changing gender roles, both Lynn and Carl instead "see" flawed personality traits in one another and vacillate between attempting to change and rejecting the other.

In helping Lynn and Carl to take a broader view of their relationship and its basis in traditional gender roles, the therapist may ask a series of reflective questions.

Therapist (*exploring gender roles in marriage*):   Before you were married, would you each tell me what you thought a husband should do and what a wife should do?

Therapist (*exploring gender beliefs in parenting*):   Before you found out that Lynn was pregnant, would you each tell me what you thought a father should do and what a mother should do?

Therapist (*exploring family of origin gender influences*):   What types of roles existed in your parents' marriages? What were your fathers' responsibilities? What were your mother's responsibilities?

These and similar questions open up for discussion the issue of gender roles and expectations. Notice, the therapist is not asking anyone to change but is attempting to heighten each partner's awareness of gender. Within the context of couples therapy, each partner has the opportunity to explore his or her biases with the therapist while the other partner listens. Potential impasses are addressed as each partner verbalizes his or her position. Change is more likely to occur when covert agendas are made overt.

Although the therapist's beliefs also fall along the traditional–egalitarian dimension, his or her beliefs are left at the door. The therapist's task is to increase the couple's goodness of fit and reciprocity equilibrium and not to shape the couple to fit the therapist's ideology. This is not done to accept a traditional inequality power differential between men and women but to have the therapist assist the partners to look at their patterns and determine for themselves what they find mutually satisfying.

Content Themes

While transferences and countertransferences and gender issues are present to one degree or another in every case and may contribute to treatment impasse, a third factor, content themes, is unique to individual couples. As a basis for an impasse, these themes are not mentioned in the initial complaints. The therapist may have a sense that there is more than meets the eye, but the couple has not revealed the issue.

The content theme may not be initially exposed for a variety of reasons. One partner may fear the other's anger if the issue were to be revealed. Shame or embarrassment may fuel the cover-up. Or, the partners may be unaware of the issue's impact on their relationship. Regardless, these themes may fuel potential impasses.

Physical Abuse

As a covert theme underlying and hindering therapeutic progress, violence in a marriage is a hidden powder keg primed for an explosion. Unless therapy has been court ordered or the couple present violence as their chief reason for seeking therapy, the extent and fear of physical abuse is frequently hidden from the therapist. It may emerge at a later stage of therapy or may be the issue creating the impasse. (For the purposes of our discussion, we are assuming a situation where the man physically abuses his female partner. Although the pattern of abuse may be reversed in some situations, the abusive relationship is more characteristically male to female.)

In these situations, the therapist has had a gnawing feeling that he or she does not possess all the pieces to the couple's puzzle. There are hints something is amiss as the woman sits on the edge of her chair when the man's temperature is rising or as he shoots her a glance when she starts to raise a topic. But still, the couple avoid directly labeling the issue. The woman avoids it out of fear of retribution, and the man does not want to air dirty laundry. As the impasse builds, the therapist is left probing an unknown but highly sensitive area. The following section highlights recent research into this area and emphasizes the clinical implications for the couples therapist.

Although most men struggle with the issues of intimacy and dependency in relationships, abusive husbands manifest more extreme reactions to these emotional themes. Typically having observed their father's abuse of their mother or having been themselves the victims of abuse, potential abusers seek extreme and exclusive intimacy with their mates (Campbell, 1993). In the early stage of a relationship, this need may take the form of possessiveness and obsessive jealousy. The woman may initially mistake the male's possessiveness for passion; however, his jealousy soon begins to isolate her from other relationships.

Although guarding the exclusiveness of the relationship, the man fears the loss of control and engulfment of a dependent relationship. This rise in anxiety coupled with a perceived lack of deference on his mate's part sets the stage for violence. Aggression, whether verbal or physical, creates a safer emotional distance for the man as the partners become antagonists. Moreover, aggression reasserts the man's dominance and control over his partner (Campbell, 1993).

The women in these relationships may hold themselves responsible for their mate's unhappiness and displeasure. Also, as the relationship becomes more and more noncommunicative in ways other than the violent outbreaks, women may also initiate aggression in response to their loneliness (Campbell, 1993).

In an investigation of distressed violent and nonviolent couples, Jacobson, Gottman, Waltz, Rushe, Babock, and Holtzworth-Munroe (1994) did not find significant differences between the groups in husbands' or wives' anger. However, the violent couples evidenced higher levels of contempt and belligerence in their communication. The researchers considered contempt a form of psychological abuse and belligerence a highly provocative form of emotional aggression.

Extrapolating from the study, diagnostic signs of potential violence are: (1) excessive jealousy and controlling behavior on the male's part, (2) a woman's isolation from family and friends because of the man's jealousy and need for control, (3) anger alone (a necessary but insufficient sign of potential violence), and (4) anger coupled with a high level of contempt and belligerence in the couple's communication patterns.

In an attempt to discriminate more fully the various types of abusers, Gottman, et al. (1995) examined physiological correlates to abuse. Specifically, differences in heart rate reactivity were found to discriminate between two types of abusers. Type 1 men became more belligerent and contemptuous as their heart rates decreased during marital conflict. On the other hand, the heart rates of Type 2 men increased during marital conflict.

Biographical information showed that Type 1 men, although no more violent in their marriages than Type 2 men in terms of the frequency of violence, committed the more serious assaults—for example, kicking and hitting their wives with a fist (Jacobson, Gottman, & Shortt, 1995). Also, they were generally more violent outside the marriage in terms of friends, strangers, and co-workers, and they were more likely to be diagnosed as antisocial, drug dependent, and aggressive-sadistic.

Interactional patterns also differed for the two types. Type 1 men, coinciding with the decrease in heart rate, began the interactions with a high frequency of aggressive behavior, but the frequency dropped as the interaction continued. Type 2 men, however, fit a more frequent pattern of increasingly aggressive behaviors in the escalating argument with their wives and thus elevating their heart rate. To explain this difference, the researchers hypothesized that Type 1 men's heart rates lowered as the men focused their attention on manipulating or controlling their wives. For the interaction, the husband's fully directed anger heightens the wife's fear and reduces her own expression of anger. Perhaps the man's threatening tone or stare produces enough fear in the wife that she withdraws from the conflict.

The researchers further hypothesized differing flash points for the violence. Type 1 men struck back when they believed their wives were trying to control them. Even the wives' reasonable requests for cooperation or respect were perceived as attempts at control. Surprisingly, Type 1 men were not threatened by increasingly independent moves by their wives as long as the women remained submissive and passive to the men's wishes.

In contrast, Type 2 men were more likely to be threatened by their wives' increasing independence. They fear abandonment. As their heart rate increases, Type 2 men lose emotional control and become abusive. The abuse does not have the calculated manner of the Type 1 men's attempts at control, but it is instead an attempt to engage the women and keep them interacting. *Her withdrawal is the real threat.*

Thus, Type 1 men are highly controlled in a domestic dispute and become abusive to dominate the wife. In contrast, Type 2 men become abusive as they lose control emotionally. Because of these differences in emotional control and recognizing that any conclusions at this stage of the research are premature, the investigators suggested that Type 1 abusers would be less likely to respond to psychotherapy than Type 2 abusers (Gottman et al., 1995). The obvious reason is that Type 2 men may learn greater emotional control, particularly if it maintains the relationship, whereas the cold manipulation of Type 1 men suggests more severe psychopathology.

In a 2-year follow-up of separation and divorce rates, Type 1 had a 0% rate compared to Type 2's rate of 27%. Two hypotheses were offered for this finding. First, women married to Type 1 men may be too intimidated and afraid to leave the relationship. Because the woman's anger has been suppressed for so long, she may be unable to mobilize her anger to confront or implement change. Second, a significant percentage of women married to Type 1 men are themselves antisocial and may be habituated to violent relationships.

To summarize for therapeutic purposes, two types of batterers have been identified, Type 1 and Type 2. Type 1 batterers become cold and calculating in their violence as a domestic dispute escalates. Violence is used to control and intimidate. These men are also more likely to be violent outside the home. Historically, they are more likely to have seen reciprocal violence between their parents, and, diagnostically, they are likely to be antisocial, drug dependent, and aggressive-sadistic.

Type 2 batterers, on the other hand, become abusive as they lose emotional control in a domestic dispute. They are more likely to have viewed their fathers abusing their mothers. Psychologically, they fear abandonment. Violence is a response to being emotionally overloaded and fearing the partner's withdrawal.

In terms of the couples' relationships, the partners in Type 1 relationships are enmeshed in their violence. The women, more often than not, do not end the relationships, either out of fear and intimidation or because of their own collusion in the violence. Thus, because of the severe pathology of the batterers and the enmeshment of the partners, couples therapy has a poor prognosis.

Women married to Type 2 batterers are more likely to end the relationship. Still, a positive prognosis is more likely with these couples when more effective problem-solving strategies evolve and the batterer gains an appreciation for his fear of abandonment. In these cases, couples therapy has a much improved prognosis, particularly if both parties are committed and motivated.

Nevertheless, once violence is woven into a relationship the prospects for successful psychotherapy diminish. Walker (1995) did not recommend family systems therapy as the initial treatment in battering relationships. She argued that because of the power inequities in the battering relationship, women enter therapy not as equal partners with their mates but as victims who fear retribution outside the therapy sessions and thus who cannot participate honestly. In these cases, therapy does little more than support the status quo as the woman sits passively, afraid of confronting her husband.

Consequently, for Walker (1995) couples therapy is appropriate only after the batterer completes an offender-specific treatment program or evidences the following behavior: he has (1) accepted responsibility for the violence, (2) stopped the violent behavior, (3) learned new skills to manage anger and conflict, (4) addressed key family of origin issues, and (5) learned new gender role patterns.

While Walker (1995) presents an ideal format for addressing spousal abuse, these types of individual treatment programs are few and far between and may not be available to the average couple or therapist. However, Walker's basic point needs underlining: The batterer must accept responsibility for his actions and address his actions in individual treatment before couples therapy is introduced. Couples therapy can begin to heal the wounds to the marriage only after the batterer has begun significant change.

Thus, if violence in the relationship is a hidden agenda, couples therapy will more than likely reach an impasse. While the male may attempt to control the sessions through overt or passive-aggressive tactics, his wife will sit silently guarding her statements. In these situations, the therapist is left with the difficult task of uncovering the impasse issues and advising the couple concerning the next appropriate step.

DRUG ABUSE

Drug abuse, particularly alcohol abuse, is so woven into some couples' lives that it can be obscured by the more obvious presenting problems. Even though alcohol may be a central organizing dynamic in many cases, therapists often overlook or fail to ask about drug usage (Treadway, 1987). Unfortunately, it may only be at times of impasse that a therapist looks more closely at the issue of drug abuse and its ramifications for the couple.

One way of conceptualizing a couple's drug abuse dynamic is to envision a triangle with the drug, for example alcohol, as the third point. Thus, alcohol may serve as a distance regulator for the couple. The alcoholic may turn to it and distance him- or herself from his or her spouse when stress builds in the marital relationship. Or, arguments over alcohol may distract the couple from other issues. For example, instead of quarreling over intimacy issues, the couple is on more familiar turf when arguing over drinking patterns.

Steinglass, Bennett, Wolin, and Reiss (1987) suggested that it is possible for the entire family to become an alcoholic system. In the alcoholic family system, the family accommodates to one or more of its members' alcohol abuse but at great cost to the family's emotional growth.

More specifically, in a systemic perspective of an "alcoholic marriage," both partners may collude in the alcohol problem. While the alcoholic has the presenting problem, the spouse's behavior is seen as maintaining (enabling) the problem—for example, making excuses for the alcoholic's behavior, correcting the alcoholic's mistakes. This is portrayed as an over- and underfunctioning couple dynamic.

Accordingly, the systemic model would hypothesize that the relationship's tenuous balance is maintained by alcohol abuse and that if the alcoholic quit drinking the spouse would decompensate with a physical or emotional illness. Again, the assumption is that both partners collude in meeting mutual, dysfunctional needs.

Although the systemic view offers a parsimoniously appealing clinical model, research fails to support the over/underfunctioning dynamic as the norm for the "alcoholic marriage" (McCrady & Hay, 1987). Instead, research suggests that during abstinence from alcohol both members of the couple improve significantly in their enjoyment of the relationship (Nirenberg, Liepman, Begin, Doolittle, & Broffman, 1990). Thus, instead of viewing the members of the couple as conspiring in the alcohol abuse, an alternative hypothesis is that alcohol abuse creates or exacerbates marital problems (Noel, McCrady, Stout, & Fisher-Nelson, 1991).

As always, the impact of gender further expands the clinical picture. In a study of couples married on average at least 15 years where one spouse is an admitted alcoholic seeking outpatient alcohol/marital therapy, the gender differences found are summarized below (Noel et al., 1991):

1. Male alcoholics were drinking before the marriage, whereas female alcoholics began after the marriage and developed alcohol problems later than men. In the study, women married at 24 years of age began regular drinking at age 29.5. They began to experience drinking problems about 41 years of age and on average sought treatment 4 years later. Men, on the other hand, married at 27 years of age had begun regular drinking about age 20.5. They began to experience drinking problems about age 33 and sought treatment 9 years later.

2. Couples where the wife was an alcoholic were more satisfied with the relationship than couples with an alcoholic husband.

3. Alcoholic wives exhibited more positive communication with their husbands whereas alcoholic husbands were more negative toward their wives.

4. Overall, marriages of alcoholic husbands were more disruptive than marriages of alcoholic wives.

The finding that couples with an alcoholic wife are more satisfied with their relationships than couples with an alcoholic husband is intriguing. From a gender-role perspective, one may speculate that alcoholic wives maintain traditional gender roles. Her alcoholism maintains her submissive position in respect to her husband. But, male alcoholics may fail to adequately fulfill male/husband roles; for example, they may fail to provide an adequate income. We may further speculate that when seeking treatment a woman may be asking for help with her husband's drinking, but when the wife drinks the man is less likely to seek treatment.

Regardless of one's theoretical position or the gender of the abuser, when confronted with an impasse involving drug abuse a therapist must ponder several questions:

Should I work with the presenting problem and let the substance abuse emerge during the course of treatment?
Should I address the issue directly?
Should I encourage the nonabusing partner to address the issue?
Is drinking the "real" problem or simply another manifestation of a dysfunctional relationship?

In answering these questions, the therapist assesses the power of denial and the role of responsibility.

Denial is typically at the heart of the impasse. In a frequent scenario, the couple has entered therapy with a series of mutual complaints but little progress has been made. Drug abuse has been studiously avoided, and because the couple has not brought up the issue neither does the therapist. Nevertheless, the impasse suggests to the therapist that significant issues are being avoided. Even in those cases where drug abuse is the presenting issue, the history of broken promises and failed attempts at change underscores the couple's denial of the seriousness of the abuse. Unfortunately, the stronger the denial, the poorer the prognosis for therapy.

Besides assessing the extent and the power of denial in the couple's dynamics, a therapist must also look inside and determine to what degree he or she is responsible for change. For example, is it the therapist's job to confront the alcohol abuse? Is the therapist's job to support the more functional spouse by encouraging his or her confrontation of the abusing partner? Does the therapist refuse to see the couple until the abusing spouse enters an alcohol program? Until that happens, does the therapist offer individual therapy to the nonabusing partner—an individual therapy designed to educate the partner concerning alcoholism and reducing his or her emotional distress?

In answering the question of responsibility, a therapist may be guided by a theoretical model, professional training, or personal history. Suffice it to say, there is no one right way. Instead, we offer some guidelines to assist the therapist in addressing three common impasse patterns involving drug abuse:

1. *Hidden agenda*—In these cases, the members of the couple have presented other issues and have avoided raising the issue of drug abuse. The therapist may have suspicions during the course of treatment, but the couple never opens up the issue. Consequently, the therapist opts to focus on the couple's presenting problem, but therapy soon bogs down.

Because the therapist suspects substance abuse, he or she is left searching for an opening into this area. The extent of the denial alone hints at the power of the issue for the couple. Consequently, a direct confrontation would probably lead to an indignant denial and, if the issue is pushed further, the couple's unilateral termination of therapy. Instead, the therapist may backtrack and explore more of the family of origin dynamics specifically related to substance abuse.

Therapist: It occurs to me that I neglected to ask all my questions concerning your families. If you would bear with me, I need to ask a few more. For example, what were the patterns of alcohol usage or were there any family members who abused alcohol?

By exploring the family of origin themes, the therapist is bringing up the issue of substance abuse but distances the issue from current dynamics. In doing so, the therapist attempts to bring the past into the present.

Therapist: Carl, you describe your father as very quiet, but to help fill out my picture of him, did he drink at all?

Carl: Well, he liked a few beers at night.

Therapist: How much is a few?

Carl: I don't know, maybe a couple.

Therapist: Do you drink in a similar way?

Carl: Maybe; I like a few beers now and again.

Although not as forthcoming as one might wish, Carl has opened up the issue of his drinking. The past is now present and the therapist can now pursue the issue by asking more questions of Carl and bringing Lynn into the discussion.

Therapist: Lynn, before I ask you about your family, I was wondering if Carl's description of his drinking matches your perception.

2. *Unilateral concern*—More typically the case, one member of the couple brings in the other member because of his or her drug abuse. While the partner details the abuse, the alcoholic, for example, sits passively or belligerently belittles and minimizes the complaints. The partner with the complaint lays out the problem for the therapist to solve. For the therapist, this is a lose-lose position. If the therapist allies with the concerned partner, therapy resembles a tag-team wrestling match against the abuser. (The alcoholic always wins because only he or she can truly stop drinking.)

If, however, the therapist, by minimizing the complaints, attempts to engage and ally with the alcoholic as a means of establishing rapport, the concerned spouse becomes even more concerned. It appears after all of his or her efforts to coerce the partner into treatment, the therapist is not taking the substance abuse seriously. Worse yet, it looks like the therapist is believing the abusive partner's excuses and explanation.

In these cases, the therapist usually stands at a fork in the road: ally with the concerned partner and make substance abuse the chief therapeutic issue or put the issue on the shelf while exploring the couple's dynamics. There are pros and cons to each choice. The alliance with one spouse directly threatens the abusing partner and raises his or her resistance to therapy. But by not focusing on the substance abuse the concerned spouse may feel defeated.

Walking a fine line between the two choices, the therapist acknowledges the issue while exploring the couple's other dynamics.

Therapist: Clearly, the use of alcohol has been a continuing issue in your relationship. My concern is that it has come to dominate your marriage to the point where you both have lost sight of one another. What I would like to do is put the issue of alcohol on the shelf for a short period of time. I would like to spend a few sessions talking about other issues in your relationship. We will return to this issue of alcohol after I have a more complete picture of who you each are and who you are together.

3. *Bilateral concern but with repeated failures*—The couple present the drug abuse as the central issue but also describe a history of failed attempts at change. Therapy is a roller-coaster ride of high hopes and drop-offs into reality as the abuser with all good intentions makes promises that he or she inevitably breaks. The abuser maintains that he or she could stop at any time.

In cases where substance abuse is clearly identified by both partners, the therapist would be justified in insisting that couples therapy will be effective only after successful individual rehabilitation or concurrent with individual treatments (O'Farrell, 1991).

However, in situations where the abuser resists individual rehabilitation, rather than refuse treatment, the therapist may draw up a contract with the couple.

Therapist (*to the abusing partner*):   Although acknowledging that alcohol is a significant issue in your marriage, you also say that you do not abuse it and have complete control over it. It is not my job nor do I wish to judge whether or not you drink too much. Instead, in order for the therapy to work and to avoid endless discussion of did you or did you not drink too much, let's draw up a contract. I would like you and your partner to establish a maximum daily limit on your alcohol intake, something that you both agree on. I will merely ask each session how the contract has held up since the last time we met.

Notice, the therapist has created a win-win situation. First, the couple are asked to negotiate an agreement on an issue central to their dynamics. This alone is a therapeutic intervention. More importantly, if the abuser upholds the agreement, a significant step has been taken. But, even if the abuser violates the contract, the therapist is in a stronger position to insist on rehabilitation. If the abuser still refuses a rehabilitation program, the therapist can offer individual treatment to the partner.

Therapist: From both of your accounts, our contract has been broken several times. It is clear to me that little will change in your relationship as long as alcohol dominates your marriage. If you [abuser] will not enter rehabilitation, then the best I can do is offer individual therapy to your partner and help her [or him] decide what she [or he] wishes to do with this issue.

Sexuality and Intimacy

Although perhaps not the bricks in a couple's relationship, sexuality is certainly a key element in the mortar that holds the bricks together. Why we are drawn sexually toward one person and not another is a question probably best left to poets. Still, it is fair to say that every intimate relationship, at least initially, possesses a passionate "chemical" reaction.

Sometimes, as therapists sitting with a highly conflicted couple, we can forget that at one time a passionate fire burned between the two partners. The flame may now be reduced to a smoldering ember barely visible to the eye or, unfortunately, in some cases the flame has been replaced by a chilling coldness. Yet ironically, sex is the only thing some couples can agree on.

Rarely is the couple's sex life their chief complaint. Instead, communication or arguments over time spent together hint at a gap between the partners, an emotional gap suggesting a sexual gap. Moreover, the anger spilling over in a session may hint at a frustrated sex life. The couple may not know how to openly and comfortably talk about sex, or they may have argued about it so much that it has become a taboo topic.

Therapists also differ in their own comfort level with the issue. Some therapists easily ask about a couple's sexual functioning in the first session. The sexual inquiries are asked in the same tone as "Who does the grocery shopping?" For other therapists, because they themselves are uneasy about the topic or because they are not sure what to do if or when the issue comes up, they avoid the subject. If, however, sex is a central theme for the couple that is left unaddressed, then even after some initial therapeutic gains in other areas an impasse looms on the horizon.

Before offering guidelines on managing this potential impasse, we first need to acknowledge the influence of gender roles on a couple's sexual functioning. This is followed by a conceptual model for viewing sex and intimacy within the couple's context.

In their study of American couples, Blumstein and Schwartz (1991) found that heterosexual couples suffer from "male only" and "female only" gender-role prescriptions with regards to sexual functioning. Men are expected to be the sexual aggressor and feel the need to perform. Women, on the other hand, are required to be more passive and as a result may feel restrained and not in control of their own experience. Moreover, the stereotyped characteristics of male aggression and female passivity create a circular mythology whereby it is believed that men need sex more than women.

It is easy to imagine any number of sexual impasses in a couple's relationship flowing out of the gender-role prescriptions. A man might grow tired of always initiating sex and may wish his mate would do so. A woman may deny her own sexual desires in the name of "proper" behavior. Another woman may be angry and feel rejected because her husband does not fulfill his aggressor role as frequently as she might like. Another man may be a very inconsiderate lover believing his mate is not "really" interested in sex and over the years his belief becomes a self-fulfilling prophecy as his wife, feeling chronically used and sexually ignored, loses interest in sex.

Along the same lines, men and women learn different ways of being physically close. "Just hold me," the woman says. "But, I thought you wanted to have sex," says the man. Whereas women may seek closeness without any sexual intent, for many men sex is the chief means of obtaining intimacy. It is in the sexual embrace that they may feel intimately connected to their partners.

Both roles may also mitigate against a mutually satisfying sexual relationship. Because men are valued more for what they do than for who they are, male sexuality emphasizes skill and performance (Meth & Pacsik, 1990). Thus, a male's attention may remain focused on himself whereupon he asks his partner, "So, how was that?" Or, translated to male terminology, "How was I?" In contrast, the female passive sexual role denies the woman full authority over her sexuality. The role dictates responsiveness to the partner's initiatives.

For couples therapists, however, the discussion of sexuality is not an abstract debate but a difficult chicken or egg question. Are the couple's sexual problems an outgrowth of their emotional dynamics? Are the sexual difficulties the root of the couple's problems? Or, is sex used as a weapon in the couple's war with one another? For example, is the withholding of sex a form of punishment for an earlier transgression?

As a means of conceptualizing the role of sexuality in a relationship, Schnarch (1991) proposed an integration of sexual and couples therapy. Distancing himself from traditional sex therapy with its focus on "pathology" and sexual dysfunction, Schnarch believed sexual difficulties are a process in the relationship rather than a personal defect. In addressing the above chicken or egg dilemma of couples therapists, Schnarch (1991) observed, "The relationship between sexual and non-sexual problems is complex: (a) each can be a manifestation of the other, (b) each can have relatively unique etiology, and (c) the interaction of the two often creates such an enmeshed system that 'chicken and egg' distinctions become a moot point" (p. 146). Thus, to separate sexual functioning from the relationship is an arbitrary distinction. Rather, sexual functioning is embedded within the couple's intimate relationship.

In conceptualizing couples' sexual difficulties, Schnarch builds on Bowen's concept of the differentiation of self (Kerr & Bowen, 1988) (see chapter 6). Briefly, a person's level of differentiation is reflected in the ability to maintain one's sense of self in close proximity to a partner. The more differentiated one is, the more one is able to enjoy both intimacy and aloneness. Intimacy is achieved without sacrificing a sense of self. When alone, the well-differentiated individual possesses the capacity for self-validation.

The less differentiated the partner, the more the relationship sparks anxious ambivalence. In the intimacy of the relationship, the less differentiated individual is drawn to fusion with the partner—"If you don't love me, I am nothing." However, the movement toward fusion ignites a fear of engulfment—"I will be swallowed up and I will be controlled." Thus, the couple's relationship resembles the movement of an accordion. At any given moment, the partners may be moving toward or away from one another. Their arguments, therefore, may actually serve the purpose of creating distance when the fear of fusion is too great. But also, when the emotional distance becomes too great and a fear of aloneness takes over, arguments serve to bring the partners back in contact with one another.

For Schnarch (1991), the partners' level of differentiation determines their capacity for intimacy. He defined intimacy as the unilateral capacity of the individual to maintain a clearly defined identity as one and one's partner disclose "core aspects of self." In other words, a couple's level of intimacy is reflected in the partners' ability to share their unique thoughts and feelings without eliciting anxiety or control in one another. For example, Lynn could go out to dinner with a girlfriend without Carl retaliating with passive-aggressiveness. Likewise, it would be all right for Carl to watch the "big game" on television without Lynn feeling rejected. Or, more specifically, Lynn and Carl could discuss their feelings about one another and their relationship without setting off anxiety alarms and generating defensive patterns.

The anxiety based in each partner's level of differentiation spills over into the sexual relationship (Schnarch, 1991). Sexual boredom, for instance, is seen as a systemic defense against intimacy and eroticism. Thus, within the interrelationship of emotional and sexual functioning, sexual difficulties reflect both the partners' individual and the couples' dynamics. For example, if Lynn and Carl are uneasy discussing their differences with one another and they both are ambivalent in the intimacy of their relationship, one wonders how this is mirrored in their sex life. Or, alternatively, one wonders to what degree they each were predisposed toward sexual difficulties because of their respective levels of differentiation.

As a means of exploring and responding to potential sexual impasses, we offer the following guidelines:

1. Impasses may be avoided and a great deal of time saved if the issue of sexuality is explored during the assessment phase of treatment. But, because sexuality is a tender, awkward issue for many couples, the therapist must time his or her questions to match the couple's comfort level. Although assessing the couple's dynamics is of primary importance in the beginning of therapy, equally important is establishing a working therapeutic alliance with the couple. If, for example, the partners shift uneasily in their chairs and become defensive as the therapist explores their sexual functioning, the therapist needs to listen to these signals and move off the topic. It is better to put the issue on the shelf for the time being than to risk offending one or both partners.

2. Once the issue is introduced, however, understanding each partner's myths of sexuality deepens the therapist's understanding of the couple. Myths may reflect cultural beliefs about men's and women's sexuality or more personal myths originating from the respective families of origin. More importantly, exploring the partners' myths of one another's sexuality not only opens up the issue but also is a window into the couple's capacity for intimacy.

3. Unless it is the couple's chief complaint, sexuality should be initially addressed as a manifestation of the couple's dynamics. Thus, rather than struggle with the chicken or egg question, assume the couple's sexuality is determined by the partners' capacity for intimacy.

4. Although the couple have not identified sex as a reason for beginning therapy and they appear defensive when the issue is brought up, listen for hints that open the door into the area.

Lynn: I don't feel close to Carl any more.

Therapist: What do you feel like when the two of you are sexually intimate?

5. Once the issue has been brought up, assess the extent of the problem:

> Has the couple experienced difficulties from the beginning of the rela-
> tionship?
> When did the sexual difficulties emerge?
> Did other stresses coincide with the sexual problems?
> Have they been able to talk about it, have they ignored it, or have they
> been afraid to bring it up?
> How have they tried to remedy the situation?

6.   If the relationship dynamics have improved and the couple has made progress in communication and problem resolution but the sexual difficulties linger, then a referral to a sex therapist may be appropriate. This is done, however, only with an understanding and agreement on everyone's part—the therapist and the members of the couple. As part of the agreement, the sexual difficulties are clearly defined and the couple is motivated to pursue sex therapy.

7.   In order to develop a comfortable approach to sexuality in couples therapy, the therapist needs to address the questions of normality and gender. What is "normal" sexuality for a couple? What is "normal" sexuality for men? What is "normal" sexuality for women? By clarifying one's own myths concerning sexuality, a therapist is in a better position to communicate his or her beliefs as well as to facilitate a couple's exploration of the topic.

8. Above all else, sexual impasses evolve because the couple and the therapist have danced around the issue. Ultimately, it is the therapist's responsibility if the issue has been avoided.

EXTRARELATIONSHIP AFFAIRS

Unbeknownst to the couples therapist, a fourth person sometimes exercises a strong influence on the treatment process. In some situations an affair is hidden from the therapist and spouse. A hidden affair almost always results in a treatment impasse because (1) the therapist is proceeding without all the pieces to the puzzle, (2) the treatment process is tainted by a basic dishonesty, and (3) the triangle created by the partners and lover works against therapeutic progress.

In other situations a therapist may be placed in a clinical dilemma when the partner in the extrarelationship affair lets the therapist in on the secret. This partner, who may profess a level of guilt over the ongoing affair, is not ready to terminate it and wants the therapist to "keep" the secret.

Finally, in a third situation, the affair has been openly acknowledged, or in many cases "discovered" by the partner, but the partner involved in the affair minimizes it or has announced that it is over. Unfortunately, as treatment progresses, it becomes painfully clear that the affair continues to greatly influence the couple's relationship.

Before offering specific responses to the impasse, extrarelationship affairs need to be placed within a conceptual context.

Moultrup (1990) defined an extramarital affair as a relationship outside of the marriage that affects the level of intimacy within the marriage, creates an emotional distance between the partners, and creates an unhealthy deficit in the level of intimacy in the marital relationship. Pittman (1989) made a distinction between adultery and infidelity. Adultery is a sexual act outside the marriage whereas infidelity is a sexual dishonesty within the marriage that may threaten the relationship.

Building upon his concept of infidelity, Pittman (1989) identified four patterns of infidelity:

1. *Accidental infidelities*—Accidental infidelities are spontaneous, unplanned sexual experiences—for example, a brief affair on a business trip. The meaning of the experience for the marital relationship depends upon how the person defines it. For example, following an accidental infidelity, a person may experience guilt, remorse, and a vague sense of anxiety. Thus, the experience possesses a negative connotation. Another person, however, may have found the experience pleasant and is able to justify what occurred as inconsequential because no one got hurt. If the latter is the definition of the experience, then the person may become a philanderer.

2. *Philanderers*—Sexual conquests are the chief motivating force for the philanderer. What is or is not occurring in the current relationship has little influence on the philanderer's behavior. The philanderer's roving eye is always on the alert for the next opportunity.

3. *Romantic affairs*—A head-over-heels attraction drives romantic affairs. That overwhelming sense of being in love leaves little room for logic and responsibilities. It is as if the participants are lost in love, ignoring or denying other emotions such as guilt or shame.

4. *Marital arrangements*—At the heart of marital arrangements are badly flawed marriages that no one wants to change. Affairs create and maintain an emotional distance that both partners collude in keeping. Both partners may know or may not really want to know about the affairs. Or, in some cases, the affairs are a symptom of a stormy marriage in which the affairs are acts of revenge that inject passion and jealousy into the relationship.

In understanding the dynamic functions of extrarelationship affairs, Moultrop (1990) built on Bowen's (1978) concept of triangles. As a brief review, Bowen (1978) viewed the triangle as the fundamental unit of an emotional system where there are two inside and one outside positions. When there is tension between two people, the tension is diffused by "triangling-in" a third person. The inside position is the desired position during times of calm, but in times of tension the outside position is preferred.

The emotional triangle, therefore, is a dynamic process of shifting movements from being inside to being outside to being inside. For example, in times of stress external to the relationship—for example, a loss of a job—the partners may turn to one another for support. But as time goes by, the financial stress increases the stress between the partners. One spouse may say, "I do not think you are looking hard enough to find another job." The partner replies, "Why can't you support me through this difficult time?" It is in this setting that one or both parties may triangle-in a third person. It may be as simple as each partner turning to a friend to complain or it may also be fertile ground for an extrarelationship affair.

An affair has the effect of increasing the emotional distance between two people as a result of one partner's involvement with another person (Moultrup, 1990). Thus, extrarelationship affairs may serve to regulate distance within a relationship. Or, the affair may be a defense against or avoidance of intimacy. The philanderer described above moves from one affair to another while fleeing his or her fear of intimacy. Each affair is as shallow as the last one. Even romantic affairs suffer from illusions of intimacy. The illusion is that in the throes of love we have found a kindred spirit, someone who loves us for who we are and understands us deeply. Of course, the illusion is evident to outsiders but is never initially apparent to the lovers. It takes time for disillusions to develop.

The triangle created by an affair contains rich meanings for the individuals involved. For example, both Carl and Lynn entered marriage expecting to be faithful and emotionally close with one another. After the birth of their child and with increased financial pressures, there was less and less time for one another. The marriage began to feel less like a haven and more like a trap, a trap where individual autonomy was lost and each looked at the other resenting the demands. The early positive closeness of a new marriage was slowly being replaced by a sense of negative closeness. Worse yet, both Carl and Lynn felt incapable of changing the balance in the relationship. Within this context, an affair was just as probable as the decision to enter therapy.

Besides the various patterns and meanings of extrarelationship affairs, infidelities are most likely to occur at turning points in the relationship. For example, the most common transition points are the birth of a child and the death of a parent (Moultrup, 1990). Parenting demands pull a couple together but sometimes in negative ways. Who is going to get up with the baby arguments replace lying in bed and holding one another. Moreover, parenting responsibilities were unimaginable before the birth of the first child. For Lynn, those responsibilities take the form of guilt over working full-time. For Carl, the financial responsibilities loom heavily.

An affair may also be an attempt to remove oneself from the intense grief felt because of a significant loss in one's life. The affair not only emotionally distances a person from the pain but also serves to reaffirm one's own vitality. Any number of other transition points also have the potential to ignite an affair—for example, the loss of a job, financial pressures, or difficulties with children.

In conceptualizing affairs, however, the therapist must assess the affair's meaning. For example, it may be erroneous to automatically assume that an affair is a statement about a couple's relationship. An affair may be a unilateral act on the part of one mate. Detailed questioning may reveal a compulsive history of extrarelationship affairs. As Pittman (1989) points out, there are philanderers who will seek extrarelationship affairs regardless of the quality of the couple's relationship.

However, the meaning of an affair may be a direct reflection of the couple's relationship. A long-standing, bitter relationship is more likely than not a precursor to affairs by one or both partners. In other cases, such as the marital arrangements described above, both parties collude in "secret" affairs. Again, to successfully address the issues surrounding an affair, a therapist must first assess and understand the meaning of the affair for each partner.

On a more practical level, the question remains as to what to do when an affair surfaces in the course of couples therapy or when it is the basis of the therapeutic impasse. For example, in some cases, both partners are aware of a past affair, but the issue has been "swept under the carpet." The unresolved pain, anger, and guilt of the affair have festered and lie at the heart of the couple's current difficulties. In these cases, the affair is handled as one would any problem from the past that strongly affects the present.

More often than not, and by its very nature, an affair is a secret. It may be a secret the therapist suspects or a secret the partner tells the therapist. Either situation presents a difficult dilemma for the couples therapist and calls for a clinical judgment and decision.

In cases where one strongly suspects an affair is the basis of the impasse, the therapist may ask for individual sessions.

Therapist: I believe we have made some progress with your relationship, but I think we are stuck at this particular time. I would like to meet with you each individually to further appreciate your individual positions.

In the individual sessions, the therapist introduces the issue of affairs and offers the opportunity for the partner to address the issue.

Therapist: Carl, I know things have been pretty rough between you and Lynn. In times like this, sometimes a man can feel drawn to other women. I was wondering if you have felt anything like that?

However, if the therapist is met with a series of blanket denials but he or she still has a strong suspicion of an affair, the therapist may address the issue directly.

Therapist: Carl, I might be crazy, but I have this strong feeling that you are drawn to another woman. Am I just off base?

If the therapist is met with further denials then he or she may resume the couple's sessions but with a vague sense of unease because the impasse has still not been resolved. If, however, Carl admits to an affair, the therapist is in the awkward position of knowing a secret. In a variation on a theme, a partner has told the therapist about the affair and in so doing is dumping the question of revealing the secret in the lap of the therapist.

The basic dishonesty of secret affairs is antithetical to the norm of therapy. Still, therapists disagree as to the clinical management of a secret affair. For example, Pittman (1989) believed marriages can survive the revelation of an affair and that they should be revealed if the marriage is to become healthy. Moultrup (1990), however, argued that the therapist needs to weigh the following factors before making the decision to reveal a secret affair: (1) whether the affair occurred in the past or is currently active, (2) the dynamic meaning of the affair, (3) the current dynamics of the couple, and (4) the dynamic implications of revealing the affair at the present time.

For example, when a partner reveals the affair to the therapist, he or she may be asking for the therapist's permission to continue. Or, the partner, out of a sense of guilt, may be asking the therapist to reveal the secret. Or, the partner may wish to shock the spouse into paying attention to the issues which are still active in the relationship that first prompted the affair.

Because an affair and the accompanying secret may have multiple meanings, Moultrup (1990) cautioned a therapist to resist a dogmatic approach to extrarelationship affairs where treatment is refused until the affair is terminated and revealed. Instead, treatment will be more effective if specific interventions are postponed until the emotional meaning of the affair is ascertained.

A secret, however, places a therapist in a difficult position. As a guiding principle, it is a question of effectiveness—that is, what does the therapist need to best do his or her work. For example, some therapists may be able to adopt Moultrup's position and even while knowing the secret patiently work in individual sessions to discover the meaning of the affair while still conducting effective couples therapy. But an overall danger of this approach is that while attempting to discover the meaning of the affair, the therapist has inadvertently formed an alliance with one partner against another. In these cases, the therapist's avoidance of the affair in the couple's sessions fosters the impasse.

In managing a secret, a conservative approach is for the therapist to express his or her reservations about continuing couples therapy to the spouse involved in the extrarelationship affair. Accordingly, the therapist offers individual therapy to that spouse or offers to continue couples therapy as long as the affair-involved partner enters individual therapy with another therapist. Thus, the therapist avoids colluding in the secret by placing the responsibility for it back on the partner. The central message to the partner is:

Therapist: You have chosen to be involved in a secret affair for a variety of reasons. Individual therapy offers you the opportunity to understand your motivations for having an affair and for you to decide whether or not you wish to tell your spouse.

Case Summary

At first glance, it would appear that Lynn's and Carl's presenting complaints and dynamics are fairly straightforward. Here is a young couple overwhelmed by the birth of their first child and all the accompanying financial and child-care stresses. The conflict in gender roles is clearly seen in Lynn's request for domestic help and Carl's reluctance to help her. While family of origin dynamics would predict many of their difficulties, both Lynn and Carl report feeling loved and respected by their respective families. In many ways, these were strengths they each brought into the relationship.

Despite these inherent strengths and the partners' commitment to the relationship, therapy was resulting in limited progress. The initial gains leveled off and therapy continued, riding the wave of the early momentum.

Sensing an impasse, the therapist formed a number of hypotheses:

1. *Transference/countertransference*—Are strong individual transferences operating? Lynn is Carl's critical mother. So, regardless of Lynn's change in behavior, Carl's passive-aggressiveness is his dominant response. Likewise, Carl is Lynn's aloof, noninvolved father. Therefore, nothing Carl does is enough in Lynn's eyes.

What are Lynn's and Carl's transferences to the therapist? Is the therapist Lynn's long lost father? Is the therapist Carl's engulfing mother?

Is the therapist's countertransference an issue? Are Lynn and Carl stirring memories from the therapist's family of origin? Is the therapist's effectiveness diminishing because of his or her frustration with the lack of progress? Does he or she resent Lynn's dominance? Is he or she annoyed by Carl's passivity? Are Lynn's and Carl's dynamics too close to the therapist's own marital dynamics or do they replicate his or her parents' marriage?

2. *Gender issues*—Besides the obvious gender-role conflict concerning household chores, are more subtle gender influences at work? While Carl welcomes Lynn's working and financial support, he may also feel diminished by this. His father brought home the bacon and his mother stayed at home. Does he feel less of a man because his wife works and makes more money than he does? Does he criticize her as a means of diminishing her?

What amount of guilt does Lynn feel for leaving her baby in day care or with her mother? What does she do with her guilt? Does it take the form of anger and criticism directed toward Carl? Does she feel she is a "bad" mother for working when her baby is so young and does she resent Carl for it?

3. *Content themes*—Of the content themes discussed above, Carl acknowledged that his father liked a few beers in the evening and that he did as well. Carl saw no concern for his father's nor his own drinking pattern. While Lynn was concerned with Carl taking care of the baby after a few beers, she basically shared Carl's view that his drinking was inconsequential to the marital problems.

Still, from the therapist's perspective, Carl's basic response tendency to withdraw from conflict and his comfort with a few beers almost every evening was cause for concern. The drinking may not be a problem now, but it had the potential to become one. However, at this stage of the couple's development, neither partner expressed much concern over the issue and the therapist chose to move to other issues.

The theme of sexuality did spontaneously present itself. In a discussion of the diminished time the partners had for one another, Lynn mentioned in passing that their sex life was slowly becoming nonexistent. The remark was not lost on Carl as he quickly shot Lynn a disapproving look. Lynn saw the anger in Carl's eyes, quickly dropped the topic, and lowered her head, at which point the therapist entered the picture.

Therapist: I have found a couple's sex life really suffers when there is a baby in the house. Both people are usually dead tired from work and all the household responsibilities. Sometimes all they want to do is sit in front of the television. I was wondering how your intimacy has changed since Jenn's birth?

With this comment, the therapist attempts to further open up an area only briefly mentioned by the couple. Notice, the couple's diminished sex life is placed within a normal, expected context. If what they are experiencing is normal for couples with small children, then the topic is more open for discussion. In response to the above reframing, sexuality became a topic for therapy.

Initially, both Lynn and Carl blamed their lack of sexual intimacy on the obvious demands of a baby and work and general fatigue. However, once the issue was an accepted agenda for therapy, the therapist gathered a brief sexual history on the couple. Although both Lynn and Carl described their sex life as good, they both described it as sporadic at best. They may be intimate for several days in a row and then a week or two may pass before they were intimate again. Their sex life appeared to mirror their emotional life, which was characterized by closeness followed by imposed distance.

After exploring the facts concerning their sexual functioning, the therapist was convinced that the sexual difficulties were not a result of a lack of sexual knowledge on either spouse's part but rather a physical manifestation of the couple's underlying dynamics. Consequently, a number of clinical hypotheses were formed:

What role did suppressed anger play in the couple's current sexual pattern?
> Was Carl angry and resentful of the attention Lynn now gave the baby?
> Was Lynn angry at the overwhelming sense of burden she attributed to Carl's lack of support?
> Did either partner feel hurt and rejected by the other partner's actions?

Who blamed whom?
> Did Carl completely blame Lynn for the sexual difficulties?
> Did Lynn blame Carl?
> Did either party blame him- or herself for the problem?

How did the new responsibilities of parenthood affect the couple's sexual functioning?
> Was Carl overwhelmed by the new responsibilities of fatherhood?
> Did he worry about how he would provide for his wife's and daughter's future?
> Did Lynn worry about being a "good" mother?

Did either party bring problematic issues of intimacy into the marriage?
> How comfortable was Carl in an intimate relationship? Did he fear engulfment? What were his experiences in his family of origin and early dating relationships?
> What were Lynn's experiences in intimate relationships? What was the legacy from her parents' divorce?

While exploring these hypotheses, the therapist looked for ways of breaking the impasse and liberating the couple from their rigid stances with one another.

The next chapter is concerned with breaking the impasse, fostering a recommitment to the relationship, and moving toward termination.

Homosexual Couples

Recent books have highlighted therapeutic work with same-sex couples (Carl, 1990; Silverstein, 1990). Although there is no specific treatment approach preferable for or more effective with homosexual couples nor are homosexual couples any more vulnerable to problems and dissatisfaction than heterosexual couples, there are issues unique to working with homosexual couples (Peplau, 1993; Weisstub & Shoenfeld, 1987).

A chief issue in working with a gay or lesbian couple is the impact of a homophobic society on the individual and couple. Discrimination denies the homosexual couple the social supports heterosexual couples take for granted. A spouse may enhance the way the heterosexual employee is viewed by an employer; however, a homosexual significant other may be a liability to job advancement.

Moreover, when a man and woman publicly declare themselves a couple it is more likely a cause for celebration among friends and family. When the homosexual individual enters a relationship, it may signal a crisis for the individual or couple concerning the relationship's disclosure to friends and family (Appleby & Anastas, in press). The simple act of publicly defining themselves as "a couple" must be weighed against the potential effects of discrimination.

Also, as mentioned in Chapter 2, internalized, homophobic attitudes undermine individual self-esteem and work against establishing a healthy relationship (Fisher, 1993; Friedman, 1991). Thus, same-gender couples carry into therapy the deleterious, societal effects of discrimination and must negotiate how best to exist as a couple within the broader culture.

But besides the issues homosexual couples carry into the therapist's office, once therapy has begun, the therapist's countertransference attitudes and values may also affect the treatment process. Despite education, training and supervision, a therapist has not been spared the influence of a homophobic culture. Attitudes and values concerning homosexuality may be established long before a person even begins training as a therapist. Although a person may believe training and supervision have immuned him or her to homophobic attitudes, this may not always be the case.

Before treating a homosexual couple, the best one can do is be aware of one's personal values and feelings regarding homosexuality. Effective therapy occurs within a noncritical atmosphere fostered by the therapist. If the therapist's own attitudes or values concerning homosexuality diminish this atmosphere, then therapy is compromised. Further still, the unaware therapist may create his or her own roadblocks to therapeutic progress.

We are not arguing that every therapist should be able to effectively treat homosexual couples. Rather, a therapist should be aware of any potential biases and decide accordingly whether to begin treatment or to make a referral to someone else.

However, once therapy has begun, potential impasses may be avoided by (1) exploring, in the assessment phase, the impact of homosexual discrimination on each partner and its impact on the couple's relationship and (2) examining the roles they have created in relationship to one another and how these roles influence their sexual behavior as well as the pragmatic issues of property and finances.

Summary

If first- or second-order change interventions are effective, then therapy moves toward termination. Unfortunately, in many cases, couples therapy bogs down as the content of the sessions appears to go over the same old ground with little therapeutic movement. Other than the initial gains in the early phases of therapy, the therapist and couple find the lack of progress frustrating. While the members of the couple wonder if therapy is worth it, the therapist rushes to read more technique books hoping he or she will discover a magical technique to move therapy along.

Instead, the therapist may explore process and content themes that are possibly at the heart of the impasse. Transference and countertransference process issues left unexamined may be inhibiting progress. At other times, content themes such as drug abuse or threats of domestic violence may be obliquely mentioned or only hinted at.

Although the observable signs of an impasse—increasing apathy and frustration, the repetitive nature of the complaints, a sense that after the initial gains little progress has been made—are readily apparent to the observant therapist, the causes are left to be explored. Frequently, successfully exploring the causes is a matter of formulating the right questions and asking them at the right time.

For example, the hidden agenda of alcohol abuse may be vigorously protected by one or both partners. In some cases, the partners may not be aware of the impact of alcohol abuse on their relationship; thus, it is not seen as part of their "communication" problem. In other cases, alcohol abuse has been woven into an overall pattern of denial. In either case, exploring the issue risks raising one or both partners' defenses.

Proceeding with care, a therapist may wait for one partner to present an opening into the topic. Taking this as a signal that the alcohol abuse is a concern, the therapist begins to explore the role of alcohol in each of the partner's lives and its role in the relationship.

At other times without an opening, a therapist is left little choice other than to directly confront the issue. In these situations, therapy has ground to a slow crawl with little hope in sight, and the partners have offered few openings into deeper issues. Left on its own the impasse would dominate the sessions until one member of the couple unilaterally terminates with a series of missed appointments or by refusing further participation. Thus, after the failure of first- and second-order interventions, the therapist has little to lose by directly confronting the hidden agendas.

Breaking an impasse with direct confrontation is akin to cutting a diamond. If it is tapped with the right amount of force at the right time, it opens up wonderfully. Although the right force and the right time are a matter of experience and judgment, the therapist stands a better chance of success if the therapeutic alliances with each partner are as strong as the therapist can make them. Direct confrontation has a better chance when the partners believe the therapist truly has their best interests at heart and is acting to alleviate their pain. The following chapter will explore techniques for impasse resolution and ways to move toward termination.

CHAPTER TEN

Impasse Resolution and Movement Toward Termination

If first- or second-order interventions have been successful, then therapy progresses toward the couple's goals. As discussed in the previous chapter, process and content themes, however, may conspire to create a therapeutic impasse. The impasse may be unconscious—for example, a person's fear of intimacy may manifest itself in sexual difficulties. In other situations, the impasse is fueled by conscious decisions such as a secret extramarital affair or the couple's unexpressed ambivalence about continuing the relationship.

Regardless of the unconscious or conscious motivations behind the impasse, the experience for the therapist and couple is the same. Therapy is going nowhere. In these cases, the therapist is left with the difficult task of addressing the impasse if therapy is to progress.

Besides the specific suggestions offered for the individual content themes, the following interventions are generic responses to both process and content impasses: (1) therapist's use of self, (2) asking what if change did occur, (3) seeking solutions by accepting what is, and (4) presenting individual therapy as a treatment option.

If the process and content themes are successfully addressed, then the partners renew their commitment to the relationship. This may occur on a verbal level—"I feel much stronger about the relationship"—or nonverbally as each partner recommits to the relationship goals. In either case, this recommitment to the relationship signals a transition in therapy. Most notably, the individual partners shift from blaming to collaborating. This does not necessarily mean smooth sailing for the couple but it is an unofficial renewal of vows to one another and does begin the termination process.

Impasse Resolution Techniques

THERAPIST'S USE OF SELF

One does not have to be a highly skilled clinician to recognize an impasse; it feels like a dull toothache. After all participants experience the rise in hope in the initial stages of therapy, the true work of therapy begins. The couple's relationship is put under the microscope as the therapist probes the partners as individuals and each of their roles in creating and perpetuating the current problems. This is not necessarily a pleasant experience. The end results may be deeply satisfying, but the means to those ends may be arduous.

An impasse signals that the couple cannot or is unwilling to move forward. There is a vague awareness that the next step in therapy may mean an uncovering of conscious and unconscious agendas that appear too threatening to the couple. These agendas may loom like land mines with the ability to destroy the relationship. Consequently, the couple may, like the tide, move in or away from the issue.

An impasse is most evident as session after session covers the same ground. The issues may appear to be clearly identified and the therapist may have attempted to intervene to move the couple toward their established goals but, unfortunately, nothing changes. For example, Lynn's and Carl's requests of one another appear straightforward, but despite the therapist's initial mediations, little progress had been made. Each session begins with a veiled or not so veiled presentation of evidence that neither party has changed. Lynn still does not find Carl trying to be helpful and Carl still feels criticized.

Sometimes a couple will continue to come to the therapy sessions even though there is little, if any, progress. They may come because each secretly believes the therapist will either vindicate his or her position or change the other partner. At other times, the couple continue to come out of fear that there are no other alternatives and that without therapy the relationship may dissolve. Other couples continue to come because the partner who initiated therapy is strongly insistent that therapy should proceed and the reluctant mate continues to participate in a passive-aggressive manner.

Lynn and Carl combined all three of the above reasons. As a combination, these three motivations for continuing therapy were part of the impasse. Each wanted the other to change, each feared the relationship would end, and Carl passively resisted therapy.

Attempting to break the impasse, the therapist may use his or her own reactions to the progress of therapy—the therapist's use of self (Worden, 1994). In doing so, the therapist may address any or all the above motivations. For example:

Therapist: I have noticed that each of our sessions feels like a repeat of the last one. I could be wrong, but I believe you are each trying to persuade me that the other is at fault and that I am supposed to change the other. Am I misperceiving this?

For this intervention to succeed, a strong therapeutic alliance must be established. Without the couple's belief that the therapist is being honest and has the best interest of the couple at heart, the above comment comes across in a callous, judgmental manner. Thus, instead of being helpful, the therapist would have then put the couple on the defensive and greatly jeopardized the therapeutic alliance.

Therapist: I know I have felt frustrated trying to realize the goals we have set for therapy, but I was wondering what each of you feel so far about our sessions?

With this statement and question, the therapist is conducting a type of therapeutic inventory: Where do things currently stand? Again, the therapist is not blaming the couple for the lack of progress but rather is using personal reactions as an entree into the couple's experience of therapy. Depending upon the response, the therapist is then in a position to explore each partner's fear for the relationship.

Therapist: Lynn, because you initiated therapy, I was wondering what you feel now?

Therapist: Carl, you said earlier that you were reluctant to begin therapy, but as we have gotten into some of the issues that divide you and Lynn, I wonder what you have been thinking or feeling about therapy?

In opening up a discussion on the process of therapy itself, the therapist offers Lynn and Carl the opportunity to bring up their fears and concerns. However, if the therapist believes one or both partners are less than forthcoming or that they are unable to label their concerns, the therapist may probe the issue directly.

Therapist: People usually seek couples therapy at the most difficult times of their relationship. Usually there are hopes that the therapy will be helpful, but sometimes there are also fears of what it means if therapy does not help. I was wondering what you both worry about if we are not successful in therapy.

Finally, the passive-aggressive stance of the reluctant partner may be the chief impediment to change. Carl, for example, agreed to therapy only after Lynn continually brought it up and as a means of pacifying her complaints. He was a reluctant participant who believed and perceived that therapy would only be another forum for Lynn's complaints. For therapy to progress past this impasse, the therapist walks a fine line of addressing Carl's passive-aggressiveness but without criticizing him. To accomplish this, the therapist reframes Carl's behavior as protective of the couple.

Therapist: Carl, I know you are not a great believer is this therapy business and that you are here primarily because of Lynn's request, but I was wondering if you also thought therapy may harm the marriage or even if you thought our sessions have made things worse between you and Lynn?

Paradoxically, by directly expressing his resistance and concern about therapy, Carl is no longer in a passive-aggressive stance but is now actively shaping the process. Although Carl may have disparaging comments about therapy, it is important to respect his view and to invite him to shape the process.

Therapist: Carl, you made several good points. How do you think we can improve what we are doing in our sessions?

The use of self can be an invaluable tool in moving through the impasse. It
communicates an openness on the therapist's part: Here is how I see it, correct
me if I am wrong, what does each partner see, and what can we do about it. But,
as with any technique, it can be misused, particularly if the therapist is struggling
with negative countertransference issues toward either partner or if the therapist
believes the lack of progress reflects his or her failure as a therapist. In these
cases, the therapist may use personal reactions to judge one or both partners.

Therapist: Carl, I am continually frustrated with your behavior. You appear to
resist every possibility for change.

Once a therapist's negative countertransference issues set the agenda, then little
progress will be made. Instead, as in the above example, the therapist has labeled Carl the problem (confirming Lynn's view) and will now attempt to blame
him into changing.

Asking What If

Partners, at an impasse, typically assume polar opposite positions along one or
several issues. The tug-of-war is an attempt to change the other person or to
convince the therapist who is right and who is wrong. Partners may say they
wish for change but are either waiting for the other person to change first or
refuse to take the first step themselves. At this point, the "objective" therapist
enters the scene and rather than choosing one side over the other begins to pull
in a third direction. However, in an impasse, both partners not only pull against
one another but also begin to pull against the therapist.

Where both partners resist change, particularly the therapist's pull toward
change, the couple exists in a status quo, albeit an unsatisfactory one, that defines the relationship. Even though both partners complain about the other and
the state of the relationship, neither actively seeks to change it nor leave it.
Instead, the hostile distance between them almost appears to be their bond.

For example, imagine two people who experience difficulty with intimacy
but do not wish to be alone. They both fear and want togetherness. Their solution is to stay together but apart. Their hostility maintains their distance but does
not push the relationship to the breaking point. Enter the therapist who errs by
listening to only one part of the message—the couple's desire to be closer—
while not fully appreciating the fear just below the surface. Without appreciating
or acknowledging the fear of togetherness, attempts to bring the couple closer
together are doomed from the start.

From a defensive perspective, it is easy for each partner to blame the other
for the emotional distance rather than face up to or admit to their own fears. The
endless accusations going back and forth protect the individual's self-concepts
while sabotaging the relationship. Given these defensive motivations, an impasse

is inevitable, particularly if the therapist accepts the couple's definition of the problem—for example, "We don't communicate"—and attempts to pull the partners back together.

But rather than stay with the couple's definition of the problem, the therapist may avoid the mutual blaming by refocusing on the individuals and asking, "*What if* what you wanted came true?"

Therapist: Lynn, what if Carl started helping out more around the house. What would that do to or for you?

Lynn: Well, that would be great!

Therapist: I am sure it would be, but what would it do to or for you?

Lynn: What do you mean?

Therapist: Well, would you feel closer to Carl? Would you want to spend more time with him?

Lynn: I am not sure.

Therapist: What aren't you sure about?

Lynn: I am not sure if I would spend more time with him.

Notice, by asking each partner to entertain what it would be like to get his or her heart's desire, the therapist moves past the impasse issues to a deeper ambivalence about the relationship, a deeper ambivalence that heretofore had escaped scrutiny. What if, however, Lynn's response was in the affirmative?

Lynn: If Carl helped out more around the house, I would definitely feel closer to him and want to spend more time with him.

Therapist: I am a little confused. Do you mean the only reason you are not closer to Carl is because he does not help out around the house?

Lynn: That's right!

Therapist: What then is so important to you about Carl helping out around the house that you would pull away from him until he changed? Or, let me put it another way, Carl's helping out around the house would mean or symbolize what to you?

Lynn: That he cared.

Therapist: Cared?

Lynn: Yes, cared about me.

Therapist: Do you doubt or how long have you doubted that Carl cares about you?

Again, the therapist moves around the stated impasse—Carl's helping around the house—into the more personal and complex issues of feeling cared for. Once this area is opened up, any number of questions expand on the theme.

Therapist: When did you feel Carl cared for you?

Therapist::   How did you know he cared?

Therapist: When you feel not cared for, how do you react?

As a means of expanding themes, the therapist's questions go back and forth between observable behavior and attributes. For example, the flow of questions may contain the following sequence:

1. What behavior is observed?
2. What does that behavior mean to the observer (attributions)?
3. How do those attributions shape a response (behavior)?
4. What is the effect of the response on the significant other (behavior)?
5. How is the response interpreted by the significant other (attributions)?

Asking what if questions forces the partners to explore the deeper meanings behind their complaints. The complaint "We don't communicate" may be the surface complaint for complex, underlying feelings: Am I loved? Am I respected? Am I cared for? Asking "what if" quickly bypasses the impasse.

SOLUTIONS OUT OF ACCEPTING WHAT IS

Many times in the face of an impasse, a therapist's first response is to redouble his or her efforts. As the couple sits more and more in resentful silences, the therapist works harder, assuming greater control of the sessions by offering more and more suggestions, attempting to elicit more and more interactions, and assigning more and more homework, but to no avail. It may sometimes reach the point where the therapist dreads the upcoming session because of the effort he or she will have to extend, which will in all probability result in the familiar frustration.

In these cases, countertransference feelings abound. If these feelings are left unchecked, the therapist may begin to blame or scapegoat one of the partners—"If only he or she would change." When the impasse reaches this point, the therapist begins to mirror the partners' individual stances—three people sitting in a room waiting for someone else to change.

One can assume each partner is feeling similar things. Each has expected the therapist to work a miracle and change the partner. The longer this has not occurred, the more frustrated he or she becomes. The therapist's "objective and impartial" clinical stance is seen by each partner as "wishy-washy" and not very helpful. The couple may continue to come to the sessions, but this may be due to momentum alone and the lingering hope that the relationship can improve.

As a guidepost for couples therapists, these countertransference feelings and the building discontent of the partners, particularly later in the treatment process, signal an impasse of great proportions. It may mean the therapist does not possess all of the pieces to the puzzle as in the above content themes. It may mean there are process themes left unidentified. It may be evidence of more severe pathology than initially suspected in one or both partners. Or, it may be simple stubbornness on both spouses' part.

Still, the therapist may disengage and confront the couple with the facts.

Therapist: I think it is time we took inventory. We have been working for many
sessions now with little progress. I am beginning to feel like a dentist doing
an endless root canal. I think we need to face the fact that this may be the
best your relationship can be. That's not to blame either one of you, it is just
accepting the facts as I see them. But, I could be wrong. What do each of you
think?

On a paradoxical level, for the therapist to "accept what is" shifts the rules of
therapy. The therapist is no longer trying to change the couple nor motivate the
partners toward change. Rather, the therapist is saying, "It looks like nothing is
going to change between the two of you, so let's just accept that fact."

Although the couple's first reaction may be anger toward the therapist for
giving up, paradoxically, faced with the accusation that they cannot change, the
couple begin to argue and prove the therapist wrong. Surprisingly, the couple
return the next session with evidence of change, to which the therapist continues
the paradoxical position.

Therapist: I am glad you had a good week, but I am afraid it will not continue.

In this paradoxical intervention, the therapist continues to maintain that nothing
will change while the couple attempts to prove him or her wrong.

Paradoxical interventions, however, should be used with caution. Although
some couples are challenged to prove the therapist wrong, other couples may
hear the therapist's words as judgment and condemnation—"Even an expert is
telling us we have failed at this relationship." If this is the case, then the therapist
has violated a basic healing tenet of "cause no harm."

By also pointing out the rigid impasse, the therapist is asking the couple to look
at the state of the relationship: Is this the relationship you want? The therapist is no
longer tirelessly working to keep the relationship together but is implying that the
glue to stay together must be created by the couple. There will be no magic wands
waved or dramatic transformations by the other partner but, if they are to stay together, it will be because they begin to accept one another "warts and all."

Therapist: If the two of you are to remain together, then the only choice I see is
to accept one another. You have battled so long to change one another, I
wonder what would happen if you did accept one another?

For some people, the concept of just accepting the other person is a new
idea. For so long, they have been struggling with changing one another and
resisting the other's attempts to change them. In this struggle, each partner has
felt demeaned and lacking in some essential elements. Therapy, therefore, has
been just a continuation of this process.

Paradoxically, once the members of the couple move toward accepting one
another and cease the attempts to change one another, change begins to occur.
The change mechanism is twofold: (1) being accepted may have been what each
partner was actually fighting for, and (2) without the need to resist, each partner
may freely choose change.

Imagine two people creating a relationship but from the beginning each feeling only partially accepted by the other. Their early arguments involve criticism of one another's behavior. But, after a while, these criticisms are no longer about specific behavior—"You never pay attention to me"—but are personalized into character attacks—"You are an insensitive person." With this, the couple's grim struggle to change one another begins and eventually culminates in the therapist's office.

The idea of accepting one another is frequently greeted by relief but also suspicion. The control struggle dies hard as each partner silently thinks, "I will accept only after I am accepted." If the couple embraces acceptance, then the impasse is broken and therapy takes a new turn. The focus of the sessions is now on accepting one another. Equally important, the focus shifts from blaming the other for the lack of change to each individual looking inward: "It is my work to accept my partner."

As the responsibility for change shifts to within each individual partner, the coercive pressure directed toward the other is lessened. Without the coercive pressure to change, the partner need no longer put up defensive walls. More importantly, because he or she is no longer busy resisting, each partner is now in a position to freely change to improve the relationship. Change is much easier when a person is not being forced into it.

Individual Versus Couples Versus Family Therapy

Earlier we offered guidelines for planning interventions using individual or couples therapy. In the assessment phase of treatment, this decision is based on the couple's initial presenting problem. However, faced with a stubborn impasse and in light of issues that may have emerged while struggling through the impasse, the choice of individual versus couples therapy may again arise. In addition, family therapy may serve as an adjunct treatment to couples therapy.

As therapy progresses it may become clear that individual pathology is at the root of the couple's issues. For example, one spouse's alcohol abuse may dominate the couple's life. Although other issues have been addressed in therapy, some event always draws the discussion back to alcohol. It is at this impasse that the therapist confronts the issue.

Therapist: Although there are significant issues between the two of you, I do not believe we will get anywhere without the alcohol abuse being addressed. If we are to continue the couples sessions, I believe you [the partner abusing alcohol] must also be in an alcohol program.

Although this stance risks losing the couple, it is the therapist's honest assessment. The decision to confront the alcoholism and insist on individual treatment is weighed against the prospects of truly being able to make significant changes in the couple's relationship. Without doing so, the therapist does the couple a disservice by continuing treatment and ignoring significant individual pathology.

At other times, a member of the couple may request individual therapy. Through the process of therapy, one partner may become aware of individual issues he or she wishes to address. Therapy has helped clarify the individual agendas that are involved with but are also separate from the couple's dynamics. For instance, Carl may become increasingly aware that his need to emotionally disengage from Lynn is a consequence of his family of origin experiences. He may recognize that this is his problem and may seek individual therapy to resolve it.

When the issue of individual therapy arises, the therapist decides whether to offer it him- or herself or refer to another therapist. It is important to remember that the therapist's client is the couple's relationship. Thus, guiding the therapist's decision is a simple principle: "Will individual therapy help the couple's relationship and if I offer to be the individual therapist will that be helping the relationship?"

Implied in this question is the recognition that by being the individual therapist, the therapist risks upsetting the delicate balance in the therapeutic triangle. Individual therapy threatens to create an alliance between the therapist and one member of the couple at the expense of the couple's relationship. This alliance may become real as the therapist begins to lose impartiality or if the other partner believes he or she has been left out. Either way, couples therapy is being compromised.

Although some therapists believe they can successfully walk this tenuous tightrope of simultaneously conducting individual and couples therapy, it is our belief that there are more risks than gains in this approach. Instead, a conservative step is to refer out. In this situation, not only is the therapist free of any boundary dilemmas, but the partner seeking individual therapy has a personal forum to discuss any issue he or she may wish without fearing it will get back to the partner.

Individual therapy may also be sought following a prolonged impasse when one or both members of the couple have strong questions as to whether to continue the relationship. One spouse may not be able to live with the partner if he or she keeps drinking. One partner may not be able to stay in the relationship without an acceptable level of intimacy and sexuality. One mate may not be able to commit to the relationship as long as he or she feels demeaned by the other. In these cases, individual therapy is sought to resolve these questions and to decide if the relationship is viable.

While couples therapy may be conducted simultaneously with individual therapy or even supplanted by individual therapy, in some cases, couples therapy may be augmented by broadening the perspective to family therapy. For example, after Jenn's birth, Lynn and Carl struggled with child care and negotiating the support from Lynn's extended family. Thrown back into intense interaction with her mother, Lynn's family of origin issues were reignited. The concrete realities of child care had created additional stress on the couple relationship. Lynn assumed the burden of asking her mother for support, but this increased her anger at Carl's passivity in these matters. In order to provide concrete solutions, a few family therapy sessions involving Carl, Lynn, Lynn's mother, and Lynn's sister would serve to open lines of communication between Carl and

Lynn's family, help relieve Lynn of the full responsibility, and establish boundaries concerning child-care requests.

Expanding couples therapy into family therapy is most indicated when current, ongoing family of origin issues are directly affecting the couple's relationship. Please note that the emphasis is on *current, ongoing issues* affecting the couple. One assumes we never fully escape the influence of our families of origin on our intimate relationships and that those themes continually emerge in couples therapy. Consequently, family therapy is best employed as an adjunct to couples therapy to strengthen the couple's capacity to manage current boundaries with their respective extended families.

Commitment and Movement Toward Termination

With the resolution of the impasse, couples therapy moves rapidly toward termination. We do not necessarily mean rapidly in terms of a number of sessions, but because the key stumbling block to progress has been removed, the couple can more fruitfully work on their relationship.

Whether through first- or second-order change interventions or by the resolution of process or thematic impasses, successful couples therapy results in a recommitment of both partners to the relationship. Even if both parties enter therapy stating their strong commitment to one another, their problems are significant enough to seek counseling. Successful therapy renews and strengthens their belief in the relationship.

Although successful therapy may mean the resolution of the initial complaints, it also refers to process goals achieved during the course of therapy: (1) effective problem-solving skills and (2) consensual intimacy. During the course of therapy, the couple's problem-solving skills are continually challenged and refined. The therapist is there to guide the couple, but the skills the partners develop are their own—ones that they carry into new situations.

By consensual intimacy, we mean the contributions of each partner in defining the meaning of intimacy for the couple. Through the process of therapy, partners redefine and refine their meanings of intimacy. Again, the therapist is there to guide the couple, but the consensual definition of intimacy evolves between the partners.

It would be nice if couples therapy were a smooth process from first interview through termination but reality is often far different. Couples therapy can produce various outcomes. Some are a consequence of the therapeutic encounter, but others fall outside of the therapist's control. Although not inclusive, the following list is an attempt to highlight common patterns:

PERPETUAL IMPASSE

Unfortunately some couples remain in a constant state of impasse. It is as if their problems have become chronic and intractable. These couples have a history of entering therapy only to unilaterally terminate when the more sensitive issues are being uncovered. Every few years or at developmental stress points, these couples seek out a new therapist to triangle into the couples' distress. A new therapist not only offers hope for change but is also an opportunity for the couple to cover the same old ground with a new person.

Arguments for these couples have become almost scripted and are easily but painfully repeated. In therapy, these couples stay in treatment until the stress is reduced to within manageable limits and terminate before the more difficult issues surface. Even though these cases may be considered successful—stress levels have been reduced and the couple is functioning more effectively—a therapist is left with a gnawing feeling that very little has changed and that the couple will probably be sitting in another therapist's office in the not too distant future.

IMPASSE AS A STEP TOWARD DISSOLUTION

In these couples, one or both parties have decided to dissolve the relationship or are at least 90% sure that is what they wish to do. Couples therapy is sought as one last attempt to save the relationship. But again, one or both parties have at least one, if not both, feet outside the partnership.

Therapy is sought with the slim hope that the therapist is a magician who will raise the relationship from the dead. However, lacking a magic wand, the therapist is more often faced with poor motivation on the couple's part and an affective noninvolvement in the treatment sessions. These couples may come for several sessions until an internal, undisclosed quota is met. At this point the partners look at one another and say, "See, we tried therapy and that did not work."

Of course, therapy in these cases is doomed almost from the start. Without the personal investment in the relationship, the couples do not even address any significant issues. While these issues may be brought up, they are offered more as complaints and examples of the intolerable quality of the relationship. From the therapist's perspective, it is as if one or both partners are biding their time until they suddenly and unilaterally terminate therapy. Even if one partner is desperate to maintain the relationship, the therapist senses that the other partner is only minimally involved.

COUPLES THERAPY TO EASE THE PAIN OF SEPARATION

Sometimes one partner has decided to unilaterally end the relationship. Couples therapy is sought to ease the pain of the separation. Unfortunately, each member of the couple presents a different agenda to the therapist.

The partner who wishes to leave the relationship wants the therapist to take care of the partner being left. Therapy is sought to ease that partner's pain. The exiting partner consistently gives the clear message that the relationship is over and he or she has come to therapy to help his or her mate come to terms with this fact. (In some cases, the hidden agenda is the hope that the therapist will take care of the ex-mate, thus relieving the exiting partner of any guilt.)

Typically, the partner being left is shocked at the partner's request for separation and begs for the couple to enter therapy. He or she hopes to save the relationship. Even if this was the indifferent partner for most of their time together, at this point he or she is willing to do anything to save the relationship. The therapist is begged to change the partner's mind about leaving.

Because of the conflicting agendas, these cases are both frustrating and painful for the therapist. They are frustrating because a therapist cannot successfully address such mutually exclusive wishes. Moreover, the therapist's own behavior may vacillate between trying to salvage the relationship and easing the pain of separation.

Similar to the situations discussed above, these cases rarely move past a superficial level of therapy. The exiting partner will come to the sessions as long as he or she has hope that the other partner will finally "hear and accept" the dissolution message. If the message is never heard or accepted, then the exiting partner will unilaterally terminate therapy, believing he or she has done all that can be done. The other partner may come for a few more sessions, individually attempting to accept the dissolution, but he or she is still strongly invested in the relationship and continually hopes the exiting partner will have a change of heart.

FEAR OF DISSOLUTION AND RENEWED COMMITMENT

Lynn and Carl best fit this type. These couples may begin therapy because one member strongly pushes for it. The relationship is basically sound, but the partners have found themselves arguing more and more. The arguing has increased to a point of concern for one or both partners. They fear the dissolution of the relationship and worry that the fighting may mean just that.

Characteristically, one partner feels more strongly about beginning therapy than the other. Or, in some cases, both partners are ambivalent about beginning therapy. But in either case, it is the fear for the relationship that brings the couple into the therapist's office.

What happens once they are there, however, is determined by the therapeutic process. The skill of the therapist in building a therapeutic alliance, in accurately assessing the presenting problems, and in responding with appropriate interventions will strongly influence the outcome. If successful, then therapy moves toward termination with the partners renewing their commitment to the relationship.

COMMITMENT TO THE RELATIONSHIP

These couples are motivated to begin therapy because of the pain they are experiencing. There is no doubt of their commitment to one another nor fear of dissolving the relationship. Because of these strengths, these couples readily respond to therapy because their basic commitment sustains them through the difficult phases. Termination is the logical conclusion to improved problem-solving skills and new definitions of intimacy.

COUPLES THERAPY MOVING INTO INDIVIDUAL THERAPY

Although the couple's issues were the initial reasons for referral, during the course of assessment and the early phases of therapy it becomes clear to the therapist and the partners that individual dynamics underlie the couple's issues. Although the couple's disagreements are seen as legitimate concerns, they are superseded by individual issues.

Consequently, in the context of couples therapy, the therapist and couple together decide to shift the focus to individual dynamics with the resumption of the couples sessions at a later date. However, the key to a successful shift to individual therapy is the source of the definition. That is, the definition of the problem comes from within the individual partner and is not imposed by the therapist or mate.

Although the therapist may strongly suspect that individual dynamics are at the heart of the couple's problems, to impose this suggestion risks raising the partner's defenses and overall resistance to therapy. Ultimately, the therapist's suggestion of individual therapy is a matter of timing. First, the suggestion comes after the couple's dynamics are openly discussed and each partner is aware of his or her contribution to them. Second, the therapist establishes a therapeutic relationship with each individual partner. And finally, the individual dynamics that superseded and are negatively affecting the relationship are acknowledged by the individual partners.

Process of Termination

The issue of termination may be raised by one or both partners or by the therapist. Ideally, termination is the natural and mutually agreed-to end point of the therapeutic encounter. However, at other times, termination may be unilaterally insisted upon by one partner.

When the possibility of terminating therapy is brought up by one of the partners, it may signal defensiveness or it may be a message that the partner has changed as much as possible at this time. Regardless, the therapist is left to discern what message is being sent. For example:

Carl (*at the beginning of a session following a session where the couple's sexuality was the topic*):   Things are much better between Lynn and me and I do not see much purpose in continuing these sessions.

Therapist: I am glad to hear that but would you fill me in on what is better now than before?

With this comment, the therapist decides to build on Carl's comment and identify the positive changes that have occurred.

Therapist (*following Carl's response*):   Carl, the changes sound good, but you did not mention the topic of sex. Have the two of you talked about it since we last met?

Carl: No.

Therapist: Well, I could be wrong, but based on our discussion last week sex appears to be an important issue for the two of you. Lynn, do you have an opinion about this issue?

Notice, the therapist does not challenge Carl or accuse him of defensiveness or resistance but instead asks if there has been resolution with the issue of sex and asks Lynn to confirm this fact.

Lynn: I think we just scratched the surface and we need to discuss it more.

Therapist: Carl, I do not believe in forcing any issues with couples. Lynn would like to go further with this issue, but you may not wish to do so. If we focus more on sex, it will be because both of you wish to do so. If you do not want to go any further with it then you need to help Lynn understand your position.

The therapist is willing to accept Carl's position but puts responsibility for the decision back into the couple's hands.

As a rule of thumb, when one partner brings up the issue of termination, the therapist needs to check out if (1) both of the partners have discussed the issue and (2) if both share the same opinion. If both parties are in agreement, then the therapist begins the termination process.

Regardless of who does it or how the issue is brought up, following a logical progression of reviewing goals, clarifying reciprocal expectations, and identifying remaining problems, the work of therapy is summarized to date.

REVIEWING GOALS

A logical beginning is to review the goals established in the assessment phase. Although these goals may have changed over the course of therapy, they still serve as a starting point.

Therapist: When we first met, you each had specific concerns. Lynn, you wanted Carl to help more around the house. Carl, you wanted Lynn to stop criticizing you. I was wondering, how do you each feel about those issues now?

The answers to this question serve as a barometer for therapeutic change. Besides addressing the specific complaints, the answers also hint at changes on the process level of the relationship. For example, although Carl was helping a bit more around the house, Lynn was feeling stronger about the relationship and the future because she and Carl were now able to talk about more substantial issues—for example, sexuality and his emotional withdrawal. For his part, Carl was still sensitive to Lynn's perceived criticisms but saw them less as criticism than as legitimate requests for help.

During the course of therapy other goals may have also evolved. For example, Lynn's and Carl's basic problem-solving styles were called into question. Instead of employing personalized attributes—she is critical; he is rejecting—as a means of withdrawing from one another, therapeutic interventions blocked the withdrawal pattern and forced the couple to work through specific problems as they arose. On the most intimate level, the increased capacity to discuss their sexual relationship deepened Lynn and Carl's relationship. At termination, these goals would also be reviewed.

CLARIFYING RECIPROCAL EXPECTATIONS

Termination also offers an opportunity to draw up an informal contract concerning reciprocal expectations.

Therapist: During the course of our sessions I have frequently asked each of you what you would like from one another and what you are willing to give to the other. I would like to take a few minutes and clearly spell out those expectations. Lynn/Carl, what would you like and what are you willing to give?

After drawing up the list either mentally or on paper, the therapist asks for feedback from each partner:

Therapist: You just heard what he [or she] said. Do you agree or would you like to have heard something else?

If the partners are in agreement, then the reciprocal expectations are clarified. Disagreement, however, may signal that termination is premature. A disagreement on reciprocal expectations is practically a guarantee of problems soon after therapy ends. In fact, one could argue that therapy is not successfully completed until this basic agreement is established.

IDENTIFYING REMAINING PROBLEMS

Although therapy may end, the relationship continues to evolve. It is unrealistic to believe that all of a couple's difficulties can be resolved through therapy. Moreover, even the most successful therapy cannot immunize the couple from future problems. Thus, as therapists we are intervening at a particular time with a particular problem in a couple's development.

At termination, however, there is an opportunity to take an inventory of the couple's emotional life, specifically, what issues are still sensitive and will possibly present future problems. For example, although both Lynn and Carl were now aware of their respective patterns and had evolved new ways of problem-solving, therapy would not eliminate their basic family of origin legacies that served as their respective Achilles' heels. Lynn is still vulnerable to feeling the weight of responsibility and fear of abandonment. Carl is still sensitive to perceived criticisms and will withdraw when he is hurt or threatened. Future stressors may ignite these patterns.

It is hoped that the lessons learned in therapy will protect the relationship, but termination is a chance to buttress these safeguards.

Therapist: You both have worked hard, and the relationship is stronger because of it. But I was wondering, what will you each do when the other happens to push your sensitive button. For example, Lynn, how would you like to respond when you feel overwhelmed and fear Carl is not there for you? Carl, how would you like to respond when you feel criticized?

Finally, as a preventive measure the couple is asked to look down the road and predict future difficulties.

Therapist: Before we end I would like to look into the future. What issues might reappear in the future or what new issues might lie ahead?

Predicting future difficulties increases the partners' understanding of their own dynamics and serves as a rehearsal for when or if the problematic situations arise.

Case Summary

Testing clinical hypotheses (see case summary in Chapter 8) is a combination of clinical judgment and timing. If the therapist brings up the issue before the couple is comfortable discussing it, then he or she risks raising the couple's defenses or forcing a unilateral, premature termination. For example, Lynn was ready to discuss their sex life, but Carl was angry and defensive concerning the issue. For the therapist to push the issue before Carl was ready would risk further alienating him from the treatment process.

If, however, the couple does not spontaneously bring up or offer an opening into the impasse issue, the therapist is at a choice point: Should I bring up the issue myself in an attempt to break the ice and risk igniting anxiety that will overwhelm the couple? Unfortunately, there are no clear guidelines to offer a therapist at these points. Instead, the intangibles enter the picture, such as the quality of the therapeutic rapport with each partner, the partners' sense that the therapist is truly acting in their best interests, and a clinical judgment that the anxiety generated by this issue will not overwhelm the couple. Fortunately, Lynn had opened the door into the couple's sexuality. Still, the therapist proceeded with caution because of Carl's defensiveness.

As discussed in the previous chapter, Lynn and Carl's sex life mirrored their emotional relationship. Lynn would most likely bring up the issue; Carl would become defensive. Their capacity to constructively grapple with an issue was limited because of rapid shifts in blaming one another for their problems. Moreover, their respective levels of differentiation belied the distance they maintained with one another. Lynn feared Carl's rejection and Carl feared Lynn's engulfment. As a result, they both avoided the topic of sex.

Focusing on the couple's sexuality, the therapist accomplished two separate but intertwined goals: (1) If the impasse was to be broken, sexuality was a clear content issue to be addressed; and (2) on a process level, successfully dealing with a sensitive issue such as sexuality would by definition greatly improve the couple's capacity for intimacy and would develop communication and problem-solving skills that could generalize to other and future issues.

Employing many of the earlier mentioned techniques, the therapist focused on disrupting and breaking the dysfunctional interactional patterns while helping the couple to evolve new, more satisfying ones. Specifically, Carl was encouraged to discuss his concerns rather than withdrawing into a passive-aggressive stance. Lynn was supported in her attempts to struggle with her guilt over child care and to push past Carl's anger to more successfully resolve their issues.

As the therapist actively blocked the repetition of the dysfunctional patterns in the therapy sessions, Lynn and Carl were forced to evolve more successful means of problem solving. As the therapist helped each partner voice his or her fears and concerns in a more direct fashion, the more comfortable they each became in sharing their thoughts and feelings with one another.

Beginning therapy harboring fears that their problems may lead to divorce, both Lynn and Carl had struggled through therapy and had spontaneously renewed their commitment to the relationship. This was clearly visible by an increased emotional and sexual intimacy. It was at this point that the therapist and couple mutually agreed to terminate.

Summary

Because a couple's relationship is a work in progress, ever changing and evolving, a precise beginning and end to therapy may be difficult to distinguish. It is not uncommon to work with a couple during a crisis, helping them weather it, without fully addressing the underlying dynamics. Although no significant changes have occurred in the relationship, the couple is grateful and views therapy as very helpful.

Likewise, therapy may be an ongoing process whereby four or five sessions during a crisis may lead to more sustained couples therapy 2 years later. Maybe those four or five sessions will lead to individual therapy 1 year later. Again, because marriage, and we dare say life, is a work in progress, the therapist must remain open to the possibilities of engaging and helping a couple. The key is to remember whose agenda must dominate the session. The therapist has the responsibility to open the door into an area or issue, but it is ultimately the couple's choice whether to enter that room.

More often than not, couples enter therapy with polarized agendas for one another—Lynn wants this from Carl; Carl wants that from Lynn. Consequently, the last thing they need is for the therapist to also have hidden agendas—for example, I will help Lynn confront Carl, or Lynn must face the issue with her mother. Although the therapist may be theoretically sound in his or her view of the problem, it does little good, and perhaps some harm, if the couple does not share a similar perspective. Thus, poor couples therapy is akin to three people in a boat who are each attempting to row in a different direction. Productive therapy occurs when all three people row the same course.

REFERENCES

American Association for Marriage and Family Therapy Commission on Accreditation for Marriage and Family Therapy Education and Training. (1991). *Manual on accreditation.* Washington, DC: Author.

Anderson, S. A., Russell, C. S., & Schumm, W. A. (1983). Perceived marital quality and family life-cycle categories: A further analysis. *Journal of Marriage and the Family, 45,* 127–139.

Aneshensel, C. S., & Pearlin, L. I. (1987). Structural contexts of sex differences in stress. In R. C. Barnett, L. Biener, & G. K. Baruch (Eds.), *Gender and stress.* New York: The Free Press.

Appleby, G. A., & Anastas, J. W. (in press). *Not just a passing phase: Social work with lesbian, gay and bisexual people.* New York: Columbia University Press.

Aries, E. (1996). *Men and women in interaction: Reconsidering the differences.* New York: Oxford University Press.

Balswick, J. O., & Balswick, J. K. (1995). Gender relations and marital power. In B. B. Ingoldsby & S. Smith (Eds.), *Families in multicultural perspective.* New York: Guilford Press.

Bandura, A. (1986). *Social foundations of thought and action: A social cognitive theory.* Englewood Cliffs, NJ: Prentice-Hall.

Barnett, R. C., & Baruch, G. K. (1987). Social roles, gender, and psychological distress. In R. C. Barnett, L. Biener, & G. K. Baruch (Eds.), *Gender and stress.* New York: The Free Press.

Barnett, R. C., Brennan, R. T., Raudenbush, S. W., & Marshall, N. L. (1994). Gender and the relationship between marital-role quality and psychological distress: A study of women and men in dual-earner couples. *Psychology of Women Quarterly, 18*(1), 105–127.

Baucom, D. H., & Epstein, N. (1990). *Cognitive-behavioral marital therapy.* New York: Brunner/Mazel.

Beall, A. E. (1993). A social constructionist view of gender. In A. E. Beall & R. J. Sternberg (Eds.), *The psychology of gender.* New York: Guilford Press.

Beer, W. R. (1983). *Househusbands: Men and housework in American families.* South Hadley, MA: J. F. Bergin/Praeger.

Begley, S. (1995, March 27). Gray matters. *Newsweek, 125,* 48–54.

Bem, S. L. (1985). Androgyny and gender schema theory: A conceptual and empirical integration. In T. B. Sonderegger (Ed.), *Nebraska symposium on motivation: Vol. 32. Psychology and gender.* Lincoln: University of Nebraska Press.

Bem, S. L. (1993). *The lenses of gender: An essay on the social reproduction of male power.* New Haven: Yale University Press.

Bernard, J. (1972). *The future of marriage.* New York: Bantam Books.

Berry, J. W. (1994). Acculturative stress. In W. J. Lonner & R. S. Malpass (Eds.), *Psychology and culture*. Needham Heights, MA: Allyn & Bacon.

Bertalanffy, L. von. (1968). *General systems theory: Foundations, development, applications*. New York: George Braziller.

Best, D. L., & Williams, J. E. (1993). Cross-cultural viewpoint. In A. E. Beall & R. J. Sternberg (Eds.), *The psychology of gender*. New York: Guilford Press.

Bleier, R. (1991). Gender ideology and the brain: Sex differences research. In M. T. Notman & C. C. Nadelson, *Women and men: New perspectives on gender differences*. Washington, DC: American Psychiatric Press.

Blumstein, P., & Schwartz, P. (1983). *American couples: Money, work, sex*. New York: William Morrow.

Blumstein, P., & Schwartz, P. (1991). Money and ideology: Their impact on power and the division of household labor. In R. L. Blumberg (Ed.), *Gender, family and economy: The triple overlap*. Newbury Park, CA: Sage.

Bly, R. (1992). *Iron John*. New York: Vintage Books.

Bograd, M. (1990). Women treating men. *The Family Therapy Networker, 14*(3), 54–58.

Bowen, M. (1976). Theory in the practice of psychotherapy. In P. J. Guerin, Jr. (Ed.), *Family therapy: Theory and practice*. New York: Gardner Press.

Bowen, M. (1978). *Family therapy in clinical practice*. New York: Aronson.

Bradbury, T. N., & Fincham, F. D. (1990). Attributions in marriage: Review and critique. *Psychological Bulletin, 107*(1), 3–33.

Braverman, S. (1993). The limits of systems therapy: The problem of intimacy. *Contemporary Family Therapy an International Journal, 15*(4), 285–297.

Burggraf, C. S., & Sillars, A. (1987). A critical examination of sex differences in marital communication. *Communication Monographs, 54*(3), 276–294.

Campbell, A. (1993). *Men, women and aggression*. New York: Basic Books.

Campbell, J. L., & Johnson, M. E. (1991). Marital status and gender similarity in marital therapy. *Journal of Counseling and Development, 69*(4), 363–366.

Cancian, F. M. (1989). Love and the rise of capitalism. In B. J. Risman & P. Schwartz (Eds.), *Gender in intimate relationships: A microstructural approach*. Belmont, CA: Wadsworth.

Carl, D. (1990). *Counseling same sex couples*. New York: Norton.

Carli, L. L. (1990). Gender, language, and influence. *Journal of Personality and Social Psychology, 59*, 941–951.

Chehrazi, S. (1987). Female psychology: A review. In M. R. Walsh, *The psychology of women: Ongoing debates*. New Haven: Yale University Press.

Chess, S., & Thomas, A. (1986). *Temperament in clinical practice*. New York: Guilford Press.

Chodorow, N. (1978). *The reproduction of mothering*. Berkeley, CA: University of California Press.

Christensen, A., & Heavey, C. L. (1990). Gender and social structure in the demand/withdraw pattern of marital conflict. *Journal of Personality and Social Psychology, 59*(1), 73–81.

Cohn, L. D. (1991). Sex differences in the course of personality development: A meta-analysis. *Psychological Bulletin, 109*, 252–266.

Cross, S. E., & Markus, H. R. (1993). Gender in thought, belief, and action: A cognitive approach. In A. E. Beall & R. J. Sternberg (Eds.), *The psychology of gender*. New York: Guilford Press.

Darwin, C. (1871). *The descent of man and selection in relation to sex*. New York: Modern Library.

deShazer, S. (1994). *Words were originally magic*. New York: Norton.

Doherty, W. J. (1981). Involving the reluctant father in family therapy. In A. S. Gurman (Ed.), *Questions & answers in the practice of family therapy*. New York: Brunner/Mazel.

Dougherty, W., & Jacobson, N. (1982). Marriage and the family. In B. B. Wolman (Ed.), *Handbook of developmental psychology* (pp. 667–680). Englewood Cliffs, NJ: Prentice Hall.

Eagly, A. H. (1987). *Sex differences in social behavior: A social-role interpretation*. Hillsdale, NJ: Lawrence Erlbaum.

Edelsky, C. (1976). The acquisition of communicative competence: Recognition of linguistic correlates of sex roles. *Merrill-Palmer Quarterly, 22,* 47–59.

Edelsky, C. (1977). Acquisition of an aspect of communicative competence: Learning what it means to talk like a lady. In S. Ervin-Tripp & Mitchell-Kernan (Eds.), *Child Discourse* (pp. 225–243). New York: Academic Press.

Efran, J. S., Lukens, M. D., & Lukens, R. J. (1990). *Language, structure, and change: Frameworks of meaning in psychotherapy*. New York: Norton.

Fagot, B. I., Hagan, R., Leinback, M. D., & Kronsberg, S. (1985). Differential reactions to assertive and communicative acts of toddler boys and girls. *Child Development, 56,* 1499–1505.

Falbo, T., & Peplau, L. A. (1980). Power strategies in intimate relationships. *Journal of Personality and Social Psychology, 38,* 618–628.

Fisch, F., Weakland, J. H., & Segal, L. (1982). *The tactics of change: Doing therapy briefly*. San Francisco: Jossey-Bass.

Fisher, H. (1992). *Anatomy of love*. New York: Fawcett Columbine.

Fisher, S. K. (1993). A proposed Adlerian theoretical framework and intervention techniques for gay and lesbian couples. *Individual Psychology Journal of Adlerian Theory, 49*(3–4), 438–449.

Fogarty, T. F. (1976). Systems concepts and the dimensions of the self. In P. J. Guerin, Jr. (Ed.), *Family therapy: Theory and practice*. New York: Gardner.

Fowers, B. J. (1991). His and her marriage: A multivariate study of gender and marital satisfaction. *Sex Roles, 24*(3–4), 209–221.

Framo, J. L. (1981). The integration of marital therapy with sessions with family of origin. In A. A. Gurman & D. P. Kniskern (Eds.), *Handbook of family therapy*. New York: Brunner/Mazel.

Friedman, R. C. (1991). Couple therapy with gay couples. *Psychiatric Annals, 21*(8), 485–490.

Friedman, S. (1993). Possibility therapy with couples: Constructing time-effective solutions. *Journal of Family Psychotherapy, 4*(4), 35–52.

Gaines, T. (1981). Engaging the father in family therapy. In A. S. Gurman (Ed.), *Questions & answers in the practice of family therapy*. New York: Brunner/Mazel.

Gay, P. (Ed.) (1989). *The Freud reader*. New York: Norton.

Geis, F. (1993). Self-fulfilling prophecies: A social psychological view of gender. In A. E. Beall & R. J. Sternberg (Eds.), *The psychology of gender*. New York: Guilford Press.

Gergen, K. J. (1985). The social constructionist movement in modern psychology. *American Psychologist, 40,* 266–275.

Gerson, R., Hoffman, S., Sauls, M., & Utrici, D. (1993). Family of origin frames in couples therapy. *Journal of Marital and Family Therapy, 19*(4), 341–354.

Gilligan, C. (1982). *In a different voice: Psychological theory and women's development*. Cambridge, MA: Harvard University Press.

Giordano, J., & McGoldrick, M. (1996). Italian families. In M. Goldrick, J. Giordano, & J. K. Pearce (Eds.), *Ethnicity and family therapy (2nd ed.)*. New York: Guilford Press.

Goolishian, H., & Anderson, H. (1987). Language systems and therapy: An evolving idea. *Psychotherapy, 24*(35), 529–538.

Goolishian, H., & Anderson, H. (1990). Understanding the therapeutic process: From individuals and families to systems language. In F. W. Kaslow (Ed.), *Voices in family psychology.* Newbury Park, CA: Sage.

Gordon, B., & Allen, J. A. (1990). Helping men in couple relationships. In R. L. Meth & R. S. Pasick, (Eds.), *Men in therapy: The challenge of change.* New York: Guilford Press.

Gottman, J. M. (1993). A theory of marital dissolution and stability. *Journal of Family Psychology, 7*(1), 57–75.

Gottman, J. M. (1994a). *Why marriages succeed or fail.* New York: Simon & Schuster.

Gottman, J. M. (1994b). Why marriages fail. *The Family Therapy Networker. 18*(3), 40–48.

Gottman, J. M., Jacobson, N. S., Rushe, R. H., Shortt, J. W., Babcock, J., La Taillade, J. J., & Waltz, J. (1995). The relationship between heart rate reactivity, emotionally aggressive behavior, and general violence in batterers. *Journal of Family Psychology, 9*(3), 227–248.

Gottman, J. M., & Levenson, R. W. (1992). Marital processes predictive of later dissolution: Behavior, physiology and health. *Journal of Personality and Social Psychology, 63,* 221–233.

Gould, S. J. (1981). *The mismeasure of man.* New York: Norton.

Gray-Little, B., & Burks, N. (1993). Power and satisfaction in marriage: a review and critique. *Psychological Bulletin, 93,* 513–538.

Green, R., & Herget, M. (1991). Outcomes of systemic/strategic team consultation: III. The importance of therapist warmth and active structuring. *Family Process, 30,* 321–336.

Guerin, P. J., Fay, L. F., Burden, S. L., & Kautto, J. G. (1987). *The evaluation and treatment of marital conflict: A four-stage approach.* New York: Basic Books.

Gurman, A. S., & Kniskern, D. P. (1991). *Handbook of family therapy: Vol. 2.* New York: Brunner/Mazel.

Haas, L. L. (1995). Household division of labor in industrial societies. In B. B. Ingoldsby & S. Smith (Eds.), *Families in multicultural perspective.* New York: Guilford Press.

Hanna, S. M., & Brown, J. H. (1995). *The practice of family therapy: Key elements across models.* Pacific Grove, CA: Brooks/Cole.

Hare-Mustin, R. T. (1989). The problems of gender in family therapy theory. In M. McGoldrick, C. M. Anderson, & F. Walsh (Eds.), *Women in families: A framework for family therapy.* New York: Norton.

Hatfield, E., & Rapson, R. L. (1993). *Love, sex, and intimacy.* New York: HarperCollins.

Heavey, C., Layne, C., & Christensen, A. (1993). Gender and conflict structure in marital interactions: A replication and extension. Special section: Couples and couple therapy. *Journal of Consulting and Clinical Psychology, 61*(1), 16–27.

Holzworth-Munroe, A., & Jacobson, N. S. (1985). Causal attributions of married couples: When do they search for causes? What do they conclude when they do? *Journal of Personality and Social Psychology, 48,* 1398–1412.

Hudson, P. O., & O'Hanlon, W. H. (1991). *Rewriting love stories: Brief marital therapy.* New York: Norton.

Hyde, J. S. (1981). How large are cognitive gender differences? A meta-analysis using w and d. *American Psychologist, 36,* 892–901.

Jacobson, N. S., Gottman, J. M., and Shortt, J. W. (1995). The distinction between type 1 and type 2 batterers—further considerations: Reply to Ornduff et al. (1995), Margolin et al. (1995), and Walker (1995). *Journal of Family Psychology, 9*(3), 272–279.

Jacobson, N. S., Gottman, J. M., Waltz, J., Rushe, R., Babock, J., & Holtzworth-Munroe, A. (1994). Affect, verbal content, and psychophysiology in the arguments of couples with a violent husband. *Journal of Consulting and Clinical Psychology, 62,* 982–988.

James, D., & Drakich, J. (1993). Understanding gender differences in amount of talk: A critical review of research. In Tannen, *Gender and conversational interaction*. New York: Oxford University Press.

Jensen, L. C., McGuie, A. P., & Jensen, J. R. (1991). Do men's and women's world-view differ? *Psychological Reports, 68*, 312–314.

Jordan, J. V., Surrey, J. L., & Kaplan, A. G. (1991). Women and empathy: Implications for psychological development and psychotherapy. In J. V. Jordan, A. G. Kaplan, J. B. Miller, I. P. Stiver, & J. L. Surrey (Eds.), *Women's growth in connection: Writings from the Stone Center*. New York: Guilford Press.

Josephs, R. A., Marekus, H. R., & Tafarodi, R. W. (1992). Gender differences in the source of self-esteem. *Journal of Personality and Social Psychology, 63*, 391–402.

Kandel, D. B., Davies, M., & Raveis, V. H. (1985). The stressfulness of daily social roles for women: Marital, occupational and household roles. *Journal of Health and Social Behavior, 26*, 64–78.

Kaslow, F. W. (1981). Involving the peripheral father in family therapy. In A. S. Gurman (Ed.), *Questions & answers in the practice of family therapy*. New York: Brunner/Mazel.

Kayser (1993). *When love dies: The process of marital disaffection*. New York: Guilford Press.

Keeney, B. P., & Ross, J. M. (1985). *Mind in therapy: Constructing systemic family therapies*. New York: Basic Books.

Keller, D., & Rosen, H. (1988). Treating the gay couple within the context of their families of origin. *Family Therapy Collections, 25*, 105–119.

Kelley, H. H., & Thibaut, J. W. (1978). *Interpersonal relations: A theory of interdependence*. New York: Wiley.

Kerr, M., & Bowen, M. (1988). *Family evaluation*. New York: Norton.

Kessler, R. C., & McLeod, J. D. (1984). Sex differences in vulnerability to undesirable life events. *American Sociological Review, 49*, 620–631.

Kohlberg, L. (1981). *The philosophy of moral development*. San Francisco: Harper & Row.

Lakoff, R. T. (1990). *Talking power*. New York: Basic Books.

Lavin, T. J. (1987). Divergence and convergence in the causal attributions of married couples. *Journal of Marriage and the Family, 49*, 71–80.

Lerner, H. G. (1988). *Women in therapy*. New York: Harper & Row.

Leslie, L. A., & Clossick, M. L. (1996). Sexism in family therapy: Does training in gender make a difference? *Journal of Marital and Family Therapy, 22*(2), 253–269.

Levant, R. (1990). Psychological services designed for men: A psychoeducational approach. *Psychotherapy, 27*(3), 309–315.

Levenson, R. W., Carstensen, L. L., & Gottman, J. M. (1993). Long-term marriage: Age, gender, and satisfaction. *Psychology of Aging, 8*(2), 301–313.

Lewis, S., & Cooper, C. L. (1987). Stress in two-earner couples and stage in the life-cycle. *Journal of Occupational Psychology, 60*(4), 289–303.

Lips, H. M. (1991). *Women, men, and power*. Mountain View, CA: Mayfield.

Longman, J. (1995, May 8). As parents squirm, women happily scrum. *New York Times*, p. 1.

Lott, B., & Maluso, D. (1993). The social learning of gender. In A. E. Beall & R. J. Sternberg (Eds.), *The psychology of gender*. New York: Guilford Press.

Low, N. S. (1990). Women in couples: How their experience of relationships differs from men's. In R. Chasin, H. Grunebaum, & M. Herzig (Eds.), *One couple, four realities: Multiple perspectives on couple therapy*. New York: Guilford Press.

Luepnitz, D. A. (1988). *The family interpreted: Feminist theory in clinical practice*. New York: Basic Books.

Maccoby, E. E. (1990). *Social development*. New York: Harcourt Brace Jovanovich.

Marecek, J. (1995). Gender, politics, and psychology's ways of knowing. *American Psychologist, 50*(3), 162–163.

Marecek, J., & Johnson, M. (1980). Gender and the process of therapy. In A. Brodsky & R. T. Hare-Mustin, *Women and psychotherapy: An assessment of research and practice*. New York: Guilford Press.

McCrady, B., & Hay, W. (1987). Coping with drinking in the family. In J. Orford (Ed.), *Coping with disorder in the family*. London: Croom Holm.

McGoldrick, M. (1982). Irish families. In M. McGoldrick, J. K. Pearce, & J. Giordano, *Ethnicity and family therapy*. New York: Guilford Press.

McGoldrick, M., Anderson, C., & Walsh, R. (1989). Women in families and in family therapy. In M. McGoldrick, C. M. Anderson, & F. Walsh (Eds.), *Women in families: A framework for family therapy*. New York: Norton.

McGoldrick, M., Giordano, J., & Pearce, J. K. (1996). *Ethnicity and family therapy* (2nd ed.). New York: Guilford Press.

McGoldrick, M., & Greson, R. (1985). *Genograms in family assessment*. New York: Norton.

McGoldrick, M., Preto, N. G. , Hines, P. M., & Lee, E. (1991). Ethnicity and family therapy. In A. S. Gurman & D. P. Kniskern's *Handbook of Family Therapy* (Vol. II). New York: Brunner/Mazel.

Meth, R. L., & Pasick, R. S. (1990). *Men in therapy: The challenge of change*. New York: Guilford Press.

Meyer, S. L., Murphy, C. M., Cascardi, M., & Birns, B. (1991). Gender and relationships: Beyond the peer group. *American Psychologist, 46*, 537.

Miller, G. E., & Bradbury, T. N. (1995). Refining the association between attributions and behavior in marital interaction. *Journal of Family Psychology, 9*(2), 196–208.

Miller, J. B. (1986). *Toward a new psychology of women*. (2nd edition). Boston: Beacon Press.

Mirowsky, J., & Ross, C. E. (1987). Belief in innate sex roles: Sex stratification versus interpersonal influence in marriage. *Journal of Marriage and Family, 49* (3), 527–540.

Mischel, W. (1966). A social-learning view of sex differences in behavior. In E. E. Maccoby (Ed.), *The development of sex differences*. Stanford, CA: Stanford University Press.

Moultrup, D. J. (1990). *Husbands, wives, and lovers: The emotional system of the extramarital affair*. New York: Guilford Press.

Newberry, A. M., Alexander, J. F., & Turner, C. W. (1991). Gender as a process variable in family therapy. *Journal of Family Psychology, 5*(2), 158–175.

Newsweek, (1995, March 27). (Begsley, S. 1995. *Gray matters*.)

Nichols, M. P., & Schwartz, R. C. (1991). *Family therapy: concepts and methods* (2nd ed.). Boston: Allyn & Bacon.

Nirenberg, T., Liepman, M., Begin, A., Doolittle, R., & Broffman, T. (1990). The sexual relationship of male alcoholics and their female partners during periods of drinking and abstinence. *Journal of Studies on Alcohol, 51*, 565–568.

Noel, N. E., McCrady, B., Stout, R. L., & Fisher-Nelson, H. (1991). Gender differences in marital functioning of male and female alcoholics. *Family Dynamics of Addiction Quarterly, 1*(4), 31–38.

O'Farrell, T. J. (1991). Using couples therapy in the treatment of alcoholism. *Family Dynamics of Addiction Quarterly, 1*(4), 39–45.

Osherson, S., & Krugman, S. (1990). Men, shame, and psychotherapy. *Psychotherapy, 27*(3), 327–339.

Peplau, L. A. (1993). Lesbian and gay relationships. In L. D. Garnets & D. Kimmel (Eds.), *Psychological perspectives on lesbian and male experiences* (pp. 395–419) New York: Columbia University Press.

Philpot, C. L.(1991). Gender sensitive couples therapy: A systemic definition. *Journal of Family Psychotherapy, 2*(3), 19–40.

Phinney, J. S. (1996). When we talk about American ethnic groups, what do we mean? *American Psychologist, 51*(9), 918–927.

Piaget, J. (1965). *The moral judgment of the child.* New York: The Free Press.

Pittman, F. S. (1989). *Private lies: Infidelity and the betrayal of intimacy.* New York: Norton.

Pittman, F. S. (1993). *Man enough: Fathers, sons, and the search for masculinity.* New York: Perigee Books.

Polefrone, J. M., & Manuck, S. B. (1987). Gender differences in cardiovascular and neuroendocrine response to stressors. In R. C. Barnett, L. Biener, & G. K. Baruch (Eds.), *Gender and stress.* New York: The Free Press.

Rotundo, E. A. (1993). American manhood: *Transformations in masculinity from the revolution to the modern era.* New York: Basic Books.

Rotunno, M., & McGoldrick, M. (1982). Italian families. In M. McGoldrick, J. K. Pearce, & J. Giordano, *Ethnicity and family therapy.* New York: Guilford Press.

Sabatelli, R., & Shehan, C. L. (1993). Exchange and resource theories. In P. G. Boss, W. J. Doherty, R. LaRossa, W. R. Shumm, & S. K. Steinmetz (Eds.), *Sourcebook of family theories and methods.* New York: Plenum.

Saleebey, D. (1994). Culture, theory, and narrative: The intersection of meanings in practice. *Social Work, 39*(4), 351–359.

Scharff, D., & Scharff, J. (1987). *Object relations family therapy.* New York: Jason Aronson.

Scher, M. (1990). Effect of gender role incongruities on men's experience as clients in psychotherapy. *Psychotherapy, 27*(3), 322–339.

Schnarch, D. M. (1991). *Constructing the sexual crucible: An integration of sexual and marital therapy.* New York: Norton.

Shay, J. J. (1993). Should men treat couples? Transference, countertransference, and sociopolitical considerations. *Psychotherapy, 30*(1), 93–102.

Sherman, J. A. (1980). Therapists' attitudes and sex role stereotyping. In A. Brodsky & R.T. Hare-Mustin (Eds.), *Women and psychotherapy: An assessment of research and practice.* New York: Guilford Press.

Silverstein, C. (1990). *Gays, lesbians, and their therapists.* New York: Norton.

Slipp, L. (1984). *Object relations: A dynamic bridge between individual and family treatment.* New York: Jason Aronson.

Snodgrass, S. E. (1985). Women's intuition: The effect of subordinate role on interpersonal sensitivity. *Journal of Personality and Social Psychology, 49,* 146–155.

Snodgrass, S. E. (1992). Further effects of role versus gender on interpersonal sensitivity. *Journal of Personality and Social Psychology, 62,* 154–158.

Spence, J. T. (1985). Gender identity and its implications for the concepts of masculinity and femininity. In T. B. Sonderegger (Ed.), *Nebraska Symposium on Motivation: Vol. 32. Psychology and gender.* Lincoln: University of Nebraska Press.

Steinglass, P., Bennett, L., Wolin, S., & Reiss, D. (1987). *The alcoholic family.* New York: Basic Books.

Stiver, I. P. (1991). The meanings of "dependency" in female-male relationships. In J. V. Jordan, A. G. Kaplan, J. B. Miller, I. P. Stiver, & J. L. Surrey (Eds.), *Women's growth in connection: Writings from the Stone Center.* New York: Guilford Press.

Surrey, J. L. (1991). Relationship and empowerment. In J. V. Jordan, A. G. Kaplan, J. B. Miller, I. P. Stiver, & J. L. Surrey (Eds.), *Women's growth in connection: Writings from the Stone Center.* New York: Guilford Press.

Swain, S. (1989). Covert intimacy: Closeness in men's friendships. In B. J. Risman & P. Schwartz (Eds.), *Gender in intimate relationships.* Belmont, CA: Wadsworth.

Tannen, D. (1990). *You just don't understand: Women and men in conversation.* New York: Ballantine Books.

Tannen, D. (1993). *Gender and conversational interaction.* New York: Oxford University Press.

Tavris, C. (1982). *Anger: The misunderstood emotion.* New York: Simon & Schuster/Touchstone.

Tavris, C. (1992). *The mismeasure of woman.* New York: Simon & Schuster/Touchstone.

Thomas, A., & Chess, S. (1980). *The dynamics of psychological development.* New York: Brunner/Mazel.

Toman (1961). *Family constellation.* New York: Springer Publishing.

Torrey, E. F. (1972). *The mind game: Witchdoctors and psychiatrists.* New York: Bantam Books.

Treadway, D. (1987). The ties that bind. *The Family Therapy Networker, 11*(4), 17–23.

Ussher, J. M. (1991). Family and couples therapy with gay and lesbian clients: Acknowledging the forgotten minority. *Journal of Family Therapy, 13*(2), 131–148.

Vanfossen, B. E. (1986). Sex differences in depression: The role of spouse support. In S. E. Hobfoll (Ed.), *Stress, social support and women.* New York: Hemisphere.

Walker, L. E. (1995). Current perspectives on men who batter women—implications for intervention and treatment to stop violence against women: comment on Gottman et al. (1995). *Journal of Family Psychology, 9*(3), 264–271.

Walsh, F., & Scheinkman, M. (1989). (Fe)male: The hidden gender dimension in models of family therapy. In M. McGoldrick, C. M. Anderson, & F. Walsh (Eds.), *Women in families: A framework for family therapy.* New York: Norton.

Walters, M., Carter, R., Papp, P., & Silverstein, O. (1988). *The invisible web: Gender patterns in family relationships.* New York: Guilford Press.

Wamboldt, F.S., & Reiss, D. (1989). Defining a family heritage and a new relationship identity: Two central tasks in the making of a marriage. *Family Process, 28*(3), 317–335.

Waring, M. (1988). *If women counted: A new feminist economics.* San Francisco: Harper & Row.

Wark, L. (1994). Therapeutic change in couples therapy: Critical change incidents perceived by therapists and clients. *Contemporary Family Therapy and International Journal, 16*(1), 39–52.

Watzlawick, P., Weakland, J., & Fisch, R. (1974). *Change: Principles of problem formation and problem resolution.* New York: Norton.

Weisstub, E. B. & Shoenfeld, H. (1987). Brief goal-limited couple therapy in the treatment of homosexuals. *American Journal of Psychotherapy, 41*(1), 95–103.

Whisman, M. A., & Jacobson, N. S. (1989). Depression, marital satisfaction, and marital and personality measures of sex roles. *Journal of Marital and Family Therapy, 15,* 177–186.

Whitaker, C., & Bumberry, W. M. (1988). Dancing with the family: A symbolic–experiential approach. New York: Brunner/Mazel.

White, B. B. (1989). Gender differences in marital communication patterns. *Family Process, 28*(1), 89–106.

Williams, J. E. & Best, D. L. (1990a). *Measuring sex stereotypes: A multination study.* Newbury Park, CA: Sage.

Williams, J. E. & Best, D. L. (1990b). *Sex and psyche: Gender and self viewed cross-culturally.* Newbury Park, CA: Sage.

Worden, M. (1991). *Adolescents and their families: An introduction to assessment and intervention.* Binghamton, NY: Haworth Press.

Worden, M. (1994). *Family therapy basics.* Pacific Grove, CA: Brooks/Cole.

Zygmond, M. J. & Denton, W. (1988). Gender bias in marital therapy: A multidimensional scaling analysis. *American Journal of Family Therapy, 16*(3), 262–272.

INDEX

TO THE OWNER OF THIS BOOK:

We hope that you have found *The Gender Dance In Couples Therapy* useful. So that this book can be improved in a future edition, would you take the time to complete this sheet and return it? Thank you.

School and address: _____

Department: _____

Instructor's name: _____

1. What I like most about this book is: _____

_____

2. What I like least about this book is: _____

_____

_____

3. My general reaction to this book is: _____

_____

4. The name of the course in which I used this book is: _____

_____

5. Were all of the chapters of the book assigned for you to read? _____

   If not, which ones weren't? _____

6. In the space below, or on a separate sheet of paper, please write specific suggestions for improving this book and anything else you'd care to share about your experience in using the book.

_____

_____

_____

_____

_____

Optional:

Your name: _____ Date: _____

May Brooks/Cole quote you, either in promotion for *The Gender Dance in Couples Therapy* or in future publishing ventures?

Yes: _____ No: _____

Sincerely,

Mark Worden
Barbara Drahus Worden

FOLD HERE

NO POSTAGE
NECESSARY
IF MAILED
IN THE
UNITED STATES

BUSINESS REPLY MAIL

FIRST CLASS   PERMIT NO. 358   PACIFIC GROVE, CA

POSTAGE WILL BE PAID BY ADDRESSEE

ATT: *Mark Worden & Barbara Drahus Worden*

**Brooks/Cole Publishing Company
511 Forest Lodge Road
Pacific Grove, California 93950-9968**

FOLD HERE

Brooks/Cole is dedicated to publishing quality publications for education in the human services fields. If you are interested in learning more about our publications, please fill in your name and address and request our latest catalogue, using this prepaid mailer.

Name:_____

Street Address:_____

City, State, and Zip:_____

FOLD HERE

- -

FOLD HERE